"An auspicious and timely publication, *Play Therapy and Telemental Health* provides a critical and much needed resource. Dr. Stone has assembled an impressive panel of play therapy and telehealth professionals, who provide practical material, backed up with appropriate theory. This cutting-edge book belongs on the shelves of both practitioners and academics."
—**Daniel Sweeney, PhD,** *professor of clinical mental health counseling and clinical director of the NW Center for Play Therapy Studies at George Fox University in Portland, Oregon, USA*

"Relevant for this time of crisis and beyond, this book compiles evidence-informed foundations and interventions that answer the questions we have all been asking about play therapy in the time of telehealth practice. The question is not whether to read this important book but how soon."
—**Susan M. Carter, PhD, RPT-S,** *clinical director at the Center for Change and Growth, PLC, in Kalamazoo, Michigan, USA*

"Just as the play therapist adjusts to the minute needs of the child in the playroom, so too do they adapt and respond to major public health and safety measures in response to COVID-19. However, when one door closes, another entrance opens, and this text opens the virtual platform and digital doors into a new and exciting play-therapy world. The scope of this text links relevant theory to practice and provides pertinent discourse to critically reflect and connect to clients in a variety of contexts through telemental health. A valuable resource for those who are, or wish to be, digitally savvy play therapists."
—**Judi A. Parson, PhD, RPT-S,** *discipline lead, course director, and senior lecturer in play therapy at Deakin University, Victoria, Australia*

Play Therapy and Telemental Health

Play Therapy and Telemental Health gives clinicians the tools they need to bring their therapy sessions online.

Chapters present the fundamentals of play therapy and telemental health therapy and introduce play therapists to a variety of special populations and interventions specific to telemental health. Expert contributors discuss using a wide variety of telehealth interventions—including Virtual Sandtray®©, nature play, and EMDR—with children affected by autism, trauma, and more. Readers will learn how the fundamentals of play therapy can be expanded to provide effective treatment in web-based sessions.

This is a vital guide for any clinician working in play therapy in the 21st century.

Jessica Stone, PhD, RPT-S, is a licensed clinical psychologist and co-creator of the Virtual Sandtray®©. She is also an author, innovator, and speaker specializing in the therapeutic use of digital tools in therapy.

Play Therapy and Telemental Health

Foundations, Populations, and Interventions

Edited by Jessica Stone

NEW YORK AND LONDON

First published 2022
by Routledge
605 Third Avenue, New York, NY 10158

and by Routledge
2 Park Square, Milton Park, Abingdon, Oxon, OX14 4RN

Routledge is an imprint of the Taylor & Francis Group, an informa business

© 2022 selection and editorial matter, Jessica Stone individual chapters, the contributors

The right of Jessica Stone to be identified as the author of the editorial material, and of the authors for their individual chapters, has been asserted in accordance with sections 77 and 78 of the Copyright, Designs and Patents Act 1988.

All rights reserved. No part of this book may be reprinted or reproduced or utilised in any form or by any electronic, mechanical, or other means, now known or hereafter invented, including photocopying and recording, or in any information storage or retrieval system, without permission in writing from the publishers.

Trademark notice: Product or corporate names may be trademarks or registered trademarks, and are used only for identification and explanation without intent to infringe.

Library of Congress Cataloging-in-Publication Data
Names: Stone, Jessica (Child psychologist) editor.
Title: Play therapy and telemental health: foundations, populations, and interventions / edited by Jessica Stone.
Description: Milton Park, Abingdon, Oxon; New York, NY: Routledge, 2021. | Includes bibliographical references and index. | Summary: "Play Therapy and Telemental Health gives clinicians the tools they need to bring their therapy sessions online. Through the presented fundamentals of play therapy and telemental health therapy, the play therapist will be introduced to a variety of special populations and interventions specific to the delivery of services through telemental health. Expert contributors discuss using a wide variety of telehealth interventions- including virtual sandtray work, nature play, and more – with children affected by autism, trauma, and other issues. Readers will learn how the fundamentals they already know can be expanded to provide effective treatment in web-based sessions. This is a vital guide for any clinician working in play therapy in the 21st century"– Provided by publisher.
Identifiers: LCCN 2021004517 (print) | LCCN 2021004518 (ebook) | ISBN 9780367755584 (hardback) | ISBN 9780367755577 (paperback) | ISBN 9781003166498 (ebook)
Subjects: LCSH: Play therapy -- Technological innovations. | Psychotherapy -- Technological innovations. | Mental health services -- Technological innovations.
Classification: LCC RJ505.P6 P5283 2021 (print) | LCC RJ505.P6 (ebook) | DDC 618.92/891653–dc23
LC record available at https://lccn.loc.gov/2021004517
LC ebook record available at https://lccn.loc.gov/2021004518

ISBN: 978-0-367-75558-4 (hbk)
ISBN: 978-0-367-75557-7 (pbk)
ISBN: 978-1-003-16649-8 (ebk)

DOI: 10.4324/9781003166498

Typeset in Bembo
by MPS Limited, Dehradun

Contents

Foreword ix
JOHN W. SEYMOUR
Prologue xii
JESSICA STONE
Terminology xiv

SECTION I Foundations

   1

1 Theoretical Roots and Branches of the Evolving Field of Play Therapy   3
LYNN LOUISE WONDERS

2 Purposeful Application of Theory to Case Conceptualization and Treatment Planning   25
LYNN LOUISE WONDERS

3 Telemental Health Play Therapy   45
JESSICA STONE

4 Cultural Humility in the Telemental Health Playroom   68
CARMEN JIMENEZ-PRIDE

SECTION II Special Populations

   85

5 TraumaPlay™ and Telemental Health: Innovations Through the Screen   87
PARIS GOODYEAR-BROWN AND KATE WORLEY

viii *Contents*

6 The Power of Attachment in Telemental Health   99
   CLAIR MELLENTHIN

7 Virtual EMDR and Telemental Health Play Therapy   110
   JACKIE FLYNN

8 AutPlay® Therapy and Telemental Health: Strategies for
   Children with Autism   130
   ROBERT JASON GRANT

9 Telemental Play Therapy in Schools   144
   SONIA MURRAY

10 Neurodiverse Older Teens and Young Adults in
   Telemental Health Play   156
   KEVIN B. HULL

SECTION III Special Interventions
                                                      171

11 Using the Virtual Sandtray®© App: A Boy's Journey to
   Healing   173
   HEIDI GERARD KADUSON

12 Foundations of Virtual Playrooms   187
   RACHEL A. ALTVATER

13 Expressive Therapies in Telemental Play   201
   LESLIE BAKER

14 Nature Play Therapy and Telemental Health: How
   Green Time and Screen Time Play Well Together   217
   JAMIE LYNN LANGLEY

15 The Universe of You: Using Remote VR to Improve
   Psychoeducation Through Spatial Presence, Attention
   Allocation, and Interaction   229
   RYAN KELLY

   Conclusion   240
   JESSICA STONE
   Index   242

Foreword

John W. Seymour

For over 20 years, play therapists have been brainstorming how to incorporate digital technology into play therapy practice, sometimes drawing very different conclusions about the risks and benefits of doing so. I have witnessed, participated in, and sometimes provoked these lively collegial discussions, and have expressed my own evolving cautions and enthusiasm on the topic. As a play therapist, I found it hard to picture Virginia Axline bringing a set of virtual reality goggles to her home sessions with Dibs. Would that be her way of being really present with him in the moment? Would the goggles be a connecting point or a roadblock to her therapeutic relationship with him? At the very same time, I found it hard to picture Axline being disinterested and dismissive of Dibs had he greeted her at the door with a pair of his VR goggles and asked her to play. Wouldn't she respectfully and wholeheartedly engage him where he was at that moment in what interested him? Even if I somehow knew what she would have done (perhaps found in a long-lost chapter of Axline's book?), what would I do as a therapist when presented with this scenario? How would I intentionally and ethically incorporate digital technology with the humanity of the therapeutic relationship?

When I was growing up and learning to read, I was already learning of the tensions between humanity and technology. I loved science fiction, beginning with the adventures of teen-scientist Tom Swift, Jr. (*Tom Swift and the Visitor from Planet X*) to the classics of Jules Verne (*Twenty-Thousand Leagues Under the Sea*) and H. G. Wells (*War of the Worlds*). Science fiction provided my imagination with fascination for how humans could transform the world through science and technology, with so many possibilities for our future. Along with the tales of wonder, there were also cautionary tales of how science and technology applied carelessly could result in unexpected outcomes. Humans could embrace technological developments for the betterment of all. They also needed to watch out for the occasional killer robot. Teen inventor Tom Swift always seemed to know how to bend technology's arc toward the better direction to avoid disaster, saving our world over and over in every new book in the series. While Tom waged these technological battles for the world, my brothers and I waged our own less than successful technological skirmishes with parents over issues such as the amount of television watching that would rot your brain, or the number of battery-operated toys that were too many. My relationship with technology has always been complicated.

Fast forward, and I am a family therapist using play therapy in my work with children and families. I have slowly but surely been learning small ways to incorporate technology into my therapeutic work. I have had some very good company on this learning journey. Dr. Jessica Stone, editor of this book, along with many of the chapter authors have been my go-to resources for the last ten years on the responsible use of digital technology in harnessing the therapeutic powers of play and play therapy. I have attended their workshops, participated in their demonstrations, and raised my share of questions. Ask any one of them, and they would likely report that I have usually had more caution than enthusiasm for the topic and that I have raised more than my share of questions!

There has been a growing trend of our lives becoming even more intertwined with technology, and at some point, I imagined that technology would have a greater impact on our practice of psychotherapy, too. Whatever my personal reservations, it was time for me to do some additional reflection and study on how to do this in a professional and ethical way. At the end of 2019, I designed my own independent study to determine the status of 21st century best play therapy practices for incorporating digital technology into my play therapy practice. I would be ready when this integration occurred, and thought I had several years to prepare.

And you know what happened next: 2020, a pandemic six weeks into the year, a near-halt to face-to-face mental health services four weeks after that. Mental health professionals and the people we serve were significantly impacted, and our usual ways of helping had also been impacted. We were faced with the challenge of ethically taking care of ourselves and our clients as the world changed around us. The future I was going to study for arrived a few years early. I started an overtime scramble to respond as well and as quickly as possible. My first purchase was Dr. Stone's just-off-the-press (what timing!) *Digital Play Therapy: A Clinician's Guide to Comfort and Competence*. I had two weeks, not two years, to prepare myself personally and professionally for full-fledged digital play therapy delivered through telehealth videoconferencing. My killer robot anxiety began to return.

Eight months have passed since the first stay-at-home orders of the pandemic. I have been seeing all my clients through telehealth videoconferencing. I have been sifting through all the technological bells and whistles that I could identify as potential resources, looking for the ones that best incorporated the therapeutic powers of play and enhanced the therapeutic relationship. I have tried to be very deliberate in my observations, reflections, and choices about how to work in the online environment, quickly tossing some approaches that clearly didn't have the depth and impact of face-to-face work, and trying to make sure that I identified every way that this new medium could enhance imagination, creativity, and wonder in a way that might not have happened in an overflowing play therapy room. I have sought a lot of feedback from clients as I have worked, and I have compared a lot of experiences with my colleagues who are developing these new skills along with me. I am grateful that soon I will have the benefit of this new book to continue to guide my learning, and I am grateful for the colleagues and shared learning experiences along the way.

And yes, I will still keep my eyes open for those killer robots.

Prologue

Jessica Stone

You are about to discover why I think this book is simply amazing. If you can imagine the scene ~ in the midst of the COVID-19 pandemic a lot of my time is spent updating features for our Virtual Sandtray®© App, answering questions, writing, training, and browsing social media posts regarding the transition for play therapists from in-person, face-to-face sessions to providing telehealth sessions. For some, this has been a relatively simple transition. For most, it has been full of important considerations. From the logistics of technological delivery to the theoretical and practical implications, therapists worldwide worked to keep their client's best interests at heart, their practices afloat, and everyone's health intact. Having written a few books over time I began thinking in terms of what is needed NOW. Really, what was needed *yesterday*, but I could not do anything about yesterday at that point. I came up with a crazy idea to ask a number of knowledgeable people if they would be willing to write a chapter about their specialty and telehealth. I thought I would have quite a few people who would say they just did not have time. Would you believe it, EVERY SINGLE PERSON SAID "YES". Ultimately two people had to drop out due to extenuating circumstances and then the next level miracle happened ~ two new people stepped up with *even less time* and took on the challenge.

The purpose of this book is to provide the reader with important information and resources as we not only navigate this COVID-19 telehealth environment, but also begin building a foundation for future telehealth work. Throughout these transitions people have discovered new ways to work, new ways to connect, and new ways to implement the therapeutic powers of play. Many people will gladly go back to 100% in-person, face-to-face sessions, however, others are looking toward staying 100% telehealth, and others still are thinking about hybrid practices. Some families have benefitted greatly from telehealth; less time missed from work and less time missed from school have resulted in easier and better access to mental health services than ever before for many. For some, the screen has actually assisted with their willingness to speak about certain topics. Therapists have had unique opportunities to learn about client's environments and family dynamics like never before.

Split into three sections, *Play Therapy and Telemental Health* provides the clinician with information for a solid foundation. A historical look at play therapy, it's theories, and core tenets allows the play therapist to return to their roots and remember components which help answer "what am I doing and why am I doing it?". How these roots tie into treatment planning is next in this text for the therapist to integrate fundamentals into treatment directions that will inform the therapeutic paths to come. Telemental health play therapy fundamentals help the therapist understand how such fundamentals are congruent with providing teletherapy care. Cultural competence and humility reminds each of us to look both within ourselves and our client's lives to integrate important components in each level of care both in both approach and logistics. Once the play therapist has journeyed through the fundamentals, the next two sections, Special Populations and Special Interventions, provide the reader with researched, well-thought through considerations and interventions for immediate implementation.

This book is a true testament to the dedication each and every author has for clients everywhere and the entire field of play therapy, including the importance of providing solid information guides to all. I am humbled and I am blessed by each and every author in this book. Typically, a book takes about 18 months to go from the proposal stage to the book on the shelf. I proposed this book to my editor at Routledge and she understood the urgency; practitioners need this information as quickly as we can get it to them. She committed that if I could get the manuscript to them quickly, they will work to publish it quickly. Ultimately this book took 8.5 weeks from the time of the contract to the time the last chapter was received. A phenomenal display of dedication and my utmost respect to each author involved. On behalf of myself, Routledge, your fellow play therapists, and all our clients, a heartfelt "thank you" to you all. Jessica

Terminology

There have been many different definitions of telemedicine and different terms which have been used over the years. These include: telehealth, telemental health, teleplay, eHealth, mHealth, telebehavioral health, telepsychiatry, telecounseling, computer mediated/aided, videotherapy, and many more. Each term intends to convey a distinction specific to a population, field, use, etc. For the purpose of this text, the term "telemental health play therapy" is primarily used to reduce confusion and specifically convey the use of confidential, protected virtual platforms to provide psychological play therapy services from a distance. The following definitions of telemental health and play therapy have informed the terminology used:

Telemental Health

Telemental health or telebehavioral health is the process of providing behavioral therapy or psychotherapy remotely, typically utilizing HIPAA-compliant video conferencing or text-based messaging. The advantages of virtual delivery of psychotherapy include reduced stigmatization, increased convenience for patients, and improved provider efficiency.

(WeCounsel, 2021, para 1)

Play Therapy

Play Therapy is defined by APT as 'the systematic use of a theoretical model to establish an interpersonal process wherein trained Play Therapists use the therapeutic powers of play to help clients prevent or resolve psychosocial difficulties and achieve optimal growth and development.' Play Therapy should only be provided by licensed clinical mental health professionals with a graduate mental health degree and extensive specialized play therapy education, training and supervised experience.

(Association for Play Therapy, 2020, para 4-5)

References

Association for Play Therapy (2020). *What is play therapy?* https://www.a4pt.org/
WeCounsel (2021). *Telemental health: History.* https://www.wecounsel.com/telemental-health/

Section I
Foundations

1 Theoretical Roots and Branches of the Evolving Field of Play Therapy

Lynn Louise Wonders

There is a dynamic and rich history that tells a story of the ongoing development and evolution of theoretical orientations over the past 100 years (Karpiak et al., 2016). The field of play therapy itself has its own story from roots to branches that continue to develop and evolve. Today play therapy is considered the most appropriate way of addressing children's behavioral, emotional, and developmental problems (Ray, 2011). Research reviews using meta-analysis of play therapy outcome studies have shown play therapy to be effective when treating children's mental, emotional, and behavioral needs across a span of ages and presenting issues (Bratton et al., 2005; Leblanc & Ritchie, 2001; Lin & Bratton, 2015; Ray et al., 2015). The needs of children, however, were only first regarded in the late 19th century (Brodie, 1998; Mintz, 2006). The field of play therapy has grown and continues to evolve much like a tree with a well-established root system, a solid trunk, and branches upon branches of theoretical models and practices growing over time.

In this modern society with rapidly advancing technology, including mental health services provided over telemental health, it is more important than ever that clinicians be well rooted in theoretical foundations. Having an in-depth understanding of the history of play therapy's evolution allows therapists to have an appreciation for the origins and growth of various approaches, orientations, and interventions in order to translate services effectively to online play therapy.

While play therapy can be used across the lifespan with people of all ages and stages of development (Olson-Morrison, 2017; Kaduson, 2015), for the purposes of this chapter the focus will primarily be on history and theories related to mental health of children, providing a historical account for how play therapy came to be and how it has continued to evolve over time. We will consider four phases of the play therapy field's development. First, we will examine how children were viewed in the time that preceded the 20th century's development of child psychology as a construct. We will then look at the roots and branches of psychoanalysis with children and their parents. The third section of this chapter will view the ways play therapy emerged as an established field in and of itself with a variety of theoretical orientations. The fourth section will examine how current trends including telemental health, neuroscience, and the use of technology will inevitably shape the future of play therapy.

Views of Childhood Prior to the 20th Century

The idea that children's natural play is an essential part of childhood development can be traced back 2,500 years to classic philosophies of Plato and Aristotle (Beaumont, 1994). Despite those early glimmers of what would later come to be central to healthy child development, prior to the late 1800s in Western culture, children were generally not regarded until they were old enough to work and contribute to households and communities (Heywood, 2018). The social construct that we know as *childhood* has evolved over time. Ariès (1962) wrote about European medieval times in which children did not have a childhood because they were viewed as miniature adults. Heywood (2018) explains that the nature of the pre-industrial, medieval times was such that children were required to enter the world of adults as early on as possible for purposes of survival. As we look back on the history of childhood, it is important to acknowledge how cultural context significantly influenced the way in which children were raised, schooled, and regarded (Mintz, 2006).

While most historical accounts of childhood development are couched in Western context, there are anthropological and ethnographic studies that provide perspectives as to how children and childhood have been regarded over time examining long traditions of indigenous people around the world. Lancy (2017) examines parenting traditions of world-wide societies in comparison to those of Western culture. Basden (1966) found that the Igbo of Nigeria have historically regarded three-year-olds as self-sufficient. Dentan (1978) studied the Semai people of Malaysia who left their children to follow, play, and learn independently without direct teaching from adults. Silverman and Caughey (1980) explain how Chuuk parents of Micronesia have a long tradition of directly fostering and nurturing desirable qualities in children. Cross-cultural and transnational studies demonstrate that the needs of a particular society and environment within the cultural context informs the way adults regard children's presence and development (Bornstein et al., 2011; Ashby & Horn, 1990).

Prior to the early 20th century in European and American cultures, a child's behavioral problems were judged as immoral rather than seen as symptomatic of mental and emotional needs (Rey et al., 2015). Juvenile insanity was first recognized and differentiated from mental retardation and epilepsy in the late 19th century (Parry-Jones, 1989). G. Stanley Hall founded the first journal of child psychology in 1891 and the first society of child study in 1894 (Rey et al., 2015). In 1896, Lightner Whitmer established the first psychological clinic for children for diagnosis, assessment, and treatment (Baker, 1988). These later 19th century developments planted the seeds which would take root; growing and evolving into play therapy. In the early 1900s, there was a new trend of addressing the emotional and behavioral needs of children in school settings.

The Influence of Psychoanalysis: Roots and Branches

Psychoanalytic theory was the basis for the initial effort to understand the behavioral and emotional needs of children in the early part of the 20th century (Seymour, 2016). Sigmund Freud published his often-cited case of Little Hans in which Freud recommended the father of his young patient observe the child's play as a source of insight into the child's phobia of horses (Freud et al., 1955). Freud viewed play as a child's form of free association, the method through which psychoanalysts help patients uncover unconscious thoughts and feelings (D'Angelo & Koocher, 2011). Over the following ten years, Freud made a concerted effort to spend time observing children's play, recognizing that children imagined and explored make-believe worlds. He noted the tendency for children to reenact challenging experiences over and again through their play and concluded that it was this repetition of themes within the play that children developed mastery which led to resolution of presenting problems (Mannoni, 1970). That well-known case about Little Hans was the beginning of the pervading belief that play is a window through which a child's inner and outer world can be observed and better understood by therapists.

Though Sigmund Freud may have been the first to publish an account of the value of play for children's natural psychoanalytic process, it was Hermine Hug-Hellmuth who was the first psychoanalyst to develop techniques specifically for children distinguished from adult methods (Hug-Hellmuth, 1913; Hoffman, 2020; Plastow, 2011). Hug-Hellmuth was the first to use the term play therapy, (Hug-Hellmuth, 1913; Geissmann & Geissmann, 1998) using drawing and writing games to help her understand the unconscious mind of children (Lenormand, 2012).

Pioneering Influences of Four Significant Female Psychiatrists

Anna Freud, Melanie Klein, Margaret Mahler, and Margaret Lowenfeld all made great strides in forging the way for child psychology to become a focused field of study. Each made significant contributions that have influenced the many branches of the field of play therapy.

Anna Freud and Melanie Klein, both trained and practiced in psychoanalysis, were both heavily influenced by Hug-Hellmuth's work (Plastow, 2011). Freud and Klein both utilized play within the psychoanalytic model and both have been regarded as contemporaneous firsts to practice child psychoanalysis (Donaldson, 1996). Anna Freud (1937) is perhaps most well known for her work called *The Ego and the Mechanisms of Defence* that has had great influence on the field of psychology and the understanding of defense mechanisms. Freud opened the Hampstead Child Therapy Course and Clinic in 1952 as a center for therapy services, training, and research.

Melanie Klein was the first psychoanalysts to bring forward the theory of object relations with her observations of infants and mothers, recognizing that the early attachment of infant to mother shapes the infant's experience of future relationships (Fritscher, 2019). Object relations theory was an offshoot of Freudian psychoanalytic theory (Eddins-Folensbee, 2001). This theory went on to contribute to the development of attachment theory that now informs current attachment-based models such as Theraplay® and FirstPlay®. Klein published her work *The Psycho-Analysis of Children* (Klein, 1932) which served as seminal literature contributing significantly to clinicians' understanding of the emotional development of children (Harris, 2014).

Klein and Freud had overlapping and competing views (Edgcumbe, 2000; Viner, 1996). Klein's method focused on the application of technique while Freud's method was motivated more by theory (Donaldson, 1996). While Anna Freud held to her father's theory of child development, believing the goal when working with children was to facilitate the surfacing of unconscious feelings and beliefs in order to assist children in realizing their own insights about their problems and challenge (Donaldson, 1996), Klein expanded on Freudian practice which lead to new discoveries about the development of the infant psyche (Holder, 2018). Klein viewed a child's play as a symbolic language and as a form of free association for children (Donaldson, 1996).

In 1950, Margaret Mahler co-founded the Masters Children's Centre in Manhattan at Mount Sinai hospital where she developed the tripartite treatment model that included mothers in the treatment of her child patients. Mahler's work was focused on severe mental and emotional childhood issues with emphasis on the importance of the child's environment which she wrote about in her publication called *On child psychoses and schizophrenia: autistic and symbiotic infantile psychoses* (Mahler, 1952). Her work was particularly focused on mother–infant duality and the impact of early separation of young children from their mothers (Coates, 2004).

Margaret Lowenfeld established the Children's Clinic for the Treatment and Study of Nervous and Difficult Children in London, later named the Institute for Child Psychology, where clinicians were trained in her method known as the Lowenfeld world technique (Friedman & Mitchell, 2002). Her first book called *Play in Childhood* (Lowenfeld, 1935) was published in the United States and to this day is a referenced source in the field of child psychology and play therapy. Lowenfeld's ground-breaking discovery, that playful non-verbal techniques could replace language in helping children therapeutically, impacted the developing branches of play therapy.

Branches from Traditional Psychoanalysis

There were four particularly influential historical figures in the field of psychology who emerged from the psychoanalytic movement. Alfred Adler, Carl Jung, Otto Rank, and Erik Erikson each broke from Freud's traditional psychoanalysis to form their own independent views. These respective views paved the way for the development and practice of a variety of play therapy approaches and orientations as this section will demonstrate.

Alfred Adler's Individual Psychology

Alfred Adler believed that Freud's theories were too heavily focused on sex and preferred to place less emphasis on the unconscious and more focus on the context of social dynamics and interpersonal relationships (Hoffman, 2017). Adler founded and developed a theory he called individual psychology emphasizing the importance of social context which he purported was directly connected to an individual's internal experience and views of self and others (Adler, 1924). Adler believed all behavior has a goal and purpose (Dreikurs & Soltz, 1992). According to his theory, there are four essential elements to the formation of a person's individual personality (see Table 1.1). Adler believed people experience discouragement when those four essential and elemental experiences are not fulfilled. This can lead to a variety of socially problematic behavior (Watts & Pietrzak, 2000). He focused on relationship dynamics within families and his work went on to influence the parenting work of his follower Rudolf Dreikurs (Terner et al., 1978). In the early 1990s, Terry Kottman applied the Adlerian theoretical model to work with children and developed Adlerian Play Therapy Theory (Kottman, 2001; Mosak & Maniacci, 1999). In Adlerian play therapy, clinicians apply Adlerian theory to case conceptualization and then use a combination of non-directive and directive play therapy determined for the presenting needs of each individual child within the context of the family dynamic to bring about change to thinking, feeling, and behavioral patterns (Kottman & Meany-Walen, 2016).

Table 1.1 Adler's Four Essential Elements to Formation of Personality. A four row chart listing Adler's four essential elements of personality: people 1) need to feel a sense of belonging, 2) have goals which they move toward, 3) unique and inherently creative, 4) their life experiences are from a subjective point of view

1. People need to feel a sense of belonging
2. People have goals which they move toward
3. People are unique and inherently creative
4. People's life experiences are from a subjective point of view

Adapted from Kottman, T., & Ashby, J. (2015). Adlerian play therapy. In D. Crenshaw & A. Stewart (Eds.)., Play therapy: A comprehensive guide to theory and practice (pp. 32-47). Guilford Press.

Carl Jung's Analytical Psychology

Carl Jung was a student of Sigmund Freud and was heavily involved in the psychoanalytic movement until he came forward with his own ideas that departed from Freud's theory of infant sexuality (Donn, 2011). Jung's theory emphasized symbols and archetypes representing the personal and collective unconscious (Jung, 1964). This theory went on to influence the development of sandtray therapies. Dora Kalff (2003) developed sandplay therapy merging the earlier work of Margaret Lowenfeld's world technique in sand with Jung's theoretical principles (Turner, 2005). Jungian play therapy is based in the theory that the ability to experience transformative change is within the unconscious and that children will naturally heal by way of bringing what is repressed and unconscious to the level of consciousness through symbolic play (Green, 2014). Jung's theory asserts that a child does not have conscious awareness of repressed feelings or memory but can be vulnerable to having those repressed feelings or memories activated by conscious experiences. Symbolic play is seen as the means through which children are able to face the most difficult images or memories that lie in the unconscious and that this is the process through which healing occurs. Jungian play therapy helps children form healthy attachments and helps children to develop functional social relationships (Lilly & Heiko, 2019).

Otto Rank and the Therapeutic Relationship

Otto Rank began his career in the psychoanalytic movement going on to develop a new perspective that focused on the quality of emotional connection and relationship between analyst and patient within the present moment. Rank asserted that this foundational theory was paramount to the process of a client's individuation process (Kramer, 2019). His theory became a distinct and significant departure from the psychoanalytic movement when he established the idea of birth trauma departing from the Oedipus complex along with his assertion that emotional expression was an essential part of the therapeutic process (Stein, 2010).

Rank wrote, in his publication called *Will Therapy* that neurosis exists in the past and that resolution lies in the effort to be present in what he named *the here and now* (Rank, 1936). One of Rank's students, Jessie Taft, was at the heart of the initial humanistic psychotherapy movement applying Rank's theory to work with children in what she called *relationship therapy* (J. A. Courtney, 2020a; Taft, 1933). Carl Rogers followed and credited Rank for influencing the development of his person-centered therapy. Rogers' theory emphasized the need for the therapist to provide unconditional positive regard and empathy along with accessible and transparent presence within the therapeutic relationship (Rogers, 1967). While known mostly for his psychotherapy with adults, Carl Rogers' early career included work with the Child Study Department of the Society for Prevention of Cruelty to Children in Rochester, New York and later published a book, *The Clinical Treatment of the Problem Child* which supported using a non-directive approach with children in therapy (J. A. Courtney, 2020a). Carl Rogers had a devoted student named Virginia Axline who incorporated Rogers' person-centered therapy with children calling her work non-directive play therapy (Landreth & Sweeney, 2009; Rasmussen & Cunningham, 1995). From there, the foundation for the field of play therapy was laid. Otto Rank's break from traditional psychoanalysis, to focus on the relationship between client and clinician, was the basis for what would later be known as child-centered play therapy.

Erik Erikson's Emphasis on Human Development

Erik Erikson's career began as an art teacher at a progressive school for children founded in Vienna where his natural abilities with children so impressed Anna Freud that she urged him to study psychoanalysis (Cherry, 2020). He accepted her recommendation and went on to formally study psychoanalysis, later opening his own practice treating child patients while also teaching at the university level. His first book called *Childhood and Society* was published in 1950, and it was this book that established the core of his life's work that addressed childhood development and the influence of historical and cultural context. It was this book that introduced the interdependence of somatic and ego processes within a social context (Stevens, 2009). Erikson's theory of psychosocial development is based on the the *epigenetic principle*, which says that humans develop in a sequential pattern (Flanders, 2020). His theory suggests that people go through eight sequential stages during which a common crisis is experienced. At each psychological stage, people face these crises that require resolution so that success can be achieved in experiencing the optimal psychological quality of each stage (Cherry, 2020; Erikson, 1959). Erikson's emphasis on the influence of history and culture on one's development is a noteworthy contribution to the field of psychology (Douvan, 1997).

In Erikson's book *Toys & Reasons* (1977) he writes about children's play as an attempt to find symbolic solutions rather than only an expression of the child's challenges and problems. Erikson saw play as a vehicle through which children could create models of real-life experiences from the past, present, and those anticipated in the future (Stor, 1977). Erikson (1977) highlighted the idea that creative expression and problem resolution are two major functions of play involving both cognitive and affective processes. The integration of Erikson's psychosocial stage theory into play therapy makes it possible for therapists to develop treatment plans that include prescriptively chosen directive play-based interventions that are age and developmentally appropriate for child clients (Russ, 2003). Erikson's developmental stages are closely tied to each individual client's life experience as expressed through the play that represents the client's narrative (Turns & Kimmes, 2014). Erikson's theory has gone on to serve as a bedrock for undergraduate and graduate psychology programs throughout the world. His contribution to the field of psychology undoubtedly influenced the evolution of perspectives within the field of play therapy as clinicians give consideration to the developmental status of child clients in case conceptualization and treatment planning.

Beyond Psychoanalysis: The Emergence of Play Therapy as a Field

At the time psychoanalysis was developing a focus on treating children in the early 20th century, the construct of child guidance was also beginning to develop in the United States. A number of child guidance clinics were opening in the 1920s in various locations. The first child guidance clinic was established by neurologist William Healy (Ashby & Horn, 1990). By 1928, child guidance was growing rapidly, extending to all children, not only those seen as delinquent, with an emphasis on early intervention as preventative for greater mental health problems (Thom, 1928). Rogerson (1939) wrote about play therapy being a means not only to treat a child but also to better understand the child's problems.

There emerged a new parent education movement with a focus on the need for adjustment and mental hygiene (Grant, 1998). With the growth of the child guidance and parent education movements came a branching off from psychoanalysis and ultimately the significant emergence of an entire field devoted to play therapy.

Directive Play Therapy: A Structured Approach

David Levy served as director of research at the Institute for Child Guidance where he introduced an approach he called *release therapy* involving directive play scenarios to facilitate expression and release of unpleasant and hostile feelings. He believed that once these emotions were released, children's presenting symptoms resolved and dissipated (Levy, 1938). From Levy's work there emerged a number of notable child guidance clinicians who experimented with various ways to use play-based techniques with children over the following decade. In the early 1950s, Gove Hambridge expanded upon Levy's release therapy technique believing a relationship between the child and therapist must first be established before the presenting problem could be addressed. Hambridge named this technique structured play therapy (Johnson, 2015).

While Levy was conducting research using release therapy, Mary Cover Jones was using a behavioral therapeutic approach with children to help unlearn fears (Jones, 1924), which led to the work of Joseph Wolpe, founder of behavior therapy in the 1950s and 1960s (Wolpe, 1958; Wolpe, 1969). There was an upswell of behavioral theory focus in the field of psychology in the 1950s and 1960s and from there came the beginnings of what we now know as cognitive behavioral therapy. According to Watts and Critelli (1997), Adler's theories had a major influence on contemporary cognitive theories. Adler's assertion that perceptions and beliefs shape an individual's experience (Adler, 1924) combined with Albert Ellis' theory of rational emotive behavior therapy (Ellis, 1962) and Aaron T. Beck's cognitive therapy (Beck, 1964) have resulted in what we know today as cognitive behavioral therapy (Mosak & Maniacci, 1999). Cognitive behavioral therapy eventually became known not only as a therapy in-and-of itself but also an umbrella category for all cognitive behavioral-based therapies (Guadiano, 2008). In the 1990s, Susan Knell merged cognitive behavioral therapy with the tenets of play therapy to create cognitive behavioral play therapy. This modality, which blends the need for therapeutic relationship and the directive introduction of specific interventions, considers age and development when choosing specific interventions to address thoughts, beliefs, and behaviors. She introduced play-based activities to adapt to traditional cognitive behavioral interventions such as positive reinforcement, behavioral shaping, and systematic desensitization (Knell, 2004). Shelby and Campos (2011) went on to study the application of cognitive behavioral therapy with traumatized children specifically. Cognitive behavioral play therapy theory has greatly influenced the work of many play therapists as it is rooted in evidence-based, peer-reviewed research establishing efficacy when treating anxiety disorders and trauma.

Creative, expressive, and narrative interventions are forms of directive therapy that fall under the umbrella of play therapy. Ann Cattanach (2008) Angela Cavett (2018), and Mills and Crowley (2014) have all written about the use of narrative within play therapy. Janet Courtney's FirstPlay Kinesthetic Storytelling is integrated with numerous other expressive play-based therapies directed by the therapist to facilitate therapeutic experiences for children and families (J. A. Courtney, 2020a).

In a directive play therapy, the therapist fundamentally holds the answers, knowing what is needed and serves as a guide and teacher based upon a connected therapeutic relationship. Within therapy sessions, the clinician introduces purposeful play-based interventions in a way that is generally invitational with genuine enthusiasm. The level of direction may vary. A therapist might be lightly suggestive of a particular direction or sometimes there may be a much more structured approach to introducing a specific activity. Directive play therapy should ideally be based upon the goals and objectives of the treatment plan and an ability to explain which of therapeutic powers of play and core agents of change are the focus of the interventions (Schaefer & Drewes, 2014).

Non-directive Play Therapy: A Humanistic Approach

From the theoretical branching of Otto Rank to Jessie Taft and then from Carl Rogers to Virginia Axline, the birth of non-directive play therapy was born. Having learned from her teacher Carl Rogers, Virginia Axline adopted person-centered therapy and applied those tenets to working with children. With her publication of two books, *Play Therapy: The Inner Dynamics of Childhood* (1947) and *Dibs: In Search of Self* (1964), the foundation for the field of play therapy as it is taught in most university training programs today was laid. Axline's eight guiding principles for the therapist providing play therapy are the core for her theory in practice (*see* Table 1.2).

Axline's model was further expanded by Haim Ginott who conducted nondirective play therapy with groups. He discovered that group play therapy provided an opportunity for social engagement and exploration that are not possible with individual play therapy. Ginott renamed Axline's theory *child-centered play therapy* (Ginott, 1961).

Clark Moustakas, a student of Virginia Axline, developed variations of *relationship therapy* (Moustakas 1959; Moustakas & Schalock, 1955; Moustakas, 1997) and was responsible for much of the earliest research into the outcomes of play therapy (Landreth, 2012). Moustakas found in his work with children that it was the playful relationship and interactions between child and therapist that most vitally contributed to positive change (Moustakas, 1997).

Table 1.2 Virginia Axline's Eight Basic Principles. An eight row chart listing Axline's eight basic principles: the therapist 1) must develop a warm and friendly relationship, 2) accepts the child as they are, 3) establishes a feeling of freedom to express, 4) recognizes and reflects the expressed feelings, 5) maintains a deep respect for the child's ability to solve their problems and opportunity to do so, 6) does not direct, 7) does not rush, 8) establishes limits only to anchor work to reality and have awareness of responsibility in the relationship

1. Therapist must develop a warm and friendly relationship with the child.
2. Therapist accepts the child as they are.
3. Therapist Establishes a feeling of permission in the relationship so that the child feels free to express his or her feelings completely.
4. Therapist recognizes the feelings the child is expressing and reflects these feelings back so that the child gains insight into their behavior.
5. Therapist maintains a deep respect for the child's ability to solve his/her problems and gives the child the opportunity to do so. The child can take responsibility for making choices.
6. Therapist does not attempt to direct the child's actions or conversations in any manner. The child leads and the therapist follows.
7. Therapist does not rush the therapy process, recognizing it is a gradual process.
8. Only establishes those limitations necessary to anchor the therapy to the world of reality and to make the child aware of his/her responsibility in the relationship.

Adapted from Axline, V. M. (1969). *Play therapy*. Ballantine Books.

Garry Landreth founded the Center for Play Therapy at the University of North Texas in 1988 and began a long and rich career of practicing, writing, and teaching about child-centered play therapy. Landreth (2012) wrote about how child-centered play therapy is an entire system based on an integral belief that a child has the ability to manifest their own healing and growth without direction (p. 53). Non-directive play therapy operates from the belief that the child holds the answers for what they most need. This model provides a child an emotionally safe space to explore, express, and experience whatever the child needs with the therapist serving as an attentive, accepting witness providing expressive reflection and tracking. Verbal reflection and tracking of the child's expressions and choices within the play provides the child an experience of feeling heard, seen, and accepted just as they are. This experience in itself gives the child what is needed to form trust for the therapist and a solid foundation of rapport. When a clinician uses the purest form of non-directive play therapy, the use of a goal directed treatment plan may be seen as contradicting the theory that believes children are capable of positive and healthy growth without direction when the proper conditions are provided.

Prescriptive Play Therapy

Many transtheoretical models blend and bridge non-directive play therapy and directive play therapy with common agreement that the relationship between the child and therapist is paramount to the efficacy of the play therapy. In 1997, the *prescriptive play therapy* model was first introduced in a book called *The Playing Cure: Individualized Play Therapy for Specific Childhood Disorders* (Kaduson & Cangelosi, 1997; Kaduson et al., 2020). Prescriptive play therapy is a therapeutic approach that calls for the use of theories and techniques in a way that tailors the play therapy treatment plan to the particular needs of the individual client (Schaefer, 2001). The focus of this model is to address and resolve the specific presenting problem that brings a client into therapy (Wonders, 2020). Prescriptive play therapy calls upon the clinician to establish a goal directed treatment plan after a thorough intake, assessment, and case conceptualization process that is customized to the individual client (O'Connor et al., 2016). Stone (2020) writes about the need for clinicians to have highly developed clinical skills in order to be capable of integrating theories and applying the various principles of prescriptive play therapy effectively and successfully to a treatment plan.

Prior to the introduction and adoption of the prescriptive play therapy approach, there was an assumption that unless there was evidence to the contrary, one's chosen theoretical model was applicable and effective with most, if not all, clients (O'Connor et al., 2016). On the contrary, prescriptive play therapy purports that differing theoretical applications will be most applicable and effective with differing sets of presenting issues and differing diagnoses. A prescriptive clinician will purposefully and consciously shift theoretically in order to meet the individual client's needs and develop a customized plan for treatment accordingly (Kaduson et al., 2020).

In some ways it would seem that Adlerian play therapy is a prescriptive play therapy model in that there is room for the therapist to have flexibility with treatment planning and manner of offering interventions. The four phases of the Adlerian Play Therapy model begin with a child-centered approach and then shift to more directive play therapy interventions after rapport and client-therapist connection is well established (Kottman & Ashby, 1999).

The ecosystemic clinical child psychology play therapy model is also prescriptive, in that it is a meta-theoretical and integrative model (O'Connor & Vega, 2019). This model asserts that the therapist has an obligation to be prepared to shift along with a child's rapidly changing developmental needs and the complexity of the respective family and social systems in which the child is embedded (O'Connor, 2016). Ecosystemic play therapy "addresses the total child within the context of the child's ecosystem" (O'Connor, 2000, p. 87). This calls upon the therapist to view and approach each client as a unique amalgam, influenced and shaped by their unique ecosystem.

The tenets of non-directive play therapy that emphasize relationship, rapport, respect, and acceptance are foundational tenets for all play therapy. The practices of child-centered tracking, reflecting, returning responsibility, as well as the practice of simply holding space for the child's free expression of thoughts and feelings can be maintained even within the most directive approach to play therapy (Wonders, 2019).

Family and Parent–Child Relationships in Play Therapy

There was a significant rise of social work and family systems theory in the 1950s and 1960s bringing more attention to the quality of the relationship between parents and children (Wood, 2001). In time, consideration of the family system as context became a significantly important focus in the evolution of understanding how to best treat children using play therapy.

Murray Bowen's family systems theory was one of the first and most prominent theories to influence the field of psychology in the 1950s. His theory was based on the idea that families have patterns which indicate levels of anxiety directly related to degrees of closeness and distance between family members (Brown, 1999). He believed that in order to reduce the anxiety within the family system the therapist had to help the family members see themselves as differentiated from other family members. He also asserted that family members must experience an increase in awareness of the function of the emotions expressed within the family (Brown, 1999). One of Murray's greatest contributions was the genogram, which provided a family-tree-like diagram to help clinicians design a visual representation of the family's immediate and extended dynamics. The genogram is also useful in helping family members have increased awareness of their own system. This tool is often used by clinicians providing play therapy services in the initial intake session and the process of case conceptualization to aid in assisting child clients and their families.

Virgina Satir asserted that if one family member is painfully struggling, then all family members are, in some way, also in pain. Satir showed that through Conjoint Family Therapy, all family members can find ways to have their own needs met and thereby improve family functioning at the same time, as well as experience reduction of pain. Satir emphasized that nonverbal communication carries great weight and therefore developed particular techniques such as *family sculpting*, where each member's perspective of the family dynamic could be shown in the therapy session without using words (Satir, 1967; Kaslow, 2012). Minuchin et al. (1967) studied the subsystems within a family and specifically gave consideration to the continuum of disengagement and enmeshment, seeing the therapist as the expert needing to intervene directly to interrupt unhealthy patterns observed. Carl Whitaker, one of the pioneers of family play therapy, was a staunch advocate for including children within the process of family therapy (Gil Institute, n.d.). Eliana Gil wrote about the use of play within family therapy to provide opportunity for young children to have voice within the family system while also recognizing play as a healing agent for the entire family; helping lower defenses and contributing to stronger bonds (Gil, 2016).

With the increased focus on family systems in the 1960s, child therapy clinicians saw a need to help strengthen the parent–child relationships. Bernard and Louise Guerney developed Filial Therapy in response to this identified need (Guerney, 1964; Hutton, 2004). The Guerneys observed that often undesirable behavior on the part of parents had to do with a lack of parenting skills rather than elements of psychopathology. Observing that child-centered play therapy was effective when parents were supportive of the therapeutic process, it appeared to be a logical next step to provide training for parents in how to utilize child-centered play therapy skills with their own children (Vanfleet & Topham, 2016). In 2002, Garry Landreth developed Child Parent Relationship Therapy, a form of Filial Therapy (Bratton & Landreth, 2006; Duffy, 2008; Lindo et al., 2016,)

Kevin O'Connor's introduction of ecosystemic play therapy in 1991 as a theoretically integrative model carefully considers the entire family and social context in which a child is embedded, particularly in the initial case conceptualization process (O'Connor, 2001). Ecosystemic play therapy takes into consideration a child's developmental level at every stage of the treatment process adapting the treatment plan accordingly. This model calls upon the therapist to be prepared to shift along with the rapidly developing needs of children influenced by their complex systemic dynamics. In ecosystemic play therapy, the therapist works with various members of the child's family and social systems often serving as advocate for the child as well as therapist for the child in the playroom (O'Connor, 2016).

The focus on parent–child attachment and object relations originating from the work of Melanie Klein was later demonstrated in the works of John Bowlby and Donald Winnicott, which in turn influenced Ann Jernberg and Phyllis Booth (who created Theraplay®) (O'Connor et al., 2016). In the process of developing Theraplay®, Jernberg and Booth also borrowed and adapted the developmental work of Austin Des Lauriers and Viola Brody that focused on the intuitive, nurturing element of touch within the therapeutic experience and relationship (Jernberg & Booth, 2001). Theraplay® is a play-based, directive treatment model that attends to the quality of the attachment between parents and children and provides experiences of connecting interactions for children and parents that are facilitated by the therapist (Jernberg & Booth, 2001). Theraplay® provides opportunity for repair and healing to ruptured parent–child bonds and has been proven effective with attachment disorders (Korkeaoja & Niemi, 2012).

Developmental play therapy provides various experiential activities designed to simulate attachment connections with others, as evidenced by the aforementioned work of Viola Brody who emphasized the use of nurturing touch within the therapeutic process (Courtney, 2006). Janet Courtney (2020b) has published research and provided clinical training that carries this developmentally based work of Viola Brody forward with a model called FirstPlay® Therapy. The FirstPlay® Therapy model equips trained therapists to teach parents how to use pre-symbolic interactive play and nurturing touch to create secure attachment and enhance healthy brain development for infants.

Current and Future Trends in Play Therapy

There has recently been a strong trend in the field of play therapy wherein many child therapists are moving away from single model theoretical orientation toward integrating theoretical models (Drewes, 2011). With Schaefer and Drewes (2014) bringing forward the concept of the therapeutic powers of play in a context of an integrative and prescriptive approach to play therapy, many therapists are receiving training in trans-theoretical methods. While a therapist's theoretical orientation serves as the framework for the therapeutic process, the treatment planning, establishing of goals, and informing case conceptualization (John & Segal, 2015), it can be argued that in order to meet the specific needs of individual clients a therapist will find benefit in having a broader theoretical basis.

Today we are seeing more emphasis on understanding neuroscience and brain development with special consideration of how a child's brain is influenced and shaped by the quality of familial and social connections. The empathic presence of the therapist with a child client in conjunction with the pleasurable experience of play creates new neural pathways (Stewart et al., 2016). The repetition and ritual of play therapy within the emotional safety with the trained therapist brings calm to the child's unconscious arousal system (Gaskill, 2019). The experience of the therapist engaging and attuning with the child in play therapy provides the most essential agent for change from a neuroscience perspective (Gaskill & Perry, 2017). Hong and Mason (2016) write about how most all that happens with the process of play therapy is affecting the neurobiology of a child, and play therapists can be assured that the work of play therapy and neurobiology are indeed intertwined. As the field of play therapy continues to expand, clinicians will be learning more and more about neuroscience and how the child's rapidly developing brain is significantly influenced by the experiences had in the play therapy room.

With the necessity of the use of telemental health that began in 2020, child and family therapists who provide play therapy services have been required to learn how to broaden and deepen the means and ways of attuning, connecting, and maintaining connection with clients while providing therapeutic benefits of distance play therapy and family support services. Whereas technology was for a long time rejected as having a place in play therapy sessions, the necessity of embracing technology during the pandemic of 2020 has called the field of play therapy to stretch. The fact of the matter is that the children today have been born into this digital age (Prensky, 2001; Prensky 2012; Stephen, 2020). Clinicians providing play therapy services need to become familiar with the ways children's lives today are tied to technology and how to utilize technology with the play therapy experience (Hull, 2016). The field of play therapy is rapidly shifting to see and celebrate ways to utilize technology therapeutically while staying true to the roots of the theories that inform the work we do (Perry, 1999; Snow et al., 2009). In her book *Digital Play Therapy,* Stone (2020) cites evidence of the shared experience of technology use in relationships as beneficial, and she goes on to discuss the need for people to learn how to find balance with regard to technology use; suggesting that mental health professionals have an opportunity to assist families in striving for that sense of balance. In an evolving society that is so heavily reliant on technology, it is imperative that there be an effort made to learn how to most effectively utilize technology to best help the clients served.

Currently, there is discussion in the field of psychology and research about a potential shift in the conceptualization of mental health pathology. Researchers are questioning the traditional approach as being insufficient and are seeking a bottom-up approach to discover more, as opposed to the traditional top-down approach used in psychology. The result of these proposed shifts could be a collection of new conceptualizations and approaches to a variety of diagnoses and treatments (Michelini et al., 2020; Ross & Margolis, 2019). It will continue to be important for therapists to stay abreast of these significant shifts in thought with regard to the field's views of mental health and pathology, especially with regard to children and families.

Conclusion

In order for clinicians to provide ethical and effective play therapy services for children and their families with rapidly changing societal needs, it is essential that there be a deep and wide understanding of the theoretical underpinnings for all of play therapy. Understanding the rich history of how, when, and where play therapy first began, as well as having familiarity with the evolution of theories and practice, will be important for clinicians to be able to appreciate and justify their chosen approach and clinical interventions for the treatment of child clients and their families. In order to fully embrace the process of case conceptualization and treatment planning that will be addressed in the next chapter, clinicians must first feel firmly rooted in historical theory.

References

Adler, A. (1924). *The practice and theory of individual psychology*. Harcourt Brace.

Ariès, P. (1962). *Centuries of childhood; a social history of family life*. Knopf.

Ashby, L., & Horn, M. (1990). Before it's too late: The child guidance movement in the United States, 1922-1945. *The Journal of American History*, 77(2), 713. https://doi.org/10.2307/2079299

Axline, V. M. (1969). *Play therapy*. Ballantine Books.

Baker, D. B. (1988). The psychology of Lightner Witmer. *Professional School Psychology*, 3(2), 109–121.

Basden, G. T. (1966). *Among the Ibos of Nigeria: an account of the curious and interesting habits, customs and beliefs of a little known African people by one who has for many years lived amongst them on close and intimate terms*. https://ehrafworldcultures.yale.edu/document?id=ff26-006

Beaumont, L. (1994). Child's play in classical Athens. *History Today*, 44(8), 30–36.

Beck, A. T. (1964). Thinking and depression: Theory and therapy. *Archives of General Psychiatry*, 10, 561–571.

Bornstein, M. H., Putnick, D. L., & Lansford, J. E. (2011). Parenting attributions and attitudes in cross-cultural perspective. *Parenting*, 11(2–3), 214–237. https://doi.org/10.1080/15295192.2011.585568

Bratton, S., Ray, D., & Rhine, T. (2005). The efficacy of play therapy with children: A meta-analytic review of treatment outcomes. *Journal of Professional Psychology Research and Practice*, 36(4), 376–390.

Bratton, S. C., & Landreth, G. L. (2006). *Child parent relationship therapy (CPRT) treatment manual: A 10-session filial therapy model for training parents*. Routledge.

Brodie, B. (1998). Historical overview of health promotion for children and families in late 19th- and 20th-century America. In M. E. Broome, K. Knafl, & K. Pridham (Eds.), *Children and families in health and illness* (pp. 3–14). SAGE Publications, Inc. https://www.doi.org/10.4135/9781452243313.n1

Brown, J. (1999). Bowen family systems theory and practice: Illustration and critique. *Australian and New Zealand Journal of Family Therapy*, 20(2), 94–103. http://doi.org/10.1002/j.1467-8438.1999.tb00363.x

Cattanach, A. (2008). *Narrative approaches in play with children*. Jessica Kingsley Publishers.

Cavett, A. (2018, May 3–4). *Play therapy with children impacted by trauma: Facilitating healing through narrative* [Paper presentation]. North Dakota Psychological Association Conference, West Fargo, North Dakota.

Cherry, K. (2020, March 20). How Erik Erikson's own identity crisis shaped his theories. *Very Well Mind*. https://www.verywellmind.com/erik-erikson-biography-1902-1994-2795538

Coates, S. W. (2004). John Bowlby and Margaret S. Mahler: Their lives and theories. *Journal of the American Psychoanalytic Association*, *52*(2), 571–601. http://doi.org/10.1177/00030651040520020601

Courtney, J. A. (2006). *Assessing practitioner experiences of developmental play therapy* [Doctoral dissertation, Barry University School of Social Work]. ProQuest. https://search.proquest.com/openview/2404372e85ad800a56c27c84ad0466ab/1?pq-origsite=gscholar&cbl=18750&diss=y

Courtney, J. A. (2020a). *Healing child and family trauma through expressive and play therapies: Art, nature, storytelling, body & mindfulness*. W.W. Norton & Company.

Courtney, J. (Ed.). (2020b). *Infant play therapy*. Routledge. https://doi.org/10.4324/9780429453083

D'Angelo, E. J., & Koocher, G. P. (2011). Psychotherapy patients: Children. In J. C. Norcross, G. R. VandenBos, & D. K. Freedheim (Eds.), *History of psychotherapy: Continuity and change* (pp. 430–448). American Psychological Association.

Dentan, R. K. (1978). Notes on childhood in a nonviolent context: The Semai case. In A. Montagu (Ed.), *Learning non-aggression* (pp. 94–143). Oxford University Press.

Donaldson, G. (1996). Between practice and theory: Melanie Klein, Anna Freud and the development of child analysis. *Journal of History and Behavioral Science*, *32*(2), 160–176. https://doi.org/10.1002/(SICI)1520-6696(199604)32:2<160::AID-JHBS4>3.0.CO;2-#

Donn, L. (2011). *Freud and Jung: Years of friendship, years of loss*. CreateSpace.

Douvan, E. (1997). Erik Erikson: Critical times, critical theory. *Child Psychiatry and Human Development*, *28*, 15–21.

Dreikurs, R. M. D., & Soltz, V. R. N. (1992). *Children: The challenge*. Penguin Group.

Drewes, A. A. (2011). *Integrative play therapy*. Germany: Wiley.

Duffy, K. (2008). *Filial therapy: A comparison of child-parent relationship therapy and parent-child interaction therapy* [Doctoral dissertation, Ball State University]. Cardinal Scholar BSU. https://cardinalscholar.bsu.edu/handle/123456789/193381

Eddins-Folensbee, F. F. (2001). Theraplay: Innovations in attachment-enhancing play therapy. *Journal of the American Academy of Child & Adolescent Psychiatry*, *40*(8), 984–986. http://doi.org/10.1097/00004583-200108000-00025

Edgcumbe R. (2000). *Anna Freud*. Routledge.

Ellis, A. (1962). *Reason and emotion in psychotherapy*. Carol Publishing Corporation.

Erikson, E. H. (1959). Identity and the life cycle: Selected papers. *Psychological Issues*, *1*, 1–171.

Erikson, E. H. (1977). *Toys and reasons: Stages in the ritualization of experience*. WW Norton & Company.

Flanders, W. (2020, September 25). Epigenetic principle - Personality. *Flanders Health*. https://www.flandershealth.us/personality-2/epigenetic-principle.html#:~:text=Erikson

Freud, A. (1937). *The ego and the mechanisms of defence*. L. and Virginia Woolf at the Hogarth Press, and the Institute of Psycho-Analysis.

Freud, S., Strachey, J., & Freud, A. (1955). *The standard edition of the complete psychological works of Sigmund Freud*. London: Hogarth Press and the Institute of Psycho-Analysis.

Friedman, H. S., & Mitchell, R. R. (2002). *Sandplay: Past, present and future*. Taylor and Francis.

Fritscher, L. (2019, August 13). How the relationship with our mothers affects relations with others. *Very Well Mind*. https://www.verywellmind.com/what-is-object-relations-theory-2671995

Gaskill, R. (2019, September) Neuroscience helps play therapists go low so children can aim high. *Play Therapy* (pp. 8–10).

Gaskill, R. L., & Perry, B. D. (2017). The neurobiological power of play: Using the neurosequential model of therapeutics to guide play in the healing process. In C. A. Malchiodi & D. A. Crenshaw (Eds.), *Creative arts and play therapy for attachment problems* (pp. 178–196). Guilford Press.

Geissmann, C., & Geissmann, P. (1998). *A history of child psychoanalysis*. Routledge.

Gil Institute. (n.d.). Family therapy (and family play therapy) http://www.gilinstitute.com/services/formats/family.php

Gil, E. (2016). *Play in family therapy*. The Guilford Press.

Ginott, H. (1961). *Group psychotherapy with children: The theory and practice of play therapy*. Jason Aronson.

Grant, J. (1998). *Raising baby by the book: The education of American mothers*. Yale University Press.

Green, E. J. (2014). *The handbook of Jungian play therapy with children and adolescents*. JHU Press.

Guadiano, B. (2008). Cognitive-behavioral therapies: Achievements and challenges. *Evidence Based Mental Health*, 11(1), 5–7.

Guerney, B., Jr. (1964). Filial therapy: Description and rationale. *Journal of Consulting Psychology*, 28(4), 304–310. https://doi.org/10.1037/h0041340

Harris, P. (2014). *An analysis of Melanie Klein's The Psychoanalysis of Children*. University of Machester.

Heywood, C. (2018). *A history of childhood*. Polity.

Hoffman L. (2017). Un homme manque: Freud's engagement with Alfred Adler's masculine protest: Commentary on Balsam. *Journal of the American Psychoanalytic Association. 2017*, 65(1), 99–108. http://doi.org/10.1177/0003065117690351

Hoffman, L. (2020). How can I help you? Dimensional versus categorical distinctions in the assessment for child analysis and child psychotherapy. *Journal of Infant, Child & Adolescent Psychotherapy*, 19(1), pp. 1–15. https://doi.org/10.1080/15289168.2019.1701866

Holder, A. (2018). *Anna Freud, Melanie Klein, and the psychoanalysis of children and adolescents*. Routledge.

Hong, R., & Mason, C. M. (2016). Becoming a neurobiologically-informed play therapist. *International Journal of Play Therapy*, 25(1), 35–44. https://doi.org/10.1037/pla0000020

Hug-Hellmuth, H. (1913). *A study of the mental health of a child*. Nervous & Mental Disease Publishing Company.

Hull, K. (2016). Technology in the playroom. In K. J. O'Connor, C. E. Schaefer, & L. D. Braverman (Eds.), *Handbook of play therapy* (pp. 613–627). John Wiley & Sons Inc.

Hutton, D. (2004). Filial therapy: Shifting the balance. *Clinical Child Psychology and Psychiatry*, 9(2), 261–270. https://doi.org/10.1177/1359104504041922

Jernberg, A., & Booth, P. B. (2001). *Theraplay®: Helping parents and children build better relationships through attachment-based play* (2nd ed.). Jossey-Bass.

John, S., & Segal, D. L. (2015). Case conceptualization. In R. L. Cautin, & S. O. Lilienfeld (Eds.), *The Encyclopedia of Clinical Psychology* (pp. 1–4). Wiley. https://doi.org/10.1002/9781118625392.wbecp106

Johnson, J. (2015). The history of play therapy. In K. J. O'Connor, C. E. Schaefer, & L. D. Braverman (Eds.), *Handbook of play therapy* (pp. 17–30). John Wiley & Sons.

Jones, M. C. (1924). The elimination of children's fears. *Journal of Experimental Psychology*, 7(5), 382–390. https://doi.org/10.1037/h0072283

Jung, C. G. (1964). *Man and his symbols*. Dell.

Kaduson, H., & Cangelosi, D. M. (1997). *The playing cure: Individualized play therapy for specific childhood problems*. Jason Aronson.

Kaduson, H. (2015). Play therapy across the life span: Infants, children, adolescents, and adults. In K. J. O'Connor, C. E. Schaefer, & L. D. Braverman (Eds.) (2016), *Handbook of play therapy* (pp. 327–340). John Wiley & Sons.

Kaduson, H., Cangelosi, D. M., & Schaefer, C. E. (2020). Basic principles and core practices of prescriptive play therapy. In H. Kaduson, D. M. Cangelosi, & C. E. Schaefer (Eds.), *Prescriptive play therapy: Tailoring interventions for specific childhood problems* (pp. 3–13). The Guilford Press.

Kalff, D. M. (2003). *Sandplay: A psychotherapeutic approach to the psyche*. Temenos Press.

Karpiak, C. P., Norcross, J. C., & Wedding, D. (2016). Evolution of theory in clinical psychology. In J. C. Norcross, G. R. VandenBos, D. K. Freedheim, & B. O. Olatunji (Eds.), *APA handbooks in psychology®. APA handbook of clinical psychology: Theory and research* (pp. 3–17). American Psychological Association.

Kaslow, F. W. (2012). Appendix D: A brief history of the field of family psychology and therapy. In F. Shapiro, F. W. Kaslow, & L. Maxfield (Eds.), *Handbook of EMDR and family therapy processes* (pp. 438–454). http://doi.org/10.1002/9781118269985.app4

Klein, M. (1932). *The psychoanalysis of children. (The international psycho-analytical library, No. 22.)*. Hogarth.

Knell, S. M. (2004). *Cognitive-behavioral play therapy*. Rowman & Littlefield.

Korkeaoja, P., & Niemi, R. (2012). Treating a reactive attachment disorder with Theraplay therapy. *PsycEXTRA Dataset*. http://doi.org/10.1037/e579192013-204

Kottman, T. (2001). Adlerian play therapy. *International Journal of Play Therapy*, 10(2), 1–12. https://doi.org/10.1037/h0089476

Kottman, T., & Ashby, J. (1999). Using Adlerian personality priorities to custom-design consultation with parents of play therapy clients. *International Journal of Play Therapy*, 8(2), 77–92. http://doi.org/10.1037/h0089432

Kottman, T., & Ashby, J. S.(2015). Adlerian play therapy. In D. A. Crenshaw, & Stewart, A.L. (Eds.), *Play therapy: A comprehensive guide to theory and practice* (pp. 42–47). The Guilford Press.

Kottman, T., & Meany-Walen, K. (2016). *Partners in play: An Adlerian approach to play therapy* (3rd ed.). American Counseling Association.

Kramer, R. (2019). *The birth of relationship therapy: Carl Rogers meets Otto Rank*. Psychosozial-Verlag. https://doi.org/10.30820/9783837974690

Lancy, D. F. (2017). *Raising children: Surprising insights from other cultures*. Cambridge University Press.

Landreth, G., & Sweeney, D. (2009). Child centered play therapy. In K. J. O'Connor, & L. D. Braverman (Eds.), *Play therapy theory and practice: comparing theories and techniques* (pp. 17–21). John Wiley & Sons.

Landreth, G. L. (2012). *Play therapy: The art of the relationship* (3rd ed.). Taylor & Francis.

Leblanc, M., & Ritchie, M. (2001). A meta-analysis of play therapy outcomes. *Counselling Psychology Quarterly*, 14(2), 149–163. https://doi.org/10.1080/09515 070110059142

Lenormand, M. (2012). Hug-Hellmuth or the impasses of an objectifying conception of the infantile. *Recherches en Psychanalyse*, *13*(1), 74–86. https://doi.org/10.3917/rep.013.0074

Levy, D. M. (1938). "Release Therapy" in young children. *Psychiatry*, *1*(3), 387–390. http://doi.org/10.1080/00332747.1938.11022205

Lilly, J. & Heiko, R. (2019, September). Jungian analytical play therapy. *Play Therapy*, *14*(3), 40–42.

Lin, Y., & Bratton, S. C. (2015). A meta-analytic review of child-centered play therapy approaches. *Journal of Counseling & Development*, *93*(1), 45–58. doi: 10.1002/j.1556-6676.2015.00180.x

Lindo, N. A., Bratton, S. C., & Landreth, G. L. (2016). Child parent relationship therapy: Theory, research and intervention process. In L. A. Reddy, T. M. Files-Hall, & C. E. Schaefer (Eds.), *Empirically based play interventions for children* (pp. 241–261). American Psychological Association. https://doi.org/10.1037/14730-013

Lowenfeld, M. (1935). *Play in childhood*. V. Gollansz.

Mahler, M., (1952). On child psychoses and schizophrenia: autistic and symbiotic infantile psychoses. *Psychoanalytic Study of the Child*, 7, 288–305.

Mannoni, M. (1970). *The child, his "illness," and the others*. New York, NY: Pantheon Books.

Michelini, G., Palumbo, I. M., DeYoung, C. G., Latzman, R., & Kotov, R. (2020). Linking RDoC and HiTOP: A new interface for advancing psychiatric nosology and neuroscience. https://doi.org/10.31234/osf.io/ps7tc

Mills, J., & Crowley, R. (2014). *Therapeutic metaphors for children and the child within* (2nd ed). Routledge.

Minuchin, S., Montalvo, B., Guerney, B. G., Jr., Rosman, B., & Schumer, F. (1967). *Families of the slums*. Basic Books

Mintz, S. (2006). *Hucks raft: A history of American childhood*. Cambridge: Belknap Press of Harvard University Press.

Mosak, H., & Maniacci, M.(1999). *Primer of Adlerian psychology: The analytic – behavioural - cognitive psychology of Alfred Adler* (1st ed.). Routledge. https://doi.org/10.4324/9780203768518

Moustakas, C. E., & Schalock, H. D. (1955). An analysis of therapist-child interaction in play therapy. *Child Development*, *26*(2), 143. https://doi.org/10.2307/1126296

Moustakas, C. E. (1959). *Psychotherapy with children: The living relationship*. Harper.

Moustakas, C. E. (1997). *Relationship play therapy*. Rowman & Littlefield.

O'Connor, K. J. (2000). *The play therapy primer*. Wiley.

O'Connor, K. (2001). Ecosystemic play therapy. *International Journal of Play Therapy*, *10*(2), 33–44. https://doi.org/10.1037/h0089478

O'Connor, K. (2016). Ecosystemic play therapy. In *Handbook of play therapy* (pp. 195–223). John Wiley & Sons.

O'Connor, K. J., Schaefer, C. E., & Braverman, L. D. (2016). *Handbook of play therapy*. John Wiley & Sons.

O'Connor, K. & Vega, C. (2019). Ecosystemic play therapy. *Play Therapy*, *14*(3), 32–34.

Olson-Morrison, D. (2017). Integrative play therapy with adults with complex trauma: A developmentally-informed approach. *International Journal of Play Therapy*, *26*(3), 172–183

Parry-Jones W. L. (1989). Annotation. The history of child and adolescent psychiatry: its present day relevance. *Journal of Child Psychology and Psychiatry*, *30*, 3–11.

Perry, B. D. (1999, March). The effects of technology on the brain. *Scholastic*. https://www.scholastic.com/teachers/articles/teaching-content/effects-technology-brain

Plastow, M. (2011). Hermine Hug-Hellmuth, the first child psychoanalyst: Legacy and dilemmas. *Australasian Psychiatry*, *19*(3), 206–210. https://doi.org/10.3109/10398562.2010.526213

Prensky, M. (2001) Digital natives, digital immigrants. *On the Horizon*, *9*(5), 1–6.

Prensky, M. (2012). *From digital natives to digital wisdom: Hopeful essays for 21st century learning*. Corwin Press.

Rank, O. (1936). *Will therapy; an analysis of the therapeutic process in terms of relationship*. Knopf.

Rasmussen, L. A., & Cunningham, C. (1995). Focused play therapy and non-directive play therapy: Can they be integrated. *Journal of Child Sexual Abuse*, *4*(1), 1–20.

Ray, D. (2011). *Advanced play therapy* (1st ed.). Routledge.

Ray, D. C., Armstrong, S. A., Balkin, R. S., & Jayne, K. M. (2015). Child-centered play therapy in the schools: Review and meta-analysis. *Psychology in the Schools*, *52*(2), 107–123. https://doi.org/10.1002/pits.21798

Rey, J. M., Assumpção, F. B., Bernad, C. A., Çuhadaroğlu, F. C., Evans, B., Fung, D., Harper, G., Loidreau, L., Ono, Y., Pūras D., Remschmidt, H., Robertson, B., Rusakoskaya, O. A., & Schleimer, K. (2015). History of child and adolescent psychiatry. In J. M. Rey (Ed.), *IACAPAP e-textbook of child and adolescent mental health*. Geneva: International Association for Child and Adolescent Psychiatry and Allied Professions.

Rogers, C. R. (1967). *On becoming a person: a therapist's view of psychotherapy*. Robinson.

Rogerson, C. H. (1939). *Play therapy in childhood*. Oxford University Press.

Ross, C., & Margolis, R. (2019). Research domain criteria: Strengths, weaknesses, and potential alternatives for future psychiatric research. *Molecular Neuropsychiatry*, *5*(4), 218–236. https://doi.org/10.1159/000501797

Russ, S. W. (2003). *Play in child development and psychotherapy: Toward empirically supported practice*. Routledge.

Satir, V. (1967). *Conjoint family therapy* (2nd ed.). Science & Behavior Books.

Schaefer, C. (2001). Prescriptive play therapy. *International Journal of Play Therapy*, *10*, 57–73.

Schaefer, C. E., & Drewes, A. A. (2014). *The therapeutic powers of play: 20 core agents of change*. Wiley.

Seymour, J. W. (2016). An introduction to the field of play therapy. In K. J. O'Connor, C. E. Schaefer, & L. D. Braverman (Eds.), *Handbook of play therapy* (2nd ed., pp. 3–15). John Wiley & Sons, Incorporated.

Shelby, J., & Campos, K. G. (2011). Cognitive-behavioral play therapy for traumatized children. In A. A. Drewes, S. C. Bratton, & C. E. Schaefer (Eds.), *Integrative Play Therapy* (107–128). Wiiley. http://doi.org/10.1002/9781118094792.ch7

Silverman, M. G., & Caughey, J. L. (1980). Faanakkar: Cultural values in a micronesian society. *Man*, *15*(1), 205. https://doi.org/10.2307/2802020

Snow, M. S., Wolff, L., Hudspeth, E. F., & Etheridge, L. (2009). The practitioner as researcher: Qualitative case studies in play therapy. *International Journal of Play Therapy*, *18*(4), 240.

Stein, E. (2010). Otto Rank: pioneering ideas for social work theory and practice. *Psychoanalytic SocialWork*, *17*(2), 116131. https://www.tandfonline.com/doi/full/10.1080/15228878.2010.512535

Stephen, C. (2020). Young learners in the digital age. In L. Green, D. Holloway, K. Stevenson, T. Leaver, & L. Haddon (Eds.), *The Routledge Companion to Digital Media and Children* (pp. 57–66). Routledge. https://doi.org/10.4324/9781351004107-5

Stevens, R. (2009). *Erik H. Erikson: Explorer of identity and the life cycle*. Palgrave Macmillan.

Stewart, A. L., Field, T. A., & Echterling, L. G. (2016). Neuroscience and the magic of play therapy. *International Journal of Play Therapy*, *25*(1), 4–13. https://doi.org/10.1037/pla0000016

Stone, J. (2020). *Digital Play Therapy*. Routledge. https://doi.org/10.4324/9780429001109-4

Stor, A. (1977, April 10). The games children play. *New York Times*. The Editors of Encyclopaedia Britannica. (2020, June 11). *Erik Erikson*. https://www.britannica.com/biography/Erik-Erikson

Taft, J. (1933). *The dynamics of therapy in a controlled relationship*. Macmillan. https://doi.org/10.1037/10602-000

Terner, J. R., Pew, W. L., & Aird, R. A. (1978). *The courage to be imperfect: The life and work of Rudolf Dreikurs*.

Thom, D. (1928). Everyday problems of the everyday child. *Archives of Pediatrics & Adolescent Medicine*, *36*(1), 190. https://doi.org/10.1001/archpedi.1928.01920250201021

Turner, B. A. (2005). *The handbook of sandplay therapy*. Temenos Press.

Turns, B. A., & Kimmes, J. (2014). "I'm NOT the Problem!" Externalizing children's "Problems" using play therapy and developmental considerations. *Contemporary Family Therapy*, *36*(1), 135–147. https://doi.org/10.1007/s10591-013-9285-z

Vanfleet, R., & Topham, G. (2016). Filial therapy. In K. J. O'Connor, C. E. Schaefer, & L. D. Braverman (Eds.), *Handbook of play therapy* (pp. 135–167). John Wiley & Sons.

Viner, R. (1996). Melanie Klein and Anna Freud: The discourse of the early dispute. *Journal of the History of the Behavioral Sciences*, *32*(1), 4–15.

Watts, R. E., & Critelli, J. W. (1997). Roots of contemporary cognitive theories in the individual psychology of Alfred Adler. *Journal of Cognitive Psychotherapy*, *11*(3), 147–156. https://doi.org/10.1891/0889-8391.11.3.147

Watts, R. & Pietrzak, D. (2000). Adlerian "Encouragement" and the therapeutic process of solution-focused brief therapy. *Journal of counseling and development*, *78*, 442–447. 10.1002/j.1556-6676.2000.tb01927.x.

Wolpe, J. (1958). *Psychotherapy by reciprocal inhibition*. Stanford University Press.

Wolpe, J. (1969). *The practice of behavior therapy*. Pergamon.

Wonders, L. (2019, March 04). Resources for child centered and directive play therapy in the play room. https://wonderscounseling.com/resources-for-child-centered-and-directive-play-therapy-in-the-play-room/

Wonders, L. L. (2020). Play therapy for children with selective mutism. In H. G. Kaduson, D. Cangelosi, & C. E. Schaefer (Eds.), *Prescriptive play therapy: Tailoring interventions for specific childhood problems* (pp. 92–104). The Guilford Press.

Wood, A. (2001). The origins of family systems wok social workers contributions to the development of family theory and practice. *Australian Social Work*, *54*(3), 15–29. http://doi.org/10.1080/03124070108414329

2 Purposeful Application of Theory to Case Conceptualization and Treatment Planning

Lynn Louise Wonders

Play therapy is a form of psychotherapy based on historical theoretical models which serves to support children's mental and behavioral healing and growth through the purposeful use of play with the therapeutic relationship. In order for clinicians to provide play therapy services effectively and ethically, it is imperative that there be a substantial understanding of how seminal and historical theories are interwoven with the therapeutic powers of play, as well as applied to case formulation and treatment planning. While clinicians typically receive initial training in one or two play therapy theoretical models, it is worthwhile to dig deeper into theory itself in order to be able to understand the whole of play therapy services. Often therapists new to providing play therapy services make the error of rushing into providing treatment and interventions without first taking the time to carefully gather and consider vitally important information about the child and their familial and social systems. It is a skillful process of collecting, examining, and synthesizing a great deal of information about the client before developing an effective treatment plan. A case will be made in this chapter for utilizing *goal-directed treatment planning* while honoring the theoretical roots at the base of treatment interventions. There will be discussion of the importance of theory, and the processes of problem identification, case conceptualization, and treatment planning. This chapter will then show how therapists can be purposeful in applying theory, along with the therapeutic powers of play, to processes of case conceptualization and treatment planning in an effort to ensure the integrity of the play therapy process.

Importance of Theory

Theoretical foundation underlies the integrity of psychotherapy (Drapela, 1990) and provides therapists clarity as to what it is they are providing and the reasons therein (Norcross et al., 2013). Theories are models conceived, developed, adopted, and followed to help explain what the client is experiencing that otherwise might not be easily understood or explained

(O'Connor & Ammen, 2013). Theories enable therapists to comprehend and synthesize the experiences and expressions clients bring to therapy (Wampold, 2019). Such theories help therapists understand the actions, thoughts, and dynamics that are present within family systems so that an approach for treatment can be appropriately chosen (Drapela, 1990). Theory informs the way therapists go about understanding clients' worlds, experiences, and perspectives which helps clinicians to best understand the problems with which clients struggle. The degree to which the course of therapy will unfold spontaneously or how much it will be guided or directed by the therapist's clinical knowledge is determined by theory.

The research literature demonstrates efficacy of evidence-based theoretical models for a substantial range of psychiatric conditions (Lawver & Blankenship, 2008; Cook et al., 2017). While a number of studies have demonstrated that there is no one theoretical orientation shown to be more overall effective than others, there are studies that demonstrate select theoretical orientations are more effective with particular diagnoses (Fall et al., 2010). For example, cognitive behavioral therapy has long been established as the leading, most effective treatment model for treating anxiety with effective developmental adaptations for child clients (Comer et al., 2019; Banneyer et al., 2018). Myrick and Green (2012) make a strong case for integrating play therapy with other evidence based theoretical models for treating children with OCD and this can be applied to other diagnoses as well. Play therapy is often misunderstood by the general public, the medical community, and even much of the greater field of psychology as representing only child-centered play therapy. As demonstrated in the previous chapter, play therapy is an umbrella term for many theoretical orientations and approaches rooted in a rich and diverse psychological and psychiatric history. The efficacy of play therapy as a psychotherapy model with children and families has been studied through meta-analysis demonstrating that both non-directive play therapy and directive play therapy orientations are effective theoretical methods (Bratton et al., 2005). It is advisable for clinicians to consider the diagnostic criteria with which a client presents and then look to theoretical approaches and interventions that are rooted in evidence-based research appropriate for that particular diagnosis (American Psychological Association, 2006).

The previous chapter provided a historical overview of the origins and evolution of the theoretical models that have shaped the field of play therapy with consideration of current and future trends in the field. As discussed in the previous chapter, those theories that utilize a non-directive approach hold the fundamental belief that the client has the answers within and will naturally come to realize those answers as a result of being in an accepting, positive, therapeutic relationship without direction from the therapist (Landreth, 2012; Mullin & Rickli, 2014). On the contrary, theoretical orientations that utilize a directive approach assume the therapist is best equipped to see and understand what the problems are and the best ways to address and resolve those problems therapeutically (Leggett & Boswell, 2017). Transtheoretical and integrative approaches see benefit in potentially utilizing various theories determined by the presenting needs and social context of each individual client (Schaefer, 2001; Chang, 2013). Prescriptive play therapy specifically calls for the use of theories and techniques in a way that customizes the play therapy treatment plan to the particular needs of the individual client (Schaefer, 2001).

With closer examination, each of the seminal and historical play therapy theories provides delineating frameworks that inform the approach taken, the role in which the therapist operates, and the way the therapeutic experience will flow for the client. Some theoretical models ascribe to a purely non-directive approach, some are purely directive, and others use an integrative approach (*see* Table 2.1). While there may be differing beliefs as to whether or not the therapeutic relationship in play therapy alone is enough for the client's healing and change, the unifying theoretical tenet in all play therapy is that the relationship and rapport between therapist and client is a foundational and essential element to the therapeutic process with child clients and their caregivers (Brown et al., 2014; Lugo et al., 2017). Relational connections built on trust combined with play is what leads to positive treatment outcomes (Kottman & Meany-Walen, 2018).

Identifying the Problem

In the beginning of play therapy services, there is usually an initial problem or issue reported by caregivers. This presenting issue is what typically motivates caregivers to seek treatment for the child. When the presenting problem is identified it can then translate to a working diagnosis, which marks the beginning of the case conceptualization and treatment planning

Table 2.1 Approaches to Play Therapy Theoretical Orientations. A table with 8 rows depicting 8 play therapy theories and their approaches: Adlerian, integrative; Child Centered, non-directive; Cognitive Behavioral, directive; Developmental, directive; Ecosystemic, integrative; Gestalt, integrative; Jungian, non-directive; Object relations/attachment, directive

Theories	*Approach*
Adlerian	Integrative
Child Centered	Non-Directive
Cognitive Behavioral	Directive
Developmental	Directive
Ecosystemic	Integrative
Gestalt	Integrative
Jungian	Non-Directive
Object Relations/Attachment	Directive

processes (Schwitzer & Rubin, 2015). This first step of determining what problems are observed calls upon the clinician to note symptomatic patterns that may align with one or more diagnostic criteria as outlined in the Diagnostic and Statistical Manual – 5th edition (DSM-5) (American Psychiatric Association, 2013). While there is much discussion about the DSM-5 being problematic (Khoury, et al., 2014; Wakefield, 2016; Muller, 2017), and there is a current debate within the field of mental health as to how we go about determining and classifying diagnoses (Clark et al., 2017; Yager & Feinstein, 2017; Ross & Margolis, 2019; Michelini et al., 2020), we can utilize symptomology and diagnostic criteria as beginning points for naming the initial impression of the presenting problem. This is the beginning of clinical formulation (Jongsma & Bruce, 2010). Often caregivers come to therapy focused on the problem as they see it; eager to have the therapist quickly get to solutions. In order for the course of therapy to be successful, the child, caregiver(s), and therapist ideally will be in some level of agreement as to the identified problem that will be targeted in treatment (Zubernis & Snyder, 2015; Hawley & Weisz, 2003). While some clients have a clear idea of what the problem is that brings them to therapy, others have only a vague idea, reporting symptoms that could point to a particular diagnosis (Zubernis & Snyder, 2015). An initial working diagnosis can be determined early on. This will provide the clinician a way to then gain a greater understanding of what the client is experiencing and needing through case conceptualization (Schwitzer & Rubin, 2015). As the case conceptualization process unfolds, it is very common for the presenting problem to not represent the totality of what is happening for the client. The initial diagnosis can shift and change during the process of case conceptualization and through the course of treatment as well. In the initial intake process, the therapist will need to reassure caregivers that their concerns are heard, identify what the initial problem is, and then skillfully shift the focus of the intake session(s) to gathering vital information in order to begin the process of thorough case conceptualization.

Case Conceptualization

Case conceptualization has been recognized as integral to quality psychotherapy services (Sperry, 2010). It can, however, feel like an overwhelming process for new therapists (Neukrug & Schwitzer, 2006). The process of case conceptualization serves as a bridge between the presenting problems reported by the client and the therapist's ability to develop a plan for treatment (John & Segal, 2015; Sperry, 2010). Ray (2011) writes about case conceptualization within play therapy requiring that the therapist have a foundational capacity to understand the nature of play itself, the stages of child development, and to have the therapeutic skills for gathering and utilizing the unique knowledge of the individual client within the family context. Berman (2018) discusses how case conceptualization will direct the therapist to understanding who a client is and why they are experiencing what they are experiencing. Berman further cautions that if a clinician rushes into treatment without first engaging in a careful conceptualization process, the course of treatment may go in the wrong direction from what the client actually needs.

Case conceptualization is ideally an in-depth process that includes a thorough intake of information in various ways to best understand the client's presenting situation (Neukrug, 2020). Children are imbedded in their familial, social, and cultural systems (O'Connor & Ammen, 2013). If possible and appropriate, given the situation presented, the involvement of caregivers, family members, and other significant members of the child's social system can be very helpful to both the case formulation process and for the course of treatment (O'Connor & Ammen, 2013; Dowell & Ogles, 2010; Karver et al., 2006). As clinicians go about the process of gathering information, the therapist will ask questions regarding medical history, psycho-social history, and familial and social systems context with sensitivity to cultural influences. Cultural sensitivity requires the therapist to be self-examining of one's own cultural identity, personal beliefs, biases, and attitudes. (O'Connor & Ammen, 2013). Cultural humility calls clinicians to be introspective and receptive to the lived experience, values, and views of others (Hook et al., 2017).

The clinician will ideally strive for balance and fluidity on a continuum of objectivity and subjectivity. In seeking to understand what is happening for a client from the client's subjective life experience, the formulation process also calls for the objective lens of clinical knowledge (Hegelund, 2005; Schrank et al., 2013; Ridley et al., 2017). Even in the most objective of natural science research studies, however, the research scientist will give consideration to the phenomenological realm, which is that which cannot fully be known through objective study (Rosen, 2015). In play therapy, the therapist tunes into the child's and the caregivers' subjective experiences and expressions in order to connect, extend compassion, and seek understanding of their subjective reality. This process calls for therapists to engage with curiosity about the client's lived experiences in balance with application of clinical knowledge (Neukrug, 2020).

When caregivers initiate play therapy services for a child, they are usually expecting the clinician to lend expertise in finding resolution for the problem as they see it. As a result, the way in which the therapist approaches the caregivers from the beginning is important in order to fulfill the expectation of expertise and successfully gather important background information, while simultaneously remaining receptive and welcoming. The clinician will meet with the child, providing an emotionally safe, welcoming, and age-appropriate environment through which rapport can develop and further insight can be gained through playful interaction. When clinicians conduct the intake process with caregivers and child clients, it is important for the clinician to see that the caregivers and child are in fact the experts of their lived experience, the problems they face, and their innate strengths (Waters & Asbil, 2013). While the clinician holds a body of clinical knowledge, the client has their own knowledge that the therapist needs to strive to understand (Tervalon & Murray-Garcia, 1998). The therapist facilitates rapport through this initial process of gathering information, showing interest and concern, and this helps set a foundation of trust and connection to build upon throughout the course of treatment. The perspective gained through those initial and ongoing conversations with caregivers and observations of the child in the playroom, shapes the clinician's developing case conceptualization.

An orchestrated intake process allows the clinician to grow a full understanding of the systemic context that informs the child's world (Kronengold, 2016). Children do not develop in a vacuum as they are dependent upon the social and family systems in which they live (O'Connor & Ammen, 2013). Various restrictions may limit a clinician as to the time allotted for the initial intake process. It is, therefore, important to ask the best quality questions in the most optimal way to build rapport and trust while gathering important information. That information gathered from both the caregivers and the child in those first sessions allows the therapist to develop an understanding as to what is happening in the child's inner and outer worlds. In this first stage of the play therapy process, the therapist's theoretical orientation will influence what caregivers hear as to what they can expect from the play therapy process. Regardless of how non-directive or directive a therapist's approach is, building rapport and trust while gathering background information is an essential process (Senko & Bethany, 2019).

The temporal-contextual model for case conceptualization provides therapists a non-theoretical structure for gathering and synthesizing client information. This model takes into consideration a timeline of events and experiences, past and present, as well as environmental context, while noting the client's strengths and other characteristics (Zubernis et al., 2017). The clinician will examine the context of recent and past events in the child's life including birth experience, infancy, developmental milestones, medical and mental health history for the child and the family, historical and current family dynamics, social systems as well as cultural considerations. The therapist may inquire as to the child's temperament and the parenting styles of the parents. This comprehensive psycho-social context aids in formulating a wider view of the child's needs beyond the problem first presented by the caregivers (O'Connor & Ammen, 2013).

Schwitzer & Rubin (2015) write about an inverted pyramid model that provides a four step process for case conceptualization that can be summarized as 1) identifying the problem 2) organizing symptoms into themes and patterns 3) applying theoretical inferences, and 4) narrowing the inferences more specifically to the client's specific needs. The temporal contextual model and the inverted pyramid model work well together to provide a structured means of gathering, observing, and integrating information into a meaningful structure from which the treatment planning can begin. Once the clinician has a thorough understanding of the client's problems in the context of history, family and social systems, the groundwork has been laid to begin the process of treatment planning.

Treatment Planning

A treatment plan integrates the information from the diagnosis and case conceptualization into an actionable plan for therapy (Schwitzer & Rubin, 2015), serving as a map that shows how the client will experience change (Zubernis et al., 2017). In order for the course of therapy to be successful, the child, caregiver(s), and therapist ideally will come to agreement as to the reasons the child is in therapy (Hawley & Weisz, 2003). Through the case conceptualization process the therapist has determined an initial working diagnosis and perhaps a more refined diagnosis has emerged as further information was observed and gathered. Any underlying factors and contributors to the child's presenting issues observed will inform the specifics of the treatment plan, helping to establish treatment goals and objectives (Horowitz, 1997). Often the initial presenting problem is not the only problem that needs to be addressed in therapy. At times, the presenting issue is not actually the main consideration, rather, it may be a symptom of an underlying concern which would be important to identify and address in the course of therapy. Once information has been thoroughly gathered and assimilated through the case conceptualization process, the clinician is able to bridge the initial identified problem(s) with the scope of familial and social context in order to determine and discuss goals for therapy with the child and caregivers. Obtaining buy-in from the child and caregivers as to the therapeutic goals is an important part of the treatment planning process, largely hinging on the initial rapport that has been established (Wonders, 2020; Nock et al., 2001).

Regardless of theoretical approach, it is ideal to have special emphasis given to the family system context by actively involving caregivers in the play therapy process whenever possible. The literature supports the efficacy of parental involvement in therapy demonstrating consistent improvements in child outcomes when parents are involved in treatment across type of child mental health disorder (Lin & Bratton, 2015, Dowell & Ogles, 2010; Karver et al., 2006, Bratton et al., 2005, LeBlanc & Ritchie, 2001). Gil (2016) discusses how play in family therapy enhances the work with families and involving families in the child's play therapy enhances the therapeutic experience for the child and Gammer (2009) writes about the importance of including the child's voice in the process of understanding a family system. Daley et al. (2019) suggested that integrating structural family systems theory, attachment theory, and play therapies is a natural and important approach to consider for more in-depth research.

Despite the established benefits of having parents actively involved in a child's therapy, the literature demonstrates that caregiver participation is often lacking (Baker-Ericzén et al., 2013; Haine-Schlagel et al., 2011). When caregivers do not participate in treatment research has shown that it is less likely that the progress made in therapy sessions is carried over to the home setting (Karver et al., 2006). It is important for the therapist to make every attempt to warmly welcome caregivers to the therapeutic process from the very beginning, establish and maintain rapport and avoid causing them to feel criticized or judged as this is often a reason for lack of participation (Baker-Ericzén et al., 2013). In cases where a child's parents are unable to participate, the clinician will want to gather family history and current contextual information from all sources available and attempt to involve whomever the adults are who provide care and supervision for the child.

Treatment goals can be defined as targeted changes in action and experience, agreed upon by clients and therapist at the start of treatment (Grosse & Grawe, 2002). Katz et al. (2016) found that psychotherapy clients were more motivated when goals were formulated in such a way that promoted a new behavior or action that they valued rather than goals that centered around symptom reduction. Nurcombe (1989) contended that goal directed treatment planning should replace more intuitive treatment planning. Initially this was presented out of concern for time constraints due to managed care variables, but it was later discovered goal directed treatment planning to actually be more effective. Nurcombe provides a six-step process for goal directed treatment planning as follows:

1. Identify pivotal problems and potentials
2. Rewrite the problems/potentials as goals
3. Estimate the time required to reach each goal
4. For each goal identify at least two measurable objectives
5. For each goal {determine interventions} or treatments in accordance with the evidence base, sociocultural appropriateness, and the resources available
6. For each goal/objective identify a monitor to determine if treatment is progressing or if the goal has been attained (2014, p. 9).

Utilizing goal-directed treatment planning reinforces the integrity of play therapy by establishing a map for the therapeutic process with a means to measure efficacy of the by examining outcomes of objectives along the way. Treatment outcomes can be measured by the therapist's observations of the child's patterns of play in session as well as reports from the caregivers, and often other significant adults in the child's social system (i.e. the child's teachers). The manner in which the clinician goes about utilizing a goal directed treatment planning process will differ based on theoretical orientation, which will be further discussed in the next section of this chapter. The use of this treatment planning model can be very helpful to aid in grounding the purposeful application of theory to the therapeutic process in order to effectively measure treatment outcomes.

Applying Theory to Conceptualization and Treatment Planning

Familiarity with conceptualization models, as described previously, helps the therapist function adaptively and efficiently, so that they can use their chosen theoretical orientation to formulate a treatment plan (Betan & Binder, 2010). As previously emphasized, regardless of how non-directive or directive a therapist's approach to play therapy, the clinician's responsibility is to provide a warm, receptive, and accepting therapeutic environment for the child and caregivers from the very beginning.

Non-directive Theories

The idea of case conceptualization and treatment planning might seem to contradict theoretical basis for humanistic, non-directive theoretical orientations. After all, the theory is based in the belief that the client holds the answers and will naturally experience resolution through their play if provided the ideal environment and therapeutic relationship. There is a case to be made, however, for the use of case conceptualization and goal directed treatment planning with non-directive play therapies and a way to do so without dishonoring the tenets of the theories. Even the most non-directive theorist can find way to honor the clinical process of case formulation and treatment planning in order to support both the objective and the subjective aspects of the therapeutic process.

Child-Centered Play Therapy Theory

A therapist who ascribes to child-centered play therapy will not rush case formulation and will likely be slow to determine the goals for therapy. The theory asserts that the child is the one who holds the answers. "A powerful force exists within every child that strives continuously for self-actualization. This inherent striving is toward independence, maturity, and self-direction" (Landreth, 2012, p. 62). A child centered therapist allows the child the time and space to explore, express, and experience whatever is needed for the course of natural healing and resolution to take place. As Ray (2011) discusses, however, the therapist can be fully present *in session* without directing to allow for the child's process, but then apply just enough analysis of the observed play themes *outside of sessions* to help identify the problems the child is experiencing as part of the case conceptualization and treatment planning. Based on Nurcombe's model of goal directed treatment planning (2014) a child-centered play therapist can reframe a problem revealed in the child's thematic play into a treatment goal. The time frames for treatment plan objectives may be less specific for a child-centered therapist than they would be in a treatment plan developed by a directive play therapist. For a purely child-centered play therapist, the treatment or interventions included in the treatment plan will be use of tracking, reflecting, returning responsibility, and therapeutic limit setting as well as parent consultation sessions. Filial therapy or child parent relationship therapies are based in child-centered theory and therefore may be complementary and part of a treatment plan.

Observation of the child's play themes in session can be used to connect the caregivers to the process and progress of therapy (Ray, 2011). As the therapist observes the play themes shift and change, the problems that were previously externalized in the child's life often begin to resolve as reported by caregivers and perhaps teachers. The child-centered clinician is able to use these observations and reports as a measure of progress per the goal directed treatment plan.

Jungian Analytical Play Therapy

Similar to the child-centered theorist, a play therapist who is closely aligned with pure Jungian theory will never rush the child's process (Allan, 1997). The therapist will remain the observer allowing for whatever symbols may emerge that serve as metaphor for the child's healing and growth (Green, 2014). As Jungian analytical play therapy is analytical by name and nature, the Jungian play therapist blends the knowledge and ability to recognize archetypal themes in a child's play with patient observation and honoring the child's process (Green, 2009). Much like the child-centered play therapist, the Jungian play therapist can be purely non-directive *in session* and then apply analysis to observations made *outside of session*. The observation of initial archetypes presenting in the beginning of therapy can inform the clinician as to the problems the child grapples with, helping the therapist to conceptualize the case and then reframe those problems into goals and objectives for the therapy. Progress can be measured by tracking the thematic shifts observed while honoring the subjective, phenomenological reality of the child.

Directive Theories

Directive play therapy theories lean more on the body of clinical knowledge and skills the therapist holds to understand the nature of a child's problems and what interventions should be implemented in order for there to be resolution. There is certainly a continuum of lightly structured to heavily directive play therapy depending on the theoretical model. Even then, within the field of play therapy it is agreed upon in all theoretical models that there must be space for a therapeutic relationship to be formed and nurtured. Directive play therapy theories are highly focused with conceptualization of the case viewed through a more specific lens. These theoretical orientations provide a narrower scope to identify the nature of a child's problems and the interventions needed to actualize improvement and resolution.

Developmental Play Therapy

Viola Brody wrote about the roots of developmental play therapy theory, expressing that a child's development of self begins with awareness of the physical body and that through the therapeutic use of healthy, loving touch a child's sense of self emerges. Brody's writings emphasizes the belief loving, appropriate, therapeutic touch is central to the theory (Brody, 1997). Courtney and Siu (2018), published research that emphasized the need for clinicians to have clinical and ethical competencies in the use of touch in therapy. Courtney (2020) writes about her FirstPlay Therapy® model that uses directive teaching and facilitative interventions to help caregivers use touch with their infants and young children to enhance optimal brain development and healthy attachments. In terms of case conceptualization and treatment planning, developmental play therapy theory utilizes a process of identifying the presenting problems of children through the lens of developmental needs, deficits therein, and the use of interventions that involve purposeful, playful, safe touch. In this directive therapeutic model, the therapist holds the knowledge and skills and both educates the caregiver and facilitates interventions that include pre-symbolic play and touch. Much of the measuring of therapeutic progress will be based on the observations the therapist has of the nature of the interactions between caregiver and child.

Object Relations Play Therapy

Object relations is another attachment-based play therapy that helps young children who have suffered an attachment disruption, rupture, or trauma during early developmental stages. The therapist begins by fostering a secure therapeutic relationship with the child utilizing skills of attunement, coregulation, and empathy. Often, the interventions introduced by the therapist are playful and sensory-focused activities such as sand therapy or finger painting. These sort of sensory interventions are helpful for addressing any dysfunction of the lower brain. Caregivers are guided by the therapist to continue sensory based activities between sessions (Patton & Benedict, 2015). Though this theoretical orientation has been identified as an integrative approach, it is one that is more accurately categorized as directive in that the therapist holds the knowledge of what is needed for the child and the relationship between the child and caregiver while offering directed experiences both in session and at home. Much like developmental play therapy, the object relations therapist sees the child's presenting problems through the lens of attachment disruption or deficit so the goals and objectives for the therapy are determined with directed interventions byway of the therapist. Progress can be observed and determined by observations of the child's presentation within the therapeutic relationship and in response to the directed play activities as well as by report of caregivers.

Cognitive Behavioral Play Therapy

Cognitive behavioral play therapy is likely the most straight-forward theoretical orientation when it comes to conceptualizing and creating goal directive treatment planning. The theory is based in the belief that helping children identify and change thoughts and beliefs that are interfering with healthy functioning, the child develops a greater sense of understanding and empowerment (Knell, 1995). This play therapy theory is informed by cognitive behavioral principles and integrated in a way that is sensitive to the developmental stage and needs of the child client recognizing there will be non-verbal and verbal expressions and interactions (Knell, 2009). The process of understanding the child's presenting problem can be achieved not only by gathering a thorough psycho-social history from the parents but also through play-based assessment measures to ascertain degrees and intensity of symptomology. Interventions are determined based upon the goals and objectives established and directed by the therapist to include games and playful activities. Much of cognitive behavioral play therapy involves the therapist operating from the role of teacher, providing psychoeducation through play-based, developmentally appropriate activities. Progress is measured both in therapy sessions and by tracking behavioral measures between sessions with the help of parents and teachers.

Integrative and Prescriptive Theories

Recently there has been a strong and evolving trend in the field of play therapy whereby more and more child therapists integrating theoretical models. Many clinicians are now utilizing a prescriptive approach to play therapy which affords the ability to draw from various theoretical models to meet the needs of the given client, accessing the spectrum of therapeutic powers of play (Drewes & Cavett, 2019). There has been a growing trend in the greater field of psychotherapy and in graduate training programs for clinicians to develop an integrative model rather than operate from one single theoretical model (Jones-Smith, 2019). There are number of seminal and historical play therapy theoretical models that actually are by nature integrative.

Adlerian Play Therapy

In Adlerian play therapy child clients are seen as socially embedded and naturally driven by their goals rather than by instincts. It is a theoretical orientation that borrows from various other theories richly rooted in Adlerian theory to meet the needs of each client within the context of their familial and social systems (Kottman & Meany-Walen, 2016). An Adlerian play therapist will use a non-directive approach in the first stage of therapy allowing for the very important development of therapeutic trust and rapport and then will introduce more directive interventions in the later stages of therapy. In terms of case conceptualization, the social system in which the child is embedded would be extensively explored and caregivers who are involved in the play therapy process aid in a full understanding of the child's world and experiences. Treatment goals and objectives would likely be established within a collaborative process between the therapist, child, and caregivers. Since Adler's theory states people are naturally goal driven, the process of discussing and agreeing upon goals for therapy naturally fits with the theoretical model. Based on the theoretical lens, the overarching goals of Adlerian play therapy include: experiencing a greater connection with others in prosocial ways to gain a sense of significance and belonging and to develop healthy ways of coping with feelings of discouragement (Kottman & Meany-Walen, 2016; 2018). Adlerian play therapists, however, customize their treatment plans and interventions for specific clients, so individual therapy goals are based on the presenting problem and the underlying interpersonal and intrapersonal challenges with a special focus on amplifying the client's strengths (Kottman & Ashby, 2019).

Ecosystemic Play Therapy

The ecosystemic play therapy model is prescriptive, using a transtheoretical and integrative model (O'Connor & Vega, 2019) in which the therapist needs to shift along with a child's rapidly changing developmental needs and the complexity of the respective family and social systems in which the child is embedded (O'Connor, 2016). This theoretical model calls upon the therapist to view and approach each client as a unique amalgam; influenced and shaped by their unique ecosystem. (O'Connor, 2000, p. 87). This theoretical model relies on considerations of the comprehensive psychosocial context to formulate a wide view of the child's needs beyond the problem first presented by the caregivers (O'Connor & Ammen, 2013). Influenced by the context of the system and drawing from various theoretical play therapy approaches, goals and objectives would be determined not only by the therapist but along with the collaboration of the child and caregivers with dynamic and fluid tracking of progress along the way.

Gestalt Play Therapy

Gestalt play therapy is an experiential therapy concerned with the integrated functioning of all aspects of the child client including senses, physical body, emotions, and cognitions. This theory asserts that when a child's use of senses, body, emotions, or thoughts are not integrated, this interferes with their ability to be happily and successful engaged with the world around them (Carroll, 2009). Oaklander (2001) wrote that the goal of Gestalt play therapy is to help children regain and integrate the parts of themselves from which they've become disconnected and that it is the therapist's job to provide therapeutic experiences and opportunity for the child to achieve that goal in therapy. Carroll and Orazco (2019) write that the goal of Gestalt play therapy is for the child to experience "integrated aliveness". Here is an example of the theory driving the goal of therapy. Gestalt play therapy values a child-centered theoretical approach in order to reflect and respond to the individual child's needs, providing a warm and welcoming playful environment and trust-based therapeutic relationship. The therapist also shifts to offer directive, facilitate play-based interventions which provide the child with necessary experiences to achieve the goals of therapy. Gestalt play therapy integrates the use of child-centered play therapy and directive, structured play therapy interventions.

Prescriptive Play Therapy

Prescriptive play therapy uses theories and techniques to customize the play therapy treatment plan to the particular needs of the individual client (Schaefer, 2001). The focus of this model addresses and seeks to resolve the specific presenting problem that brings a client into therapy (Wonders, 2020). The clinician uses a goal directed treatment plan after a thorough intake, assessment, and case conceptualization process that is tailored to the client (O'Connor, 2016). In order for the therapist to be capable of successfully integrating theories and applying the principles of prescriptive play therapy, clinicians must have highly developed clinical skills and a clear understanding of the treatment planning process (Stone, 2020).

The Guiding Compass of the Therapeutic Powers of Play

It has long been established in the greater field of psychotherapy that consideration of the agents of change for the client is what helps clinicians to better understand the efficacy of therapy services (Kazdin, 2003). Schaefer and Drewes (2014) propose that play is not merely the means through which therapeutic interventions are introduced, but rather play is itself the agent of change for the child. It is further posited that there is a spectrum of play producing a variety of powers of play. The therapeutic powers of play have served as a unifying bedrock within the field of play therapy. They show serve as a way to anchor and illustrate the way play therapy is effective in helping children learn and grow regardless of what approach or theoretical orientation a therapist uses.

Schaefer & Drewes (2014) identified four over-arching powers of play illustrating that play itself: 1) facilitates communication 2) fosters emotional wellness 3) enhances social relationships, and 4) increases personal strengths.

Therapeutic Powers of Play

Figure 2.1 Therapeutic Powers of Play.
Adapted from Schaefer & Drewes (2014).

Under each of these powers of play there are 20 core agents of change named (Figure 2.1).

These core agents of change are said to be the "heart and soul" of the play therapy process (Schaefer & Drewes, 2014). By identifying the powers of play and the specific agents of change, clinicians can categorize the purposes for all interventions in the therapeutic process. Clinical supervisors can guide therapists training in play therapy with the therapeutic powers of play to provide reference points as to what is happening in the play therapy session and the purpose therein. Play therapy trainers can lean into the therapeutic powers of play to provide valid justification for the use of a particular approach, the use of a certain theoretical basis, and the implementation of interventions. Clinicians, of all theoretical orientations, can shape the treatment plan by reflecting on the span of these therapeutic powers of play and core agents of change while also using this reference point to help caregivers understand and remain invested in the play therapy process.

Conclusion

A clear understanding of one's theoretical foundation and the therapeutic powers of play will inform the processes of conceptualizing clinical cases and developing effective plans for treatment. Therapists need to be prepared to meet the fast-changing needs of an evolving society. It is critically important to sustain the integrity of play therapy services by honoring the theory that informs the processes and the stages and steps required for effective treatment of clients. As play therapy intersects with the digital age and telehealth services are widely provided, it is more important than ever that clinicians revisit theoretical foundations and clinical formulation and planning processes so that the quality of services we provide for children and families is clinically sound and beneficial.

References

Allan, J. (1997). Jungian play psychotherapy. In K. J. O'Connor and L. M. Braverman (Ed.), *Play therapy theory and practice: A comparative presentation*. (pp. 100–130). Wiley.

American Psychiatric Association. (2013). *Diagnostic and statistical manual of mental disorders (DSM-5®)*. American Psychiatric Pub.

American Psychological Association. (2006). Evidence-based practice in psychology: APA presidential task force on evidence-based practice. *American Psychologist*, 61(4), 271–285. http://doi.org/10.1037/0003-066X.61.4.271

Baker-Ericzén, M., Jenkins, M., & Haine-Schlagel, R. (2013). Therapist, parent, and youth perspectives of treatment barriers to family-focused community outpatient mental health services. *Journal of Child & Family Studies*, 22(6), 854–868. https://doi.org/10.1007/s10826-012-9644-7.

Banneyer, K. N., Bonin, L., Price, K., Goodman, W. K., & Storch, E. A. (2018). Cognitive behavioral therapy for childhood anxiety disorders: A review of recent advances. *Current Psychiatry Reports*, 20(8). https://doi.org/10.1007/s11920-018-0924-9

Berman, P. S. (2018). *Case conceptualization and treatment planning: Integrating theory with clinical practice*. SAGE Publications.

Betan, E. J., & Binder, J. L. (2010). Clinical expertise in psychotherapy: How expert therapists use theory in generating case conceptualizations and interventions. *Journal of Contemporary Psychotherapy*, 40(3), 141–152. https://doi.org/10.1007/s10879-010-9138-0

Bratton, S. C., Ray, D., Rhine, T., & Jones, L. (2005). The efficacy of play therapy with children: A meta-analytic review of treatment outcomes. *Professional Psychology: Research and Practice*, 36(4), 376.

Brody, V. A. (1997). *Dialogue of touch: Developmental play therapy*. Jason Aronson.

Brown, R. C., Parker, K. M., McLeod, B. D., & Southam-Gerow, M. A. (2014). Building a positive therapeutic relationship with the child or adolescent and parent.

Evidence-Based CBT for Anxiety and Depression in Children and Adolescents, 63–78. https://doi.org/10.1002/9781118500576.ch6

Carroll, F. (2009). Gestalt play therapy. In K. J. O'Connor & L. D. Braverman (Eds.), *Play therapy theory and practice: Comparing theories and techniques* (pp. 283–314). John Wiley & Sons Inc.

Carroll, F. & Orazco, V. (2019) Gestalt play therapy. *Play Therapy, 14*(3), 36–38.

Chang, J. (2013). Creative interventions with children: A transtheoretical approach.

Clark, L. A., Cuthbert, B., Lewis-Fernández, R., Narrow, W. E., & Reed, G. M. (2017). Three approaches to understanding and classifying mental disorder: ICD-11, DSM-5, and the National Institute of Mental Health's Research Domain Criteria (RDoC). *Psychological Science in the Public Interest, 18*(2), 72–145. https://doi.org10.1177/1529100617727266. PMID: 29211974.

Comer, J. S., Hong, N., Poznanski, B., Silva, K., & Wilson, M. (2019). Evidence base update on the treatment of early childhood anxiety and related problems. *Journal of Clinical Child & Adolescent Psychology, 48*(1), 1–15. https://doi.org/10.1080/15374416.2018.1534208

Cook, S. C., Schwartz, A. C., & Kaslow, N. J. (2017). Evidence-based psychotherapy: advantages and challenges. *Neurotherapeutics: The Journal of the American Society for Experimental NeuroTherapeutics, 14*(3), 537–545. https://doi.org/10.1007/s13311-017-0549-4

Courtney, J. A., & Siu, A. F. Y. (2018). Practitioner experiences of touch in working with children in play therapy. *International Journal of Play Therapy, 27*(2), 92–102. https://doi.org/10.1037/pla0000064

Courtney, J. A. (2020). *Infant play therapy: Foundations, models, programs, and practice*. Routledge.

Daley, L., Miller, R., Bean, R., & Oka, M. (2019). Family system play therapy: An integrative approach. *The American Journal of Family Therapy, 46*, 1–16. https://doi.org/10.1080/01926187.2019.1570386.

Dowell, K. A., & Ogles, B. M. (2010). The effects of parent participation on child psychotherapy outcome: A meta-analytic review. *Journal of Clinical Child & Adolescent Psychology, 39*(2), 151–162. https://doi.org/10.1080/15374410903532585

Drapela, V. J. (1990). The value of theories for counseling practitioners. *International Journal for the Advancement of Counselling, 13*(1), 19–26. https://doi.org/10.1007/bf00154639

Drewes, A. & Cavett, A. (2019, September). Cognitive behavioral play therapy. *Play Therapy, 14*(3), 24–26.

Fall, K. A., Holden, J. M., & Marquis, A. (2010). *Theoretical models of counseling and psychotherapy* (2nd ed.). Routledge.

Gammer, C. (2009). *The child's voice in family therapy: A systemic perspective*. W. W. Norton & Company.

Gil, E. (2016). *Play in family therapy*. The Guilford Press.

Green, E. J. (2009). Jungian analytical play therapy. In K. J. O'Connor & L. D. Braverman (Eds.), *Play therapy theory and practice: Comparing theories and techniques* (pp. 83–121). John Wiley & Sons Inc.

Green, E. J. (2014). *The handbook of Jungian play therapy with children and adolescents.* JHU Press.

Grosse, M., & Grawe, K. (2002). Bern inventory of treatment goals: Part 1. Development and first application of a taxonomy of treatment goal themes. *Psychotherapy Research, 12*(1), 79–99. https://doi.org/10.1080/713869618

Haine-Schlagel, R., Brookman-Frazee, L., Fettes, D. L., Baker-Ericzén, M., & Garland, A. F. (2011). Therapist focus on parent involvement in community-based youth psychotherapy. *Journal of Child and Family Studies*, *21*(4), 646–656. https://doi.org/10.1007/s10826-011-9517-5

Hawley, K., & Weisz, J. (2003). Child, parent and therapist (dis)agreement on target problems in outpatient therapy: The therapist's dilemma and its implications. *Journal of Consulting and Clinical Psychology*, *71*(1), 62–70. http://doi.org/10.1037/0022-006X.71.1.62

Hegelund, A. (2005). Objectivity and subjectivity in the ethnographic method. *Qualitative Health Research*, *15*(5), 647–668. https://doi.org/10.1177/1049732304273933

Hook, J. N., Davis, D., Owen, J., & DeBlaere, C. (2017). *Cultural humility: Engaging diverse identities in therapy*. American Psychological Association.

Horowitz, M. (1997). *Formulation as a basis for planning psychotherapy treatment* (1st Ed.). American Psychiatric Press.

John, S., & Segal, D. L. (2015). Case conceptualization. *The Encyclopedia of Clinical Psychology*, 1–4. https://doi.org/10.1002/9781118625392.wbecp106

Jones-Smith, E. (2019). *Theories of counseling and psychotherapy: An integrative approach*. SAGE Publications.

Jongsma, A. E., & Bruce, T. J. (2010). *Evidence-based psychotherapy treatment planning DVD workbook*. John Wiley & Sons.

Karver, M., Handelsman, J., Fields, S., & Bickman, L. (2006). Meta-analysis of therapeutic relationship variables in youth and family therapy: The evidence for different relationship variables in the child and adolescent treatment outcome literature. *Clinical Psychology Review*, *26*(1), 50–65. https://doi.org/10.1016/j.cpr.2005.09.001

Katz, B. A., Catane, S., & Yovel, I. (2016). Pushed by symptoms, pulled by values: Promotion goals increase motivation in therapeutic tasks. *Behavior Therapy*, *47*(2), 239–247. https://doi.org/10.1016/j.beth.2015.11.002

Kazdin, A. (2003). Delineating mechanisms of change in child & adolescent therapy: Methodological issues and research recommendations. *Journal of Child Psychology and Psychiatry*, *44*(8), pp. 1116–1129.

Khoury, B., Langer, E. J., & Pagnini, F. (2014). The DSM: mindful science or mindless power? A critical review. *Frontiers in Psychology*, *5*, 602. https://doi.org/10.3389/fpsyg.2014.00602

Knell, S. M. (1995). *Cognitive-behavioral play therapy*. Jason Aronson.

Knell, S. M. (2009). Cognitive-behavioral play-therapy. In K. J. O'Connor & L. D. Braverman (Eds.), *Play therapy theory and practice: Comparing theories and techniques* (2nd ed., pp. 203–236). Wiley.

Kottman, T., & Ashby, J. (2019) Adlerian play therapy. *Play Therapy*, *14*(3), 12–13.

Kottman, T., & Meany-Walen, K. K. (2018). *Doing play therapy: From building the relationship to facilitating change*. Guilford Publications.

Kottman, T., & Meany-Walen, K. (2016). *Partners in play: An Adlerian approach to play therapy*. John Wiley & Sons.

Kronengold, H. (2016). *Stories from child & adolescent psychotherapy: A curious space*. Taylor & Francis.

Landreth, G. L. (2012). *Play therapy: The art of the relationship*. Routledge.

Lawver, T., & Blankenship, K. (2008). Play therapy: A case-based example of a nondirective approach. *Psychiatry*, *5*(10), 24–28.

Lin, Y., & Bratton, S. C. (2015). A meta-analytic review of child-centered play therapy approaches. *Journal of Counseling and Development*, *93*(1), 45-58. doi: 10.1002/j.1556-6676.2015.00180.x

LeBlanc, M., & Ritchie, M.(2001). A meta-analysis of play therapy outcomes. *Counseling Psychology Quarterly, 14*, 149–163. doi: 10.1080/09515070110059142

Leggett, E. S., & Boswell, J. N. (2017). Directive play therapy. In E. S. Leggett & J. N. Boswell (Eds.), *Directive play therapy: Theories and techniques* (pp. 1–15). Springer Publishing Co.

Lugo, A. M., King, M. L., Lamphere, J. C., & McArdle, P. E. (2017). Developing procedures to improve therapist–child rapport in early intervention. *Behavior Analysis in Practice, 10*(4), 395–401. https://doi.org/10.1007/s40617-016-0165-5

Michelini, G., Palumbo, I. M., DeYoung, C. G., Latzman, R., & Kotov, R. (2020). Linking RDoC and HiTOP: A new interface for advancing psychiatric nosology and neuroscience. https://doi.org/10.31234/osf.io/ps7tc

Muller, R. J. (2017). *The Four Domains of Mental Illness*. Routledge. https://doi.org/10.4324/9781315142821-1

Mullin, J. A., & Rickli, J. M. (2014). *Child-centered play therapy workbook: A self-directed guide for professionals*. Research Press.

Myrick, A. C., & Green, E. J. (2012). Incorporating play therapy into evidence-based treatment with children affected by obsessive compulsive disorder. *International Journal of Play Therapy, 21*(2), 74–86. https://doi.org/10.1037/a0027603

Neukrug, E. (2020). *Skills and techniques for human service professionals: Counseling environment, helping skills, treatment issues*. Cognella Academic.

Neukrug, E., & Schwitzer, A. M. (2006). *Skills and tools for today's counselors and psychotherapists: From natural helping to professional counseling*. Brooks/Cole Publishing Company.

Nock, M., Kazdin, A., & Kazdin, P. (2001) Parent expectancies for child therapy: Assessment and relation to participation in treatment. *Journal of Child and Family Studies, 10* (2), 155–180.

Norcross, J. C., Pfund, R. A., & Prochaska, J. O. (2013). Psychotherapy in 2022: A Delphi poll on its future. *Professional Psychology: Research and Practice, 44*(5), 363–370. https://doi.org/10.1037/a0034633

Nurcombe, B. (1989). Goal-directed treatment planning and the principles of brief hospitalization. *Journal of American Academy of Child and Adolescent Psychiatry, 1*, 26–30. http://doi.org/10.1097/00004583-198901000-00005

Nurcombe, B. (2014). Diagnosis and treatment planning in child and adolescent mental health problems. In J. M. Rey (Ed.), *IACAPAP e-Textbook of Child and Adolescent Mental Health* (pp. 1–21). International Association for Child and Adolescent Psychiatry and Allied Professions.

Oaklander, V. (2001). Gestalt play therapy. *International Journal of Play Therapy, 10*(2), 45–55. https://doi.org/10.1037/h0089479

O'Connor, K. J. (2000). *The play therapy primer*. Wiley.

O'Connor, K. (2016). Ecosystemic play therapy. In *Handbook of play therapy* (pp. 195–223) John Wiley & Sons.

O'Connor, K. J., and Ammen, S. (2013). *Play therapy treatment planning and interventions: The ecosystemic model and workbook*(2nd ed.). Elsevier/Academic Press.

O'Connor, K., & Vega, C. (2019). Ecosystemic play therapy. *Play Therapy, 14*(3), 32–34.

Patton, S. C., & Benedict, H. E. (2015). Object relations and attachment-based play therapy. In D. A. Crenshaw & A. L. Stewart (Eds.), *Play therapy: A comprehensive guide to theory and practice* (pp. 17–31). The Guilford Press.

Ray, D. (2011). *Advanced play therapy* (1st ed.). Routledge.

Ridley, C. R., Jeffrey, C. E., & Roberson, R. B. (2017). The process of thematic mapping in case conceptualization. *Journal of Clinical Psychology*, 73(4), 393–409. https://doi.org/10.1002/jclp.22351

Rosen, S. M. (2015). Why natural science needs phenomenological philosophy. *Progress in Biophysics and Molecular Biology*, 119(3), 257.

Ross, C., & Margolis, R. (2019). Research domain criteria: Strengths, weaknesses, and potential alternatives for future psychiatric research. *Molecular Neuropsychiatry*, 5(4), 218–236. https://doi.org/10.1159/000501797

Schaefer, C. (2001). Prescriptive play therapy. *International Journal of Play Therapy*, 10, 57–73.

Schaefer, C. E., & Drewes, A. A. (2014). *The therapeutic powers of play: 20 core agents of change.* Wiley.

Schrank, B., Riches, S., Coggins, T., Tylee, A., & Slade, M. (2013). From objectivity to subjectivity: Conceptualization and measurement of well-being in mental health. *Neuropsychiatry*, 3(5), 525–534. https://doi.org/10.2217/npy.13.58

Schwitzer, A. M., & Rubin, L. C. (2015). *Diagnosis & treatment planning skills: A popular culture casebook approach.* Sage.

Senko, K., & Bethany, H. (2019). Play therapy: An illustrative case. *Innovations in Clinical Neuroscience*, 16(5-6), 38–40.

Sperry, L. (2010). *Highly effective therapy: Developing essential clinical competencies in counseling and psychotherapy.* Taylor & Francis.

Stone, J. (2020). *Digital play therapy.* Routledge. https://doi.org/10.4324/9780429001109-4

Tervalon, M., & Murray-Garcia, J. (1998). Cultural humility versus cultural competence: A critical distinction in defining physician training outcomes in multicultural education. *Journal of Health Care for the Poor and Undeserved*, 9, 117–125.

Wakefield, J. C. (2016). Diagnostic issues and controversies in DSM-5: Return of the false positives problem. *Annual Review of Clinical Psychology*, 12(1), 105–132. https://doi.org/10.1146/annurev-clinpsy-032814-112800

Wampold, B. E. (2019). Theories of psychotherapy series. *The basics of psychotherapy: An introduction to theory and practice* (2nd ed.). American Psychological Association. https://doi.org/10.1037/0000117-000

Waters, A., & Asbil, A. (2013). *Reflections on cultural humility.* American Psychological Association. www.apa.org/pi/families/resources/newsletter/2013/08/cultural-humility.

Wonders, L. L. (2020). Play therapy for children with selective mutism. In H. G. Kaduson, D. Cangelosi, & C. E. Schaefer (Eds.), *Prescriptive play therapy: Tailoring interventions for specific childhood problems* (pp. 92–104). The Guilford Press.

Yager, J., & Feinstein, R. E. (2017). Potential applications of the National Institute of mental health's research domain criteria (RDoC) to clinical psychiatric practice. *The Journal of Clinical Psychiatry*, 78(04), 423–432. https://doi.org/10.4088/jcp.15nr10476

Zubernis, L., & Snyder, M. (2015). *Case conceptualization and effective interventions: Assessing and treating mental, emotional, and behavioral disorders.* SAGE Publications.

Zubernis, L., Snyder, M., & Neale-McFall, C. (2017). Case conceptualization: Improving understanding and treatment with the temporal/contextual model. *Journal of Mental Health Counseling*, 39(3), 181–194. https://doi.org/10.17744/mehc.39.3.01

3 Telemental Health Play Therapy

Jessica Stone

> *This is a time I think we'll all remember and cherish in some way, as the time we leaned into the changes together and grew.*
>
> *(J. Flynn, personal communication, January 3, 2021)*

With the history, foundations, and treatment conceptualizations in play therapy firmly conceptualized, the play therapist can move toward adapting and applying such information to a variety of environments and platforms. In the spring of 2020 most play therapy practitioners had to transition very quickly into providing telemental health services within a very short period of time due to COVID-19. The need for human contact distancing to reduce the spread of this deadly virus led to the realizations that in-person, face-to-face sessions might not be possible for some time. In-office skills and knowledge had to be applied to digital platforms.

Once the chaos settled a bit, providers quickly recognized that there were many logistics to evaluate and decide upon. These logistics included: how will services and continuity of care be provided without the therapist and client in the same physical space? What platform should one use and how is privacy maintained? What about safety issues/concerns? What are the legal and ethical requirements on state, licensing, federal, malpractice, and professional association levels? If the therapist is "freaking out", how can they help their clients? How does one actually provide these services, as in, what do we *actually do*? The answers to these critical questions predominantly lie in key directives:

1. Apply the fundamental tenets of your training and experience to a new medium – the digital platform. This includes everything from case conceptualization and treatment planning, to direct-use interventions and collateral contact conversations.
2. Research your legal and ethical requirements and keep records of your findings.
3. Apply such findings from your research to the programs and platforms

chosen to provide services in this new medium and document how these choices meet the required criteria you have researched. Vetted resources will need to have been chosen with defined criteria in mind (i.e. HIPAA compliance).
4. Create all the appropriate legal and ethical documents needed, including specific telehealth informed consent.
5. Assess clients for appropriateness for telehealth treatment. This will include safety, diagnostic, access, socio-economic, family dynamics, and cultural considerations.
6. Seek out supervision and/or consultation from industry leaders, just as you would with any new component in your work.

This chapter intends to introduce the reader to the pre-, peri-, and post-eras of teleservices. There is a rich and surprising history of teleservices, beginning with telemedicine in the early 1900s, which informs us a bit about how we have arrived in an amazing time in history: the ability for continuity of care despite a global pandemic. The COVID-19 pandemic era of telemental health services is discussed to review the process of this rapid adoption of providing services digitally, the realizations many have experienced, and the pros and cons of such provisions. Finally, the potential future of the incorporation of teleservices in many arenas, but specifically for mental health, with be discussed.

Telemedicine

History, Pre-COVID-19

Something that might be a surprise to many is that 2006 marked the 100th anniversary of telemedicine (Strehle & Shabde, 2006). Although the term "telemedicine" came about in the 1970s by Thomas Bird from the Greek "tele" and Latin "medicus" with a translation of "healing at a distance" (p. 956), the concept was utilized as early as the beginning of the 20th century. Regarded as the first clinician to develop and apply a telemedicine technique, Dutch physiologist Willem Einthoven had his findings published in 1906 in the *Archives Internationales de Physiologie* (Strehle & Shabde, 2006; Einthoven, 1906). Results from an echocardiogram were transmitted via telephone wire over 1500 meters (Cadogan, 2020). Throughout the following 100+ years, telemedicine has been utilized in a variety of ways to provide healing at a distance.

Specifically regarding mental health services, prior to 1957 Dr. Cecil Wittson began utilizing closed circuit, one-way television to deliver psychiatric training to students in Nebraska. This was expanded to Iowa and North and South Dakota in 1957 with asynchronous, two-way communication, and in 1959 he used asynchronous video for consultations and therapy. In 1969, the first remote clinic was created through Massachusetts

General Hospital. Clinicians were providing services to children and adults from Logan International Airport which was almost three miles away from the hospital (WeCounsel, 2021; University of Nebraska, n.d.).

In 1996, an important book was published, *Telemedicine: A guide to assessing telelcommunications for health care* (Field, 1996). Forward-thinking professionals were looking toward the increased and organized use of then-current technologies to improve a number of delivery-of-care systems, including access to services. With a focus on combining technologies and innovation, telemedicine was approached and defined as "the use of electronic information and communications technologies to provide and support health care when distance separates the participants" (p. 1). A key component of the text included a project by The Institute of Medicine (IOM), which was asked to develop a framework for use in "evaluating clinical telemedicine" to "guide policy makers, reassure patients and clinicians, inform health play managers, and help those who have invested in telemedicine to identify shortcomings and improve their programs", (p. 2). At that time, the main focal points highlighted the needs of remote and rural populations and for those who could not attend in-person sessions due to poor health, mobility concerns, working from afar, or incarceration. The IOM, therefore, geared the investigations toward:

1) quality of care and health outcomes, 2) access to care, 3) health care costs and cost-effectiveness, 4) patient perceptions, and 5) clinician perceptions (Field, 1996). Ultimately the recommendations included a call for more research, more exploration, more structure, and highlighted the importance of "delineating how technical, clinical, and administrative processes are intended to work *and* determining how they are actually implemented", in order to properly evaluate the use of telehealth systems (p. 5).

Obstacles

It seems that telemedicine has faced a number of difficulties over time. While concerns regarding the quality of services when provided via tele-platforms were voiced, it appears that some other concerns were paramount. Certainly a variety of health-focused fields are steeped deeply in history and tradition (DiCarlo et al., 2021). When new techniques and modalities are presented, it is common for the adoption to be slow with numerous hiccups along the way. Additionally, businesses built around the delivery of care can have financial goals and motives regarding the delivery of such services. As described by Field, most telehealth projects from the 1960s to 1980s did not survive past their grant/trial funding; when the grant funds expired, so did the programs (1996). Why did this happen? Many reasons surrounded the costs of equipment for both the clinician and client and a lack of familiarity with the medium. The advancement of technology both in abilities and reduced cost (i.e. advanced hardware and software and increased availability for consumers) has addressed a number of concerns, however, other challenges have persisted over time, such as:

- "the rapid advance of information and telecommunications technologies" – things often change and advance quickly in technological realms.
- "a complex and often unwieldy technical infrastructure" – this can be overwhelming and difficult to create protocols and structure for individuals and organizations.
- "a diverse and sometimes dazzling array of telemedicine technologies and uses" – with so many options in hardware and software, it can be overwhelming and confusing; clinical and financial decisions can be difficult to make.
- "the initial level of cooperation that medicine at a distance often demands of independent institutions and individuals" – A sense of not wanting to "fix that which isn't broken" dominated this cooperation historically (although access to services has been a long-term concern). Prior to COVID-19, the adaptations toward adoption of tele-anything was met with resistance for a number of reasons, however, circumstances have fueled giant leaps of adoption.
- the "restructuring of the nation's health care system" – to restructure large bodies there needs to be a high level of understanding of the worth of the changes with people in power on-board to direct the necessary shifts toward the goal of structuring.

~ and last but not least,

- "the growth of investor-owned enterprises that are not much inclined to allocate resources for purposes such as clinical research that do not add to corporate profits". — Money fuels many, many things and in-person services includes a number of different needs than those provided through telesystems.

(Field, 1996, p. 4).

The World Health Organization (WHO) established a body to review the benefits of "information and communication technologies" or ICTs. This body was named the Global Observatory for eHealth, or GOe, and was tasked to evaluate the global, national, and regional status of eHealth solutions to inform policies, standards, and best practices (World Health Organization, 2010, p. 6). Surveys of WHO member states were conducted in 2005 and 2009, with the latter informed by the former. The 2009 survey was completed by 114 countries and concentrated on examining the development of four primary fields of telemedicine: teleradiology, telepathology, teledermatogy, and telepsychology. Findings included that developing countries' concerns focused heavily on lack of technical expertise, costs, and infrastructure, while the more developed countries more often cited concerns regarding patient privacy, confidentiality, perceived lack of demand, and "competing health system priorities". Essentially, what will all this cost, is it worth it, is there a need, how does it affect current systems, and how do we protect patient information? There is a strong presentation of big-business financial concerns voiced (Field, 1996; World Health Organization, 2010) and a desire for telemedicine to "strengthen – rather than compete with – other health services", (World Health Organization, 2010, p.7).

In gathering this information it becomes apparent that there has been a lot of ebb and flow included in the emergence of telehealth services. For therapists, the main arenas include clinical care aspects, theoretical appropriateness, and cost and procurement of equipment. Struggles with any large changes can include evaluations of cost and performance (defined as appropriate for any environment):

1. Is the change more costly and performs less-well?
2. Is the change more costly and performs as well?
3. Is it less costly and performs better?
4. Less costly and performs as well?
5. More costly and performs better?
6. Less costly and performs less-well? (Field, 1996).

Some of these are obvious; if something is more expensive and performs the same or less-well, then the changes are not worth making and will most likely have undesired results. Other options become more murky depending on the criteria of all involved. The lingering questions include *how and by whom* decisions regarding performance and worth are made. Historically, implementing telehealth on a large scale has been brought up and buried based on different motivations and perceived needs. COVID-19 certainly changed a lot of motivations and perceived needs, and therefore the analytic process above has taken on new meaning.

More Recent Times

The Lewin Group, Inc. worked to update the 1996 IOM report in 2000. They found that while "patient satisfaction with telemedicine has consistently been demonstrated to be high" (p. 2), certain components continued to impede the wide adoption of such services (Lewin Group, Inc. HHS −10-97-0012, 2000). Impediments continue to include allocation of resources along with research complications and reimbursement difficulties. These continue to mirror early issues – the clinician needs to find worth in the expanded methods of rendering services, including maintaining professional integrity; the governmental and insurance bodies need to recognize worth in the promotion and reimbursement of such services so they are not allocating resources for undemonstrated services; researchers need to identify worth in standardizing terms and modes of evaluation; and patients need to experience worth in the non-traditional modes of service delivery. Consumers (patients/clients) have frequently voiced positives regarding the teleservice options (Simpson et al., in press; Gustke et al., 2000). Historically it has fallen to providers, financial systems, and researchers to invest time, thought, energy, and money into the greater implementation of teleservices for the people who need it the most – the clients.

A key component in all of this is client satisfaction, which has repeatedly proven to be high (Field, 1996; Robinson et al., 2015; Gustke et al., 2000; Batastini et al., 2020; Rosic et al., 2020). Batastini et al.'s recent meta-analysis of two decades worth of research regarding the comparison of patient satisfaction of services, when delivered via telehealth and in person, yielded supportive results for telehealth services. With a focus on understanding how much one's physical presence in the room mattered, they found high levels of satisfaction with telehealth across this vast span of 57 research studies. For an independent example with specifics, a research study conducted by Gustke et al. was conducted with 495 subjects receiving telemedicine services (which included mental health). This yielded results such as: 99% endorsing: "I was able to communicate adequately with the specialist", 98.2% endorsing: "I was comfortable that the specialist was able to understand what was bothering me today", 98.7% endorsing: "Telemedicine made it easier to get medical care today", and with only 3.3% endorsing "The next time I would prefer to see the specialist in person despite the possible inconvenience", (2000, p. 9).

Moving Forward

As we move forward, we must ask ourselves: if consumer satisfaction is high, why have various fields dismissed and avoided the incorporation of telehealth into typical practice for so long? Within play therapy, we also need to ask these types of questions and develop criteria specific to the process of working with minors. Research to date has predominately focused on adult satisfaction with telehealth services and interactions. Since play therapists typically see children, how do these trends translate to the delivery of telehealth services with children in general and in play therapy specifically? Anecdotal evidence from this author includes a practice which transitioned to 100% telehealth at the beginning of the COVID-19 restrictions and has retained previous clients and added new ones throughout. Many clients have stated they would like to continue telemental health sessions overall with periodic in-person, in-office sessions when it is possible to do so.

These research explorations concerning children will be more complicated for play therapists as minors have caregivers who bring their own sets of perceptions, needs, and opinions and the dynamics between each will need to be carefully dissected to have true information. At a minimum, the client-therapist, family-therapist, caregiver/parent-therapist, the client alone, and the caregiver(s)/parent(s) alone dynamics will need to be accounted for and carefully assessed as the criteria for satisfaction may be quite different for each.

Telehealth, COVID-19

As indicated by the history of telemedicine and other teleservices, adoption of such mediums has been historically slow for a number of reasons. In particular, the cost–benefit needs analyses did not motivate movement toward global use of teleservices. Some practitioners were utilizing teleservices prior to COVID-19, however, they were often regarded as either operating "on the fringe" of their profession or serving a very niche population, such as therapists providing services to people in very rural environments or with specific diagnoses. The disparity discussed above between low provider adoption/offering and high consumer satisfaction is one to highlight and explore as we move forward and broaden the conceptualizations of these service offerings.

Growth

Use of and interest in telehealth grew dramatically in 2020 due to the needs for human contact distancing during the COVID-19 pandemic. Fair Health (2020a) tracked and compared some key information regarding telehealth in April 2019 and April 2020 in the United States. In April 2019, the percentage of telehealth usage for the USA was 0.15% and for April 2020 it was 13.00%. This is an average increase in telehealth usage of 8335.51%. Initially the northeastern regional area of the United States experienced an influx of COVID-19 cases before much of the USA and their regional telehealth usage rose by a staggering 26,209% increase in usage (Fair Health, 2020a; 2020b). The American Psychological Association (APA) surveyed their members to find that 75% of clinicians were exclusively seeing clients remotely during the pandemic (Edwards-Ashman, 2021). Play therapy specific resource arenas also experienced phenomenal increases in members and usage. For instance, a Facebook group called "Tele-PLAY Therapy Resources and Support" created by Cara Gruhala on March 14, 2020, increased to 24,010 members within the first month (C. Gruhala, personal communication, January 2, 2021). As of January 2021, the group has grown to 36,100 members. The group's mission includes "To connect mental health providers using play-based interventions in a supportive community for the purpose of exploring tele-mental health services for children" (Facebook, 2021). Other groups have experienced similar rapid member growth. The high usage and sought-after support indicates enormous shifts in telehealth service deliveries and clinician needs.

In addition to the increase in telehealth usage, Fair Health also looked at the types of appointments telehealth services utilized with comparisons of the same months between years. To stay consistent with the above April information, we can look at some break downs of this dramatic increase in telehealth usage. A comparison of the top five Current Procedural Terminology (CPT) procedure codes yields additional drastic differences: in April 2019 the top five CPT codes used via telehealth were 99441, physician telephone patient service, 5–10 minutes; 98960, education and training for patient self-management; 99213, established patient office or other outpatient visit, 30 minutes; 99444 physician follow-up appointment (seen in last seven days); 99201, new patient or other outpatient visit, ten minutes. In April 2020, the landscape was remarkably different: 99213, same as above, 15-minute physician appointment; 99214, established patient, 25 minutes; 90837, psychotherapy 60 minutes; 90834, psychotherapy 45 minutes; and 99442 physician telephone patient service, 11–20 minutes (Fair Health, 2020a). Basically, prior to COVID-19 telehealth was primarily used for quick follow-up and educational physician visits and that landscape quickly changed to include full psychotherapy sessions within the top five CPT codes used in 2020. A tremendous number of mental health providers and clients switched to telemental health services within an incredibly short amount of time.

Rapid Adoption

This dramatic increase in usage and rapid change in service structure and medium was not without concern. With the "should we or shouldn't we" dilemma pushed to the side in the immediate days of COVID-19 lockdowns, the predominant concerns continued to surround privacy, security, accessibility, appropriateness for particular disorders, and provider payment (Calkins, 2021; O'Brien & McNicholas, 2020; DiCarlo et al., 2021). Temporary provisions addressed many of these concerns, along with developer advancements to programs used within telemental health sessions for longer term use.

The rapid shift was stressful and hectic for many clinicians, however, it is important to recognize that for some clients, the telehealth modality may be a preferred and superior service. Telehealth may actually yield more positive results for some clients and their families (Simpson et al., in press; DiCarlo et al., 2021). Some clients find entering into the therapist's environment comforting; it is the container to hold them and their important expressions. For others, one's own environment, one's own control of the environment, comfort items, and physical distance allows freedoms to express. Intimacy and proximity can be comforting or it can be intimidating and even remind one of unsafe, traumatizing situations/experiences. The "virtual space of the session instills a feeling of 'protection'" for some, particularly when they have difficult subjects to discuss (DiCarlo et al., 2021, p. 3). Telemental health can even be useful as a titration process for clients with a goal of in-person sessions at some future point. People are different and have different needs; it is important for clinicians to incorporate the client's needs into the equation, not merely insist on the clinician's comfort level dictating the environment.

Yellowlees et al. (2020) transformed their UC Davis Health psychiatry department from in-person, in-office services to 100% telehealth in three days. Their article, *Rapid Conversion of an Outpatient Psychiatric Clinic to a 100% Virtual Telepsychiatry Clinic in Response to COVID-19*, provides a blueprint for short time frame clinic conversions to telehealth. The key components for such a conversion include:

1. Commit to a plan – employ decisive action and formulate, enact, and commit to a plan
2. Communicate with all the staff – create subgroups to implement specific components of the plan, communication is paramount regarding any concerns or needs
3. Notify all clients who have scheduled appointments
4. Ensure all providers and staff have the appropriate equipment and training
5. Consider the beginning days a trial period where needs and operations are evaluated and altered as appropriate/possible (Yellowlees et al., 2020, p. 750).

Clients reported relief and appreciation for the opportunity to attend virtual sessions and as of July 2020 numerous had expressed a desire to continue telemental health sessions after restrictions are lifted. This is an important concept – clients were appreciative and responded positively to the organized approach of this clinic to meet the needs of clients, maintain the continuity of care, and address the necessary health requirements. As we know from many other scenarios, the strength and attitude of the leader in a situation often sets the tone for others and in this clinic the clients felt supported by the changes and approach. Clinic concerns included: contacting clients, clients without access to the necessary equipment (phone sessions were also offered), technology difficulties for clinicians, and ensuring HIPAA compliant platforms were used (Yellowlees, 2020).

Due Diligence

As clinicians, the process of due diligence confirms that we are working to avoid harm in our actions, decisions, and policies. According to Merriam-Webster, due diligence means:

1. "law: the care that a reasonable person exercises to avoid harm to other persons or their property"
2. "business: research and analysis of a company or organization done in preparation for a business transaction" (Merriam-Webster, 2021, para 1).

As clinicians we need to attend to the therapeutic components of utilizing a new medium, and as licensed professionals we also have to attend to the regulatory, ethical, and legal components as well. With any rapid changes or decision making it is important to slow down and work through the due diligence components to ensure everyone is as protected as possible.

Rules and Requirements

Mental health providers answer to a number of governing bodies, including but not limited to: state, federal, malpractice insurance, licensing, and professional organizations. When working through the due diligence process, each of the bodies which oversee the clinician's scope should be contacted and that contact should be documented. It is advised that clinicians create a document which details each component and allows for a compilation of key items which need to be addressed and/or maintained.

Maheu, a leader in knowledge, training, and resources in telebehavioral health, delineates key recommendations for the telehealth practitioner:

1. Understand your telehealth liability on a state level. Subscribe to publications and updates to ensure you are current. Determine if you will need to become licensed in other states to provide services outside of your current licensure. Some states are offering temporary licensure and other bodies, such as PSYPACT is offering multi-state licensure reciprocity. "We need permanent improvements to regulations so licensed therapists can more easily practice across state lines and meet the growing needs of remote patient populations", (Pennic, 2020).
2. Confirm that your professional liability insurance covers the services you are providing and/or want to provide and the locations involved. Determine if you will need any additional coverage and/or training to qualify for the coverage. Obtain any requirements, coverages, limitations, specifications, etc. in writing from your professional liability insurance company.
3. Research and understand any accepted standards of care for your particular field. Resources can include: state licensing board, ethics boards of professional organizations (local and national), peers with whom you consult formally as needed.
4. Provide clients with written information regarding unexpected occurrences during telehealth sessions. This can include anything from

technological difficulties to safety plans. This will be included in your informed consent.
5. Inform clients verbally and in writing if you are delivering any type of innovative services that have not been established by validated research. Consent forms should include "advantages and limitations of telehealth service delivery, including inherent deficiencies in the electronic equipment possibly interfering with diagnosis or treatment issues related to equipment failure; choice of venue waivers to resolve issues of jurisdiction; a brief description of equipment and services to be delivered and the purpose benefits, potential risks and other consequences of serviced delivered" (p. 79). Be sure to consult your legal and ethical resources regarding the contents of your informed consent and have each client/caregiver/custodian sign the document.
6. Be sure to document all clinical information to "provide evidence that treatment is consistent with the standard of care" (p. 79). This includes all intake materials and supporting documents. Any photographs and/or video footage of clients, particularly minors, should be handled with proper protections and ethical considerations in place.
7. If you have staff, ensure that they are up-to-date with the structure and requirements put in place by your organization.
8. Keep documentation of all courses attended, particularly for telehealth. Confirm that the courses include legal and ethical considerations. Attend courses over time to remain up to date.
9. Identify and use proper protections in all transmissions and storage of a client information, i.e. encrypted email, record storage, HIPAA compliant platforms, etc. Research and understand potential breaches of confidentiality and security, storage and retrieval of records and any supervision protocols. Include this information in your informed consent.
10. Document your efforts to seek guidance from your peers, ethical boards, etc., including sharing your informed consent, strategies regarding all services delivered, handling of all patient information, records, and materials, and so forth. Documentation of such efforts shows your due diligence process for your practice.
11. Seek supervision and consultation from leaders in the telehealth arena and document any interactions in writing. If you have consulted regarding a specific topic, document any recommendations and your rationale for following or not following the recommendations.
12. Investment in well-designed systems with security at the forefront will deter potential privacy abuses.

(adapted from Maheu, 2020, pp. 78-80).

HIPAA Compliant Platform

Despite the governmental provisionally relaxed guidelines of 2019, clinicians should utilize platforms and services which protect any collected personal health information (PHI) connected to clients. These relaxed provisions are set to expire January 20, 2021, although they may be extended. However, it is important for clinicians to use protected mediums irregardless of special allowances. In the United States, the Health Insurance Portability and Accountability Act of 1996, also known as HIPAA, establishes the guidelines for mental health professionals (and others) and the protection of any PHI. Platforms which collect PHI and have been certified as HIPAA compliant will often offer a Business Associate Agreement (BAA). A clinician who utilizes PHI collecting platforms which are HIPAA compliant, have a signed BAA with the company, and has informed the client/family of any potential risks is actively working toward the necessary due diligence.

Informed Consent

Informed consent is essentially an agreement between the clinician and the client/client's caregiver(s) regarding the risks and benefits to the proposed treatment. Organizational and legal consultation should inform the contents of the informed consent a clinician utilizes. These protections are predominately in place for the client, however, they also afford protections for the therapist. The American Psychological Association (2020) provides an example of important informed consent aspects for psychologists here: https://www.apa.org/practice/programs/dmhi/research-information/informed-consent-checklist. Be sure to research your appropriate organizations for your informed consent. Advocate for yourself and your practice, even if you work for an agency. Be sure that the paperwork provided to your clients conveys the necessary material and information for both in-person, in-office sessions and telemental health offerings.

Accessibility

For many years, concerns about access to mental health services have been discussed. Location, physical difficulties, socio-economic concerns, cultural factors, health issues, family dynamics, and safety issues can all influence and effect a person's ability to attend mental health treatment appointments. For some, the closest mental health services are 100 miles away and for others they might as well be (Weir, 2021). Underserved communities are woven throughout the United States with a variety of etiologies. Needs of the clients must be taken into account when formulating and implementing a treatment plan.

Digital Divide

> Digital divide, term that describes the uneven distribution of information and communication technologies (ICTs) in society. The digital divide encompasses differences in both access (first-level digital divide) and usage (second-level digital divide) of computers and the Internet between (1) industrialized and developing countries (global divide), (2) various socioeconomic groups within single nation-states (social divide), and (3) different kinds of users with regard to their political engagement on the Internet (democratic divide). In general, those differences are believed to reinforce social inequalities and to cause a persisting information or knowledge gap amid those people with access to and using the new media ("haves") and those people without ("have-nots").
>
> (Britannica, 2021, para 1)

The digital divide concepts are critical for the telemental health clinician to consider. The distribution of hardware access is uneven and cannot be taken for granted. A digital divide exists throughout the world where some people will have access to phones, smartphones, computers, tablets, etc., and some will not. Geographical and economic realities will greatly impact these accessibility concerns (O'Brien & McNicholas, 2020). "It is prudent that clinicians take these factors into account and strive to ensure equitable access to care for all of their patients", (p. 252). Creativity will be important in these situations. Approaches can include lending items to clients (e.g. play therapy materials provided for sessions, including craft materials, books, older smartphones which can access Wi-Fi, etc.), creating treatment interventions which utilize the items they have access to, applying for grants to provide clients with materials, etc.

Needs of the People

The National Alliance on Mental Illness (NAMI) reports that one in five adults in the United States experiences mental illness each year and one in 20 adults experiences serious mental illness. Additionally, one of every six youths (aged 6–17) experiences a mental health disorder, 50% of lifelong mental illness begins by age 14 and 75% by age 24, and suicide is the second leading cause of death for people aged 10–34 (National Alliance on Mental Health, 2020). A 2017 survey revealed that 39.7 million American adults have some type of untreated substance use issue and/or mental health disorder (U.S. Government Accountability Office, 2019). The survey revealed that many people do not think they need treatment or it is not accessible. This echoes a study by Kessler et al. (2001) which found that "situational barriers, financial barriers, thinking the problem would get better by itself, wanting to solve the problem on one's own, and being scared about hospitalization against one's will" were deterrents to receiving

58 Jessica Stone

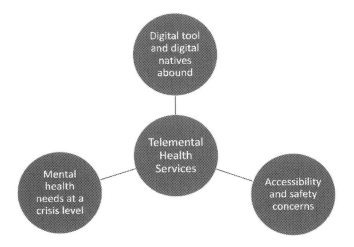

Figure 3.1 Circumstance Trifecta Leading to Telemental Health Incorporation.

mental health treatment. This 20-year span of mirrored findings indicates that the United States has a long-standing issue of poor accessibility to mental health services and a high level of need.

Adults who have untreated mental health concerns were once children who most likely could have benefitted from mental health treatment; *conservative* numbers report one in seven children experience child abuse and/or neglect (according to statistics for 2018) (Center for Disease Control, 2020). The mental health field, including play therapists, must unite to advocate for and provide services to clients with integrity and flexibility. Telemental health is an important option to offer people, even beyond pandemic conditions. It may not work for all, but it is a fundamental option to provide. Given the trifecta upon us: 1) accessibility and safety concerns, 2) digital tools and digital natives abound, and 3) mental health needs at a crisis level, we are in need of additional options in addition to the traditional. Please see Figure 3.1.

Telemental Health Play Therapy

Telemental health play therapy is here to stay. The delivery of play therapy services has forever been altered and client experience, research, and therapeutic gains will inform the future of our field. Telemental health play therapy, as defined in the beginning of this book, will expand the reaches of play therapy services to people for whom and places in which the traditional services were difficult or impossible.

Therapeutic Alliance

One of the key components of therapy is the therapeutic alliance. Prior to COVID-19 many clinicians did not believe the alliance and connection could be achieved via teleservices. Thankfully that has overwhelmingly not been the case, with many positive aspects of telemental health services being recognized and realized. The unique experience of *literally* entering the client's world, seeing their environment, any interactions that take place, their family pets, their special blanket or stuffed animal, and, in some cases, the absolute lack of these important things; being invited into these arenas has added value to the play therapy process. Straus and O'Neil (2020), wrote an article entitled *Playing Together Apart*. This article discussed the telemental health experience of clinicians in New England early in the pandemic. One of the cases discussed included Tony who brought pillows and blankets into a cardboard box, created a fort, and he and the therapist (on the phone) hid together.

> *He looked right at her, nose to nose, whispering, "Okay, now we're in a safe place. The virus can't find us here!" They virtually cuddled for the rest of the session while Tony, sometimes a small fearful boy, bravely sheltered a beloved adult inside his safe place.*
>
> (Straus & O'Neil, 2020, p. 34).

In this new era of service delivery, perhaps it is time to rethink and redefine the components of therapeutic alliance/rapport. Rapport and relationship are widely regarded as core elements of the play therapy process. Stone (2020), defines rapport as "a mutual, empathetic, harmonious, and friendly connection of participants based on mutual interest" (p. 40). Based on the findings over time regarding client satisfaction with teleservices, we are left wondering what components of the therapeutic interaction contribute to or detract from the building and maintenance of rapport? How do the findings that clients feel the rapport is built/maintained over teleservices support or alter previously held beliefs? We can explore a variety of components including: what is really needed to build/maintain rapport? Who brings what to the dynamic and what effects does each component contribute (or not)? When we identify the answers to these types of questions we can begin to understand how to implement/address these components in a variety of environments. We may not like the answers which contradict long-held beliefs, but discovering and identifying what works can help shape and inform the future of our field.

> *In many cases, we clearly need to move ahead and adopt some technology, despite a limited amount of information regarding the full impact of technological change. This is the dilemma: either we become part of the development of these new systems, tools, protocols and guidelines for their use – or others will do it for us.*
>
> (Maheu, 2020, p. 78)

Digital Tools

The inclusion of digital tools in therapy has long been thought to be counterproductive regarding therapeutic alliance, which, according to Baker (2019), and the numerous studies discussed previously in the chapter regarding client satisfaction, is simply not true. Miclea et al. found that a hybrid approach to clinician-client interaction which includes teleservices, telephone, email, and/or texting was as effective as face-to-face therapy or medication (2010).

"The integration of telepsychology with other technological innovations (e.g. mobile apps, virtual reality, big data, and artificial intelligence [AI]) opens up interesting future perspectives for the improvement of mental health assistance", (DiCarlo et al., 2021, p. 1).

Digital Play Therapy™, as described by Stone (2020), introduces a fundamental structure for the therapeutic use of digital tools in play therapy. With underpinnings which include the therapeutic powers of play (Schaefer & Drewes, 2014), prescriptive play therapy, and the 5Cs of digital play therapy (DPT), the clinician can feel confident in the tenets included in this approach. The 5Cs of DPT include: competency, culture, comfort, congruence, and capability. Applying these fundamental play therapy tenets, along with the traditional ones included in the first two chapters of this text, will allow the play therapist to formulate clinically sound and effect treatment plans and interventions. Please refer to the text, *Digital Play Therapy* for more detailed information (Stone, 2020; in press).

Two Types of Telemental Health Play Therapy Deliveries

Telemental health play therapy can be delivered in two distinct ways: asynchronous and synchronous.

> *Synchronous programs take place in real time and are a live 2-way interaction between the patient and healthcare provider. This includes virtual appointments that are conducted using the patient's smartphone, tablet, or computer with a camera. When using a smartphone or tablet, patients must first download an app that connects them with a provider.*
>
> *Asynchronous programs, also known as "store and forward" applications, are not live and involve the transfer of images, videos, and other clinical information that a healthcare provider views and responds to at a later time. In this case, patients may wear medical devices to monitor and track health information (e.g. blood pressure) in a personal health application that they forward to their healthcare provider.*
>
> (Mahar et al., 2018, p. 939).

Virtual sessions via a HIPAA compliant platform are considered a synchronous service delivery. Anything that is left to be read, replied to, or future actions taken at another time would be considered asynchronous, i.e. an email or text message (HIPAA compliance applies to asynchronous delivery as well). As mentioned above, findings by Baker (2019), Miclea et al. (2010), and DiCarlo et al. (2021), found that a combination of synchronous and asynchronous therapeutic services served clients well.

"What do we actually do?"

Much of this chapter has focused on the historical experiences and views regarding telehealth services and the importance of the integration into play therapy both for the immediate human-distancing needs and beyond. The clinician who has done their due diligence, has met or aspired toward the 5Cs of digital play therapy, and secured their appropriate hardware and software, can still find themselves in front of their device wondering what to do.

Ultimately, the play therapist who has a firm grasp on their therapeutic fundamentals and approach, and has a solid working knowledge of the client and their needs, will create powerful treatment plans to use as the case moves forward. The sessions, whether they be in-office, face-to-face or via telemental health play therapy, will implement the treatment plan utilizing vetted tools (digital or otherwise) which aim to activate the identified therapeutic powers of play. Whether the play is parallel or involves co-play, the therapist provides the materials, the client uses what they have, or they meet in a video game, the client and clinician can interact in meaningful, powerful, connecting ways.

The identified components in the treatment plan and case conceptualization will not only inform the treatment trajectory but also communication with caregivers and any collateral contacts. These key aspects of the treatment will create a solid foundation from which to provide the treatment, have discussion with others, and in writing any case notes and/or reports. Each step of the process builds the foundation for the next – the theoretical underpinnings, the case conceptualization, the knowledge of the history, foundations, and research of telehealth, the inclusion of any mitigating circumstances, the legal and ethical considerations and documentation, and ultimately the service delivery all work together to provide a solid base for the educated, informed, flexible play therapist – and all of this benefits the clients we serve.

After COVID-19

At some point the world will be released of the pandemic restrictions and a new day-to-day "normal" will be achieved. For some this will include hopes of returning to as-close-to pre-pandemic functioning as possible. For others, the pandemic has restructured priorities, goals, work, habits, interests, and more. Others still will navigate the new-found freedoms and experiences toward some hybrid existence – a little of the old, a little of the new, a bit of growth and recovery, with anything in between mixed in.

Similarly, therapists have had a plethora of responses to the shifts brought about by 2019. Many therapists have expressed distress with the transition to telemental health and returned to (or never stopped) in-person sessions despite the risks; others have already abandoned their offices with a preference for telehealth, and yet others are unsure what the future holds, with probable hybrid offerings of services on the horizon.

Clients and their families have also experienced differences through these changes. Parents who once had to leave work, pick up a child from school, drive to a session, wait for the session to finish, bring the child back to school, and finally return to work might be reluctant to return to that process now that the child has had months of telesessions which took a fraction of the time to attend. Employers may also prefer (or demand) parents advocate for telesessions as well. Some schools are providing private areas for sessions to occur so parents do not have to leave work at all and students end up missing less instructional time; they only miss the session time and not the travel time. If telesessions are productive and working toward the treatment goals, is the insistence on in-office sessions in the best interest of the client? Has the client regressed by not having in-office sessions? These (and many more) are important inquires to inform how future treatment will look. Again, for some the answer is a resounding "Yes!" it is absolutely worth it to return to in-office sessions! For others the option of telehealth removes many of the obstacles or frustrations associated with traditional treatment. Others still will benefit from exploration of the options, pros and cons of each, and a flexible, customized treatment protocol can be created.

Telemental health services are certainly robust with ways to meet the needs of many during a pandemic and physical distancing requirements, however, a rich history indicates the markers of a strong future and ongoing use. Treatment options and access to specialists will expand exponentially for clients and their families. The more research, structure, experience, and regulatory guidance provided, the more comfortable clinicians will become with long term use (O'Brien & McNicholas, 2020).

Looking Toward the Future

Landscape

Hofer, the CEO at *AbleTo*, one of the many virtual therapy service providers at this time, delineated six teletherapy and mental health predictions and trends to watch and prepare for (Pennic, 2020). A service provider business owner, Hofer certainly has his industry in mind, however, we can benefit from some thought-provoking components of his outlook.

A key component will be research and outcome measurements. This will allow industries to have increased confidence in the implemented treatment approaches. The following quote includes a call for "rigorous, evidence-based standards for measuring patient outcomes".

> The healthcare industry has made progress toward increasing access to mental health care and defining what quality care looks like. Now in 2021, the industry needs to focus on how we measure that quality. With mental health becoming an incredibly hot market and so much funding pouring in for new entrants, many leaders are concerned with the lack of rigorous, evidence-based standards for measuring patient outcomes. (para 1).

Market share is certainly a concern for all businesses – even for therapists. How do we receive referrals? How do we project the services we provide into the community? Hofer offers "organizations that don't show evidence-based rigor and good quality clinical care will fade, while those providing sound mental health care will succeed", (para 2). Know what you are doing and why you are doing it. Project and integrate all that is included in Digital Play Therapy's 5Cs and your practice will succeed.

One of the primary focal points in mental health treatment at this time is flexibility. The prescriptive play therapy approach is quite congruent with this outlook as it allows the clinician to tailor the therapeutic process to the needs of the client. No longer will the "one size fits all" approach be tolerated, nor should it be. "Mental health is not one condition requiring one solution; it encompasses a heterogeneous group of complex conditions that require different interventions", (Pennic, 2020, para 5). Moving forward we must focus on respecting people's unique and collective needs and experiences and provide services which respect both. We need to create "a solution set that can address the complexity and nuances of mental health. The market needs to be more mindful of this over the course of the next year and avoid trying to oversimplify mental health", (para 5).

A hopeful prediction is one of attention to inequalities and accessibility. "Telehealth, like COVID, has laid bare underlying inequities that have long existed in the healthcare system", (para 7). A therapist must not only have an understanding of the complex needs of a client and their family and their access to resources, but also the ability to attend sessions. Looking forward as clinicians and a field, how do we improve our reach? Hofer hopes that "In 2021, we will see a larger focus on ensuring quality mental health care reaches all populations in need, with greater emphasis on access and cost-effectiveness", (Pennic, 2020, para 7).

Clinician challenges, including self-care and acknowledgement of clinician boundaries, difficulties, and needs, is paramount. During the pandemic clinicians have been faced with great multidimensional changes.

Keeping the therapeutic tenets a priority, while simultaneously managing logistics, finances, family needs, health, personal needs, online schooling, professional requirements, and more, has posed challenges for even the most seasoned professional. "… clinicians are facing unprecedented challenges during this pandemic. For months, they've been supporting patients struggling with the impacts of COVID while they are living through it themselves—working from home, seeing patients virtually, juggling their own personal and family lives" (Pennic, 2020, para 10).

Ultimately it is the relationships that drive healing. Feeling heard, understood, seen, and accepted opens the doors of strength, resilience, and connection (Stone, 2020). One of the most profound realizations throughout this pandemic-driven shift has been about connection – that connection can happen through a screen, through a text, and/or through a phone as long as we are truly present on fundamental levels.

> *While technology is driving so much positive change in healthcare and in mental health, we need to remember the value of the human connection. Clinical interventions depend on real people delivering care, and the voices of both patients and providers need to guide our approach to care delivery, including through technology like telehealth or virtual therapy. The relationships that providers and patients create with one another are the key driver of care, and technology should complement that human connection, not replace it.*
>
> (Pennic, 2020, para 8).

Needs

Predominate future needs include training for current and incoming mental health providers and well-constructed, well-conducted research. Prior to the swift and broad transformation to telemental health services, very few trainings were offered regarding telehealth. This lack of education and experience contributes to apprehension and negative views of alternate forms of treatment delivery (Altvater et al., 2018).

Conclusion

While no one would wish that the COVID-19 pandemic occurred, we are fortunate to have 100+ years of telemedicine history and advances at our disposal. This rich background affords us the luxury of options regarding mental health service offerings and the ability to maintain continuity of care. The implications and long-lasting impacts of telemental health services are far-reaching. Positive byproducts of this scenario include drastic shifts and advancements in the options to be offered to clients and taught to clinicians. Current clinicians are witnessing and participating in a defining moment in mental health history.

Well thought through approaches which incorporate evidence based interventions, combined with experience, culminate into powerful future treatment possibilities.

References

Altvater, R. A., Singer, R. R., & Gil, E. (2018). Part 2: A qualitative examination of play therapy and technology training and ethics. *International Journal of Play Therapy*, 27(1), 46–55. doi:10.1037/pla0000057

American Psychological Association (2020). Informed consent checklist for telepsychological services. https://www.apa.org/practice/programs/dmhi/research-information/informed-consent-checklist

Baker, L. (2019). Therapy in the digital age. In J. Stone (Ed.), *Integrating technology into modern therapies* (pp. 37–47). Routledge.

Batastini, A. B., Paprzycki, P., Jones, A. C. T., & MacLean, N. (2021). Are videoconferenced mental and behavioral health services just as good as in-person? A meta-analysis of a fast-growing practice. *Clinical Psychology Review*, 83, 1–99.

Britannica (2021). *Digital divide*. https://www.britannica.com/topic/digital-divide

Cadogan, M. (2020). *Willem Einthoven*. https://litfl.com/willem-einthoven/

Calkins, H. (2021, January/February). Online therapy is here to stay. *Monitor on Psychology*, 52(1), 78–82.

Center for Disease Control (CDC) (2020). *Preventing child abuse and neglect*. https://www.cdc.gov/violenceprevention/childabuseandneglect/fastfact.html

DiCarlo, F., Sociali, A., Picutti, E., Pettorruso, M., Vellante, F., Verrastro, V., Martinotti, G., & di Giannantonio, M. (2021). Telepsychiatry and other cutting edge technologies in COVID-19 pandemic: Bridging the distance in mental health assistance. *International Journal of Clinical Practice*, 75, Art. no. e13716. https://doi.org/10.1111/ijcp.13716

Edwards-Ashman, J. (2021, January/February). Advocacy will help secure expanded telehealth coverage. *Monitor on Psychology*, 52(1), 83–85.

Einthoven, W. (1906). (H. W. Blackburn, Trans.). *The Telecardiogram*. (Original work published 1955). https://www.sciencedirect.com/sdfe/pdf/download/eid/1-s2.0-0002870357903678/first-page-pdf

Fair Health (2020a). Monthly telehealth regional tracker, Apr. 2020. https://s3.amazonaws.com/media2.fairhealth.org/infographic/telehealth/apr-2020-national-telehealth.pdf

Fair Health (2020b). Media outlets reference our data. https://www.fairhealth.org/press-release/telehealth-claim-lines-increase-8-336-percent-nationally-from-april-2019-to-april-2020

Facebook, 2021. Tele-play therapy resources and support group. https://www.facebook.com/groups/2377497079019547/about

Field, M. J. (1996). *Telemedicine: A guide to assessing telecommunications for health care*. National Academy Press.

Gustke, S. S., Balch, D. C., West, V. L., & Rogers, L. O. (2000). Patient satisfaction with telemedicine. *Telemedicine Journal*, 6(1), 5–13.

Kessler, R. C., Berglund, P. A., Bruce, M. L., Koch, J. R., Laska, Leaf, P. J., Manderscheid, R. W., Rosenheck, R. A., Walters, E. E., & Wang, P. S. (2001). The prevalence and correlates of untreated serious mental illness. https://www.thefreelibrary.com/The+prevalence+and+correlates+of+untreated+serious+mental+illness....-a087430349

Lewin Group, Inc. HHS −10-97-0012 (2000). *Assessment of approaches to evaluating medicine: Final report*. https://aspe.hhs.gov/system/files/pdf/139216/index.pdf

Mahar, J. H., Rosencrance, G. J., & Rasmussen, P. A. (2018). Telemedicine: Past, present, and future. *Cleveland Clinic Journal of Medicine, 85* (12) 938–942. doi: https://doi.org/10.3949/ccjm.85a.17062 https://www.ccjm.org/content/85/12/938

Maheu, M. M. (2020). Telehealth: Risk management in the re-tooling of health care. *Law & Governance, 7*(1), 78–80. https://www.longwoods.com/content/16422//telehealth-risk-management-in-the-re-tooling-of-health-care

Merriam-Webster (2021). Due diligence. https://www.merriam-webster.com/dictionary/due%20diligence

Miclea, M., Miclea, S., Ciuca, A., $ Budău, O. (2010). Computer-mediated psychotherapy: Present and prospects. A developer perspective. *Cognition, Brain, Behavior: An interdisciplinary journal, 14*(3), 185–208.

National Alliance on Mental Health (2020). *Mental health by the numbers*. https://www.nami.org/mhstats

O'Brien, M., & McNicholas, F. (2020, May 21). The use of telepsychiatry during COVID-19 and beyond. *Irish Journal of Psychological Medicine, 37* (4), 250-255. https://www.cambridge.org/core/journals/irish-journal-of-psychological-medicine/article/use-of-telepsychiatry-during-covid19-and-beyond/C748863E9950F24FF7BFF3277CA93628

Pennic, F. (2020, December 30). 6 Mental health & teletherapy predictions; Trends to watch in 2021. HIT Consultant. https://hitconsultant.net/2020/12/30/mental-health-teletherapy-predictions-trends-2021/

Robinson, J. D., Turner, J. W., Wood, K. (2015). Patient perceptions of acute care telemedicine: A pilot investigation. *Health Communication, 30*(12), 1269–1276.

Rosic, T., Lubert, S., & Samaan, Z. (2020). . https://pubmed.ncbi.nlm.nih.gov/32799956/Virtual psychiatric care fast-tracked: Reflections inspired by the COVID-19 pandemic

Schaefer, C. E., & Drewes, A. A. (2014). *The therapeutic powers of play: 20 core agents of change* (2nd ed). Wiley.

Simpson, S., Richardson, L., Pietrabissa, G., Castelnuovo, G., & Reid, C. (in press). *Videotherapy and therapy alliance in COVID-19* [Manuscript submitted for publication]. doi: 10.1002/cpp.2521

Stone, J. (in press). *Digital play therapy: A clinician's guide to comfort and competence* (2nd ed). Routledge.

Strehle, E. M. & Shabde, N. (2006). One hundred years of telemedicine: Does this new technology have a place in paediatrics? *Arch Dis Child, 91*, 956–959. doi: 10.1136/adc.2006.099622 http://www2.hawaii.edu/~strev/ICS614/materials/Strehle%20Shabde%20One%20hundred%20years%20of%20telemedicine%202006.pdf

Straus, M. & O'Neil, K. (2020, May/June). Playing together apart. *Psychotherapy Networker, 44*(3), 32–37.

University of Nebraska (n.d.). *Cecil L. Wittson*. https://archives.nebraska.edu/agents/people/1473

U.S. Government Accountability Office (2019). *Behavioral health: Research on health care costs of untreated conditions is limited*. https://www.gao.gov/products/gao-19-274

World Health Organization (2010). *Telemedicine opportunities and developments in member states.* https://www.who.int/goe/publications/goe_telemedicine_2010.pdf

WeCounsel (2021). *Telemental health: History.* https://www.wecounsel.com/telemental-health/

Weir, K. (2021, January/February). There's a new push to reach underserved communities. *Monitor on Psychology, 52*(1), 64–67.

Yellowlees, P., Nakagawa, K., Pakyurek, M., Hanson, A., Elder, J., & Kales, H. (2020). Rapid conversion of an outpatient psychiatric clinic to a 100% virtual telepsychiatry clinic in response to COVID-19. *Psychiatric Services, 71*(7), 749–752.

4 Cultural Humility in the Telemental Health Playroom

Carmen Jimenez-Pride

Culture and Diversity

Culture and diversity are complex, ever changing, and evolving. Historically, culture and diversity have been limited to the color of one's skin, ethnicity, or celebrated religious holidays. Diverse and cultural groups are not homogeneous despite shared or common history, attributes, or practices. Individuals are part of multiple subgroups and have multiple social identities within these subgroups. The concept of culture and diversity are broader than what traditionally extends to outward appearances or displays.

Subjective experiences such as age, gender, sexual orientation, dis(ability), socioeconomic status, generation, marital status, interests, education, occupation, hobbies etc., should also be considered when discussing culture and diversity. This chapter will explore Culture and Diversity, and how these terms play out in today's society with the telemental health services. We will explore the importance of Cultural Competence and Cultural Humility as they relate to what may be a technical divide, as all clients may not have Internet and/or other technological resources. The practitioner's goal will be to step away from what they think they know and explore what may be new cultural norms in telemental health services, expounded on throughout this chapter.

Culture

In 2017, Zimmerman asserted that

> *"Culture is the characteristics and knowledge of a particular group of people encompassing language, religion, cuisine, social habits, music and arts"* (para.1). Taking a deeper dive in the concept of culture Cristina De Rossi, anthropologist, stated *"Culture encompasses religion, food, what we wear, how we wear it, our language marriage, music, what we believe is right or wrong, how we sit at the table, how we greet visitors, how we behave with loved ones, and million other things"*.
>
> (Zimmerman, 2017, para. 3)

DOI: 10.4324/9781003166498-4

Merriam-Webster (2020a) has multiple definitions for the word culture:

- The customary beliefs, social forms, and material traits of a racial, religious, or social group.
- The set of shared attitudes, values, goals, and practices that characterizes an institution or organization.
- The set of values, conventions or social practices associated with a particular field, activity, or societal characteristics.
- Acquaintance with and taste in fine arts, humanities, and broad aspects of science as distinguished from vocational and technical skills. (Merriam-Webster, 2020a, para 1)

Culture, as defined, is a term that is often used and comes with a broad meaning that spans across multiple systems. Hudspeth (2016) stated "as mental health practitioners and researchers, we are taught to consider cultural uniqueness when working with clients" (p. 113). Based on the multiple definitions of culture and the idea of the various multicultural subgroups that individuals can belong to, practitioners should look outside of what may be deemed as the norm when evaluating and working with their client populations. Equally important is evaluating one's self to identify personal membership to various multicultural subgroups. Looking past generalized subgroups will assist the practitioner to develop a more intentional therapeutic relationship with their clients; evaluating cultural similarities and connections and allowing the clients to feel seen and heard within the therapeutic environment.

An embracing of the cultural uniqueness allows practitioners to gain a level of insight and understanding beneficial to the wholistic view of the client. The term culture leads us into a commonly related term which is diversity.

Diversity

Diversity is defined as "the inclusion of different types of people (such as people of different races or cultures) in a group or organization" (Merriam-Webster, 2020b, para 1)

> *Diversity is any dimension that can be used to differentiate groups and people from one another. In a nutshell, it's about empowering people by respecting and appreciating what makes them different, in terms of age, gender, ethnicity, religion, disability, sexual orientation, education, and national origin. Diversity allows for the exploration of these differences in a safe, positive, and nurturing environment. It means understanding one another by surpassing simple tolerance to ensure people truly value their differences.*
> (Global Diversity Practice, 2020, para.1)

Diversity as a construct does not always involve cultural differences. There can be the existence of culture without diversity, and then there is what we see more often with clients, which is cultural diversity. An example of this would be groups holding onto the foundational principles of their culture, while allowing changes, or incorporating the world around them. Other examples may include those who have grown up in strict communities, not allowing technology or agreeing with the idea of therapy, now integrating some technological services and engaging in more therapeutic interventions.

Cultural Diversity

According to Belfield (2012) culture can be considered a lens that individuals utilize to evaluate things within their environments. "Cultural diversity is important because our country, workplaces, and schools increasingly consist of various cultural, racial and ethnic groups" (Belfield, 2012, para. 6)

> *Cultural diversity, or sometimes referred to as multiculturalism, is a quality of diverse and many different cultures. Cultural Diversity a system that recognizes and respects the existence and presence of diverse groups of people within a society. The system values their socio-cultural differences and encourages each individual to celebrate it. An environment with diverse cultures also inspires everyone within the society to make significant contribution to empower their cultural identity as well as others.*
>
> (M. J., 2020, para 5-7)

The acknowledgment of our cultural differences within the practice setting allows for a greater respect and understanding to grow between client and practitioner. The onus will be on the practitioner to facilitate an environment even through the telemental health medium, that allows clients to see and feel respected on the basis on their cultural diversity. This is done by recognizing that many cultures may exist within a practitioners personal and professional life. Also, recognizing that cultural subgroups may or may not be diverse. Practitioners' respect of the cultural differences in relationships with clients, families, and colleagues is imperative. Practitioners must acknowledge that individuals have the right to cultural expressions and develop an understanding that one's cultural expression is valid. This may require a practitioner to practice without a firm understanding of the role of the client in a particular subgroup or a firm understanding of the importance or value of the cultural expression to the client. The ability of the practitioner to maintain respect for the client continues to shape the therapeutic relationship; allowing the client to develop a level of trust and comfort to assist the practitioner with deepening their understanding of the client, their roles within the subgroups, and their cultural expressions.

Practitioners operating within their professional code of ethics must remain cognizant of how services are practiced and open the opportunity for the practitioner to value what cultures clients bring to the table. For example, the practitioner operates with a concept that the client's beliefs, traditions, and practices are valuable for their cultural identity and their membership in culturally diverse subgroups.

Allowing space to understand others in terms of their cultural diversity shows a level of respect needed in the growth of the therapeutic relationship. Another concept to keep in mind is that of cultural humility and the relationship of cultural diversity and cultural humility.

Culturally Competent Best Practices

Mental health Practitioners are ethically obligated to engage in culturally competent best practices by increasing their cultural awareness. Practitioners, based on their professional code of ethics and the Association of Play Therapy (APT), are both encouraged and obligated to gain an understanding of the diverse populations they serve. The Association for Play Therapy (APT) best practices states "Play therapists are expected to adhere to any and all state and/or federal laws, state licensing board requirements and the legal and ethical codes promulgated by their primary professional organizations" (Association for Play Therapy, 2019a, p. 2).

As stated in APT best practices, to adhere to legal and ethical codes the National Association of Social Workers standards on culturally competent practices are outlined in the organization's code of ethics.

> *Social workers treat each person in a caring and respectful fashion, mindful of individual differences and cultural and ethnic diversity. Social workers promote clients' socially responsible self-determination. Social workers seek to enhance clients' capacity and opportunity to change and to address their own needs. Social workers are cognizant of their dual responsibility to clients and to the broader society. They seek to resolve conflicts between clients' interests and the broader society's interests in a socially responsible manner consistent with the values, ethical principles, and ethical standards of the profession.*
> (National Association of Social Workers, 2017, p 6)

Although every Practitioner will not fall under the ethical code of the National Association for Social Workers (NASW), the value and ethical principles are relatable across counselor, psychologist, and marriage and family therapist professional organizations. Each organization maintains a set of ethical principles, standards, or bylaws for the licensed practitioner to follow. When not following these identified guidelines the practitioner places themselves at risk of not operating within the best practice and can risk the therapeutic relationship with the client.

When looking at the dynamics within the world today it becomes imperative that practitioners develop an understanding of how culture and diversity play a role in their therapeutic practices (Kottman & Meany-Walen, 2016). Looking beyond the presenting problem is a concept that requires the therapist not only to look at the reasons for therapeutic services but also look at the client in terms of culture and diversity. When looking beyond the presenting problem the practitioner is creating a deeper healing space for the clients and families served. Furthermore looking beyond, the presenting problem requires the practitioner to move away from the mentality of "I do not see" that includes color, race, ethnicity, religion, sex, gender, etc. When operating within the "I do not see" mentality this will leave your clients not feeling seen within their therapeutic healing space. Respecting and valuing the culture and diversity of the client by taking a deeper dive into their client's historical family narratives, inter-general trauma, true cultural identities, values, norms, and traditions will continue to strengthen the therapeutic relationship and increase the opportunity for healing. Also, these practices can assist the client and family with developing a sense of belonging in their healing space (Kottman & Meany-Walen, 2016). Practitioners are charged with approaching each client practicing cultural competence. To successfully fulfill the charge, the practitioners must have a working knowledge of culture and diversity, along with an understanding of how to practice cultural humility within the therapeutic setting.

Cultural Humility

The concept of cultural humility was developed by Melanie Tervalon and Jann Murray-Garcia (Tervalon & Murray-Garcia, 1998) to address inequities in the field of healthcare. The concept of cultural humility has expanded since 1998 across various fields of practice. Cultural humility goes beyond the concept of cultural competence. Cultural humility is having an awareness of one's own cultural heritage, the influences of culture on attitudes beliefs and experiences, also recognizing the power dynamics and taking action (Asbill & Water, 2013). Summarizing the differences between the two, cultural competence can be summarized as the knowledge and cultural humility can be summarized as actions.

Cultural humility and cultural diversity often work hand in hand; practitioners must be aware of possible limitations or challenges with practicing cultural humility. Conflict may arise during the building or maintaining of the therapeutic relationship, which must be addressed in order to continue the therapeutic relationship and maintain a healthy therapeutic setting. The practitioner must recognize the value difference or the conflict within the practitioner client relationship.

In understanding cultural humility, it's important to understand that there will be therapeutic relationships in which your values, and those of your client, line up and allow for the setting of therapeutic goals and thus therapy moves forward in an easy manner. And then there are those times when there is conflict between values is so great that goal setting and moving forward with the therapeutic relationship is challenged (Davis et al., 2017). Recognizing these value difference and how cultural diversity play a role is vital in elevating this conflict and understanding why the conflict happens, thus helping to create a bond of inclusion and understanding.

Cultural Competence

Cultural competence is the ability to interact with people across various cultures, having a positive attitude toward cultural differences, gaining knowledge of different cultural practices and world views, and gaining and practicing skills to interact across cultures (National Association of Social Workers, 2015). When embracing cultural competence, mental health professionals are invited to form a moral and ethical space to meet people where they are, accept who they are, and engage in learning their behaviors, abilities, and practice from their point of view. Mental health professionals are to sit with the very essence of culture and learn its functionality for that particular subgroup.

Cultural competence is recognized as the ability to have an understanding of people from other cultures along with the ability to interact with them. Just as with the importance of culture, diversity, and cultural humility; being culturally competent requires a level of understanding of one's owns culture, having a desire and willingness to learn, value, and respect other's cultural subgroups, beliefs, and practices.

Defining cultural competency is seen as one of the most fundamental challenges to advancing the discussion about cultural competency in the field. Cultural competency is a practice that is required for practitioners based on their professional organizations' code of ethics or best practices. This concept is also sought out by mental health organizations, schools, communities, social, and professional organizations.

Suggested by Gil (2005) there are three steps that can be used to become culturally competent. Step one requires the therapist to build a sensitivity by learning about others and how they view the world. Step two requires the therapist to obtain knowledge responsibly with a focus on increasing one's knowledge of self and the limitations of self. Step three requires the therapist to not only gain the knowledge but utilize the knowledge to change their behaviors. Practicing cultural competence as a therapist will require the therapist to develop a practice of seeking supervision, consultation, and training to continue in their areas of weakness (Morrison Bennett & Eberts, 2014, p. 17).

Cultural Competence, Cultural Humility, and Telemental Health Play Therapy

Telehealth is the practice of providing clinical services on a technology platform (Chaet et al., 2017). "Technology has become an integral part of our daily lives" as stated by Altvater (2019, p. 10). The use of technology and technological products continues to increase in one's personal and professional lives. Technology is not only increasing in the mental health field but also within the practice of play therapy (Altvater et al., 2018). When thinking about the relationship between technology and play therapy first thoughts are the use of technological items within the playroom setting, but what happens when the playroom becomes technology? This requires the practitioner to show a demonstration of flexibility and adaptability to the circumstances of the client's way of life and living environment when providing play therapy services by telehealth (Mellenthin, 2020).

There is no current evidence-based research on cultural humility within the practice of play therapy nor the practice of telemental health play therapy. Although, discussions around this topic continues to increase bringing awareness to the practice of cultural humility within the play therapy setting. There is still work that is needed in this area such as continued evidence-based research, and increased conversations among the play therapy community and mental health community. Also, clinical professional's evaluating self and their privileges, biases, and roles and how that impacts the diverse communities they serve. Identifying the need for cultural humility with the practice of telehealth play therapy services will require the play therapist to have increased knowledge of cultural competence and become aware of the impact of cultural differences on the delivery of teleplay therapy services.

> *When appropriate, social workers shall advocate for access to technology and resources for individuals, families, groups and communities who have difficulty accessing them because they are a member of a vulnerable population such as people with disabilities, limited proficiency in English, limited financial means, lack of familiarity with technology, or other challenges.*
> (National Association of Social Workers, 2017, p. 26)

In 2017, the National Association of Social Workers, in conjunction with Association of Social Work Boards, Council on Social Work Education, Clinical Social Work Association published the Standards for Technology in Social Work Practice. This publication provided social workers with a set of standards focused on the use of technology in practice. In 2019, the Association for Play Therapy published the Ethical Considerations for Implementing Telehealth Health in Play Therapy (Association for Play Therapy, 2019b). Both publications discuss best practices and ethical consideration for practice of telemental health play therapy. Various professional organizations have published guidelines for speaking to ethical and best practices regarding telemental health services. None of the professional organizations go into detail regarding the practice of cultural humility while providing telemental health services.

Cultural Considerations and Limitations in Telehealth Play Therapy

Internet

The internet operates as the connector between the play therapist and client. The internet may appear as an accessible resource used to reach a large portion of the population that is often free in public locations, offered with mobile service plans, and home phone plans (Kazdin & Blasé, 2011). Although internet is a widely accessible resource, there are populations that may not have access to internet services making telehealth play therapy services out of reach. Cultural considerations would include not assuming that all individuals have access to internet services. Practicing cultural humility would require the play therapist to take a deeper dive into their assumptions and views held about of populations they serve, and how their bias toward clients who do not have internet services affects the therapeutic relations and work with the client.

Hardware and Software

With the increasing use of technology within the mental health field, computers, tablets, and mobile phones are utilized almost daily in the practice. Play therapist are utilizing technological hardware to participate in trainings, research, and providing telemental health play therapy services (Mathews, 2020) while certain populations may not have access to these technological items. Celano and Neuman (2010) stated "low-income children often lack home computers and struggle to get the computer time they need to achieve the skills necessary to be competitive" (p. 68). Other factors such as cultural practices can result in limited technological resources within the home setting. When there is a lack of hardware, the utilization of software is nonexistent.

Although a focus is on the lack of resources to obtain needed hardware and software, there are also aspects such as lack of skill to operate the software and hardware. The lack of skill can resonate with the child and adult making moving forward with telemental health services a challenge. When there is a lack of skill or resources, the risk for resistance increases. Cultural considerations would include reviewing the cultural practices of the client to develop an awareness also developing an awareness of the client's resources. Practicing cultural humility would require the play therapist to recognize their resources based on cultural differences and take action.

Materials

Providing play therapy services in a brick-and-mortar location can be considered an advantage over telemental health play therapy in regard to the materials. Children will have the ability to come into a structured environment with selected toys and items to engage in the play therapy healing process. Providing telemental health play therapy does not have the same advantage. Individuals receiving services are highly likely to be within their home environment and, based on the client's resources, there may be limitations in the materials available. Practicing cultural humility can include the play therapist's actions while preparing to engage a client in telemental health play therapy and taking in consideration their resources, environment, and other cultural considerations.

Privacy Considerations

Cultural dynamics of the populations receiving telemental health play therapy can include factors that can affect the privacy and confidentiality. According to Fisher and ProQuest Ebooks (2013) confidentiality within a therapy setting is an ethical duty for all mental health professionals and requires privacy of the information shared between the client and play therapist.

When you provide therapy in an office setting, therapists have the ability to provide an adequate private and confidential space. When conducting telemental health play therapy sessions, play therapists rely on clients and families to assist in maintaining privacy and confidentiality within the client setting. Often the therapeutic services take place in a child's home where private space can be limited. Working with diverse families requires therapist to understand and be aware of how culture may play a role in who is present in the child home and the composition of family members (Park et al., 2019).

Cultural Telehealth Play Therapy Interventions

The use of play therapy with children is dated back to early 1900s utilizing small basic materials such as wooden figures, paper, and paint (Landreth, 2012). Today, play therapists can hold space for clients in well stocked playrooms with intentional toys and materials that can be used for directive and nondirective play therapy interventions. Providing telemental health play therapy requires the play therapist to be more intentional with planning and engaging in play therapy secessions. When providing play therapy interventions, it is important to have an understanding of the clients being served, along with having a toolbox of play therapy interventions that can maintain engagement on a telehealth platform.

Bibliotherapy

Bibliotherapy is the use of books within the therapeutic setting. This is used as a tool to assist children with gaining insight, metaphors, and learning alternatives to handle life situations (Kottman & Meany-Walen, 2016). In telemental health play therapy, the play therapist can share their screen while utilizing an eBook to allow the child to see the book while the therapist reads or the child reads. The play therapist can traditionally read the book to the client or utilize YouTube to play the video reading of the book. Methods to be culturally diverse while practicing bibliotherapy include utilizing books with characters representing various cultural groups and practices.

The practice of increasing emotional literacy will give children a vocabulary of feelings and emotions to use to express self when sharing their hard stories (Goodyear-Brown, 2019). Emotional literacy also increases both verbal and non-verbal communication. When focusing on emotional literary utilizing multicultural feelings charts, animal's expressions and colors are methods to practice cultural diversity.

You can choose books to help children see reflections of their self, family, and experiences. Books can also be utilized to increase emotional literacy by teaching in a creative interactive way. The following books are resources:

- Peek -a- Boo at the Zoo (Dixon, 2018)
- No, No, Elizabeth (Jimenez, 2017)
- Elizabeth Makes a Friend (Jimenez, 2019)
- Olli's Outie (Easter, 2018)
- When I Grow Up (McEachern, 2017)
- Despite the Height (Latta, 2017)
- Jamie is Jaimie (Moradian, 2018)
- Elizabeth Makes a Friend (Jimenez, 2019)
- Antiracist Baby (Kendi, 2020)
- The Family Book (Parr, 2003)
- Focus on Feelings (Jimenez-Pride, 2018)
- Jack Feels (Flynn, 2017)
- Healing Feelings (Baker, 2017)
- Double Dip Feelings (Cain, 2001)

Expressive Arts

"The expressive arts combine the visual arts, movement, drama, music, writing, and other creative processes to foster deep personal growth and community development (International Expressive Arts Therapy Association, 2017, para 3)". Expressive arts interventions utilized in play therapy setting can increase interactions and engagement while providing virtual services. With the base definition of culture, expressive arts interventions will allow the client an opportunity to take pride in their racial and/or social identity. According Goicoechea et al. (2014) a client taking pride in their racial identity helps clients cope with discrimination and decreasing the risk of internalizing negative stereotypes. Expressive arts in telemental health with little to no material items can relieve the pressure of the family having materials or the therapist providing materials.

Creative drawing activities are directive prompts to engage children in storytelling and expressions of self. The creative drawing activities can be achieved during a telemental health play therapy session by the therapist proving the client with prompt and giving them a short time to create a drawing to express themselves. Creative drawing activities can be utilized to give visual expression to thoughts, feelings, and beliefs.

Music

According to Dansereau (2015) musical instruments are both structured and unstructured; children have the ability to create their own instrument or become an instrument during the telemental health session. Music can show up in all cultural backgrounds and give child the ability to express their thoughts and feelings in a nonverbal way. Utilizing music during a telemental health play therapy session can engage the client in sessions. Therapists practicing cultural humility while engaging in telemental health play therapy should become aware of their own bias surrounding music. Also, the therapist can be intentional regarding types of music played and instruments utilized within the office setting.

Case Example

Basic Information and Background

Peyton, an eight-year-old an African American female, was referred for therapy due to signs of depression and increasing defiant behaviors within the school and home setting. Peyton lived with her mother and grandmother and attended a Title I elementary school. Peyton entered therapy with a previous diagnosis of Adjustment Disorder with Mixed Disturbance of Emotions and Conduct. Peyton has been participating in outpatient play therapy for two months within the office setting prior to transitioning to telemental health services.

Presenting Concerns and Family Information

During the initial assessment Peyton's mother reported that Peyton had started disconnecting from her school friends and activities she used to love and demonstrated defiant behaviors within the school and home setting. Peyton's behaviors have included: not following directions, talking back to teachers and adults, and aggressive outbursts. Peyton presented with challenges of expressing her thoughts and feelings. She often stated "I do not know" when discussing her behavioral choices and feelings toward people and situations. She lives with her mother and grandmother. Peyton has limited contact with her father and does not speak of him often. Her mother works fulltime while her grandmother is the primary caregiver during afterschool hours.

Transition to Telemental Health Play Therapy

Peyton attended therapy sessions bi-monthly within the in-person office setting, utilizing the Internal Family Systems model. Internal Family Systems (IFS) focuses on assisting the client with identifying their internal parts, increasing knowledge of how their internal system, and how that system interacts with external systems (Schwartz & Sweezy, 2020). Peyton did not receive therapy services for four weeks due to transitioning to virtual learning. The play therapist was contacted by the mother to resume therapy services to focus on Peyton having challenges with transitioning from the traditional school environment to a learn-at-home model. Her mother verbalized Peyton does not put effort into her schoolwork and often has missed assignments. She also shared Peyton is disrespectful to her teacher and peers online. Peyton has also increased her defiant behaviors within the home setting.

Peyton's school did not provide their students with hardcopy books or technology resources at the time of transition. Peyton's family was able to purchase a laptop and began receiving free low speed internet services from their local phone service provider. Due to the mother's work schedule Peyton's grandmother, with limited technology skills, provides assistance during the school day.

At the start of telemental health services, the play therapist mailed the following items to the family:

- Crayons and markers
- Blank paper
- Journal
- Focus on Feelings®© Feelings Poster
- Popsicle Sticks
- Glue
- Index Cards

First Session

Peyton presented with resistance during the initial telemental health play therapy session when directed to create a picture expressing her feelings toward learning from home. Peyton did not look directly at the screen and would randomly look around the room during the telemental health play therapy session. Peyton drew random shapes on her paper and did not provide any context to her drawing. Peyton would respond in a low voice when asked questions.

Second Session Progress

Peyton did not respond verbally during the session. The play therapist gave options of writing thoughts and paper or typing thoughts within the chat feature on the virtual platform. She shared by utilizing the chat that her grandmother would not leave the room during her last therapy session and live school sessions. Peyton shared that her grandmother talks on the phone loudly and repeats things she has said in class to her mother. The play therapist engaged Peyton in written discussion to assist with identifying her needs to engage in therapy services. She expressed wanting the play therapist to talk with her mother about her grandmother's behaviors.

The play therapist followed up the mother and discussed the importance of confidently and privacy during the telemental health sessions. The play therapist discussed the difference in the dynamic of receiving services within the office setting versus telemental health services. The mother verbalized she did not have an understanding of the importance of Peyton having privacy during her sessions. She further shared her mother does not leave the room due to her belief of children do not need privacy.

The mother discussed a plan of action to increase a sense of privacy within the home setting. The mother shared her plan to talk to her mother about giving Peyton privacy during her therapy session by allowing her to go into her room.

Third Session Progress

At the start of the session Peyton reported being in the room alone. Peyton's verbal engagement was increased, and she appeared engaged in the telemental health session. She shared having a discussion with her mother about her needs for school and therapy. Peyton verbalized feeling more confident with discussing the issues and needs with her mother after her mother shared understanding there is a difference between services within the office setting and virtual setting.

During the duration of telemental health therapy services Peyton was able to make progress on her goals by increasing her verbal response of thoughts and feelings and decreasing defiant behaviors within the home setting and school setting. Peyton's attitude toward virtual learning shifted and her grades improved.

Practicing Cultural Humility in Telemental Health Play Therapy

Culture includes multiple groups of people coming together with shared likes, values, ethics, and practices requiring all play therapist to become aware of their level of cultural competence and understanding of cultural diversity. The beginning steps to increase awareness is for the play therapist to welcome diversity into their practice setting and methods by evaluating their current practices and start becoming aware of their personal beliefs. Practicing cultural humility starts prior to any contact with the client by the play therapist becoming aware of their own biases and privileges and how that can impact the delivery telemental health play therapy services.

Practicing cultural humility requires a level of honesty with self and noticing the areas that may conflict with professional code of ethical principles and governing boards their practices of cultural diversity and being willing to take steps to make changes in their personal lives and professional life.

The following questions are sample questions for the practitioner to ask self.

- What are my views regarding culturally based issues my clients or their families face?
- Have I turned clients away based on their racial identity?
- Do I have negative assumptions about a cultural group?
- Have I turned clients away based on their sexual orientation?
- Do I recognize my privilege that I was born with?
- Do I recognize my privilege that I have gained?
- Have I turned clients away based on my feeling to adequately serve that particular population?
- Do I ensure I am not thinking or acting from a egocentric view of the world?
- Have I attempted to gain real world knowledge and experience of a culture versus only what is read in academic text?

The following questions are sample questions to learn more about the cultural and family dynamics that may impact telemental health play therapy services. It is recommended to ask these questions during the initial assessment or during the transition meeting for telemental health play therapy.

- What is your understanding of telemental health services?
- Are there any spiritual or religious practices that will need consideration regarding telemental health services?
- Who are your community supports?
- Share any cultural issues or concerns you may have that our practice should be aware of.
- Are there any family dynamics that can impact telemental health services?
- Is there a place in your home that private and can be used during the telemental health session?
- Do you have technology that can be utilized during telemental health sessions?
- Will maintaining technology services be a strain on your/ the family income?

Conclusion

Practicing cultural humility while conducting telemental health services requires the play therapist to gain a greater awareness about the clients they are serving to assure therapeutic services are received ethically and effectively. Having an awareness of self and how one's own beliefs and bias can impact how services are being delivered. Play therapists have the unique opportunity to hold space utilizing creative play therapy approaches to facilitate clients going from hurt to healed.

References

Altvater, R. A., Singer, R. R., & Gil, E. (2018). Part 2: A qualitative examination of play therapy and technology training and ethics. *International Journal of Play Therapy*, 27(1), 46–55. doi:10.1037/pla0000057

Altvater, R. (2019). Research-informed technological transitions in psychotherapy. In J. Stone (Ed.), *Integrating Technology into Modern Therapies* (pp. 11–23). Routledge.

Asbill, L. & Water, A., (2013, August). *Reflections on cultural: Given the complexity of multiculturalism, it is beneficial to understand cultural competency as a process rather than an end product*. American Psychological Association. https://www.apa.org/pi/families/resources/newsletter/2013/08/cultural-humility

Association for Play Therapy (APT) (2019a). *Play therapy best practices*. https://cdn.ymaws.com/www.a4pt.org/resource/resmgr/publications/best_practices_-_sept_2019.pdf

Association for Play Therapy (APT) (2019b). *Ethical considerations for implementing telemental health in play therapy: A reflective exercise for play therapists based on the association for play therapy's best practice guidelines*. https://cdn.ymaws.com/www.a4pt.org/resource/resmgr/telehealth/Dugan_Ray_SKN_-_Telemental_H.pdf

Baker, L. (2017). *Healing feelings: A healing story for children coping with a grownup's mental illness*. Yorkshire Publishing

Belfield, L. D. (2012, December 18). *What is cultural diversity?* https://www.purdueglobal.edu/blog/social-behavioral-sciences/what-is-cultural-diversity

Cain, B. (2001). *Double-dip feelings*. Magination Press

Celano, D. & Neuman, S. B. (2010). A matter of computer time: Low-income children often lack home computers and struggle to get the computer time they need to achieve the skills necessary to be competitive. *Phi Delta Kappa*, 92(2), 68.

Chaet, D., Clearfield, R., Sabin, J. E., & Skimming, K., (2017). Ethical practice in telehealth and telemedicine. *Journal of General Internal Medicine: JGIM*, 32(10), 1136–1140. doi:10.1007/s11606-017-4082-2

Dansereau, D. R. (2015). Young children's interactions with sound-producing objects. *Journal of Research in Music Education*, 63(1), 28–46.

Davis, D., DeBlaere, C., Hook, J., & Owen, J. (2017). Navigating value differecenes and conflicts. In *Cultural Humility: Engaging Diverse Identities in Therapy* (pp. 162–163). Washington: American Psychological Association.

Dixon, K. (2018). *Peek-a-Boo at the Zoo*. Warren Publishing

Easter, S. (2018). *Ollie's Outie*. Warren Publishing

Fisher, M. A., & ProQuest Ebooks. (2013). *The ethics of conditional confidentiality: A practice model for mental health professionals*. Oxford University Press.

Flynn, J. (2017). *Jack feels: An emotional literacy resource*. CreateSpace Independent Publishing

Gil, E. (2005). From sensitively to competence in working across cultures. In E. Gil & A. A. Drewes (Eds.), *Cultural issues in play therapy* (pp. 3–25). New York, NY: Guildford Press.

Global Diversity Practice (2020). *What is diversity and inclusion?* https://globaldiversitypractice.com/what-is-diversity-inclusion

Goicoechea, J., Wagner, K., Yahalom, J., & Medina, T. (2014). Group counseling for at-risk African American youth: A collaboration between therapists and artists. *Journal of Creativity in Mental Health*, 9(1), 69–82. https://doi.org/10.1080/15401383.2013.864961

Goodyear-Brown, P. (2019). *Trauma and play therapy: Helping children heal*. Routledge.

Hudspeth, E. F. (2016). Play therapy applications with diverse cultures. *International Journal of Play Therapy*, 25(3), 113. https://doi.org/10.1037/pla0000030

International Expressive Arts Therapy Association (2017). *About us*. https://www.ieata.org/
Jimenez, C. (2017). *No, no Elizabeth*. Warren Publishing
Jimenez, C. (2019). *Elizabeth makes a friend*. Warren Publishing
Jimenez-Pride, C. (2018). *Focus on feelings*. Play Therapy with Carmen Publishing
Kazdin, A. E., & Blasé S. L. (2011). Rebooting psychotherapy research and practice to reduce the burden of mental illness. *Perspectives on Psychological Science*, 6(1), 21–37. doi: 10.1177/1745691610393527
Kendi, I. (2020). *Antiracist baby*. Penguin Random House
Kottman, T. & Meany-Walen, K. (2016). *Partners in play: An Adlerian approach to play therapy* (3rd ed). American Counseling Association
Landreth, G. L. (2012). *Play therapy: The art of relationship* (3rd ed.). Routledge/Taylor & Francis Group.
Latta, I. (2017). *Despite the height*. Warren Publishing
M. J. (2020, December 9). *Cultural diversity - how & why diverse culture makes our world better?* Diversity. Social. https://diversity.social/cultural-diversity/#gsc.tab=0
Mathews, E. B. (2020). Computer use in mental health treatment: Understanding collaborative documentation and its effect on the therapeutic alliance. *Psychotherapy (Chicago, Ill.)*, 57(2), 119–128. doi:10.1037/pst0000254
McEachern, J. (2017). *When I grow up*. Warren Publishing
Merriam-Webster (2020a). *Culture*. https://www.merriam-webster.com/dictionary/culture
Merriam-Webster (2020b). *Diversity*. https://www.merriam-webster.com/dictionary/diversity
Mellenthin, C. (2020, December). The therapeutic powers of play at work in the age of telehealth. *Play Therapy*, 15(4), 20.
Moradian, A. (2018). *Jamie is Jamie*. Free Spirit Publishing
Morrison Bennett, M., & Eberts, S. (2014). Self-expression. In C. Schaefer, & A. Drewes (Eds.), *The Therapeutic Powers of Play: 20 Core Agents of Change* (pp. 17–18). Hobeken: John Wiley & Sons Inc.
National Association of Social Workers (2017). *Code of ethics*. https://www.socialworkers.org/about/ethics/code-of-ethics/code-of-ethics-english
National Association of Social Workers (2015). *Standards and indicators cultural competence in social work practice*. https://www.socialworkers.org/LinkClick.aspx?fileticket=7dVckZAYUmk%3D&portalid=0
Park, S. S., Wiemers, E. E., & Seltzer, J. A. (2019). The family safety net of black and white multigenerational families. *Population & Development Review*, 45(2), 351–378. https://doi.org/10.1111/padr.12233
Parr, T. (2003). *The family book*. Little Brown and Company
Schwartz, R. C. & Sweezy, M. (2020). *Internal family systems therapy* (2nd ed.). The Guildford Press
Tervalon, M., & Murray-Garcia, J. (1998). Cultural humility versus cultural competence: A critical distinction in defining physician training outcomes in multicultural education. *Journal of HealthCare for the Poor and Underserved*, 9, 117–125.
Zimmerman, K. A. (2017, July 13). *What is culture?* Live Science. https://www.livescience.com/21478-what-is-culture-definition-of-culture.html

Section II
Special Populations

5 TraumaPlay™ and Telemental Health: Innovations Through the Screen

Paris Goodyear-Brown and Kate Worley

TraumaPlay™ is a flexibly sequential play therapy model for working with traumatized and attachment disturbed children, teens, and their caregiving systems. These systems may include biological parents, foster parents, teachers, babysitters, and even soccer coaches. TraumaPlay is informed by our current understandings of the neurobiology of play and trauma and is built on the power of one to heal the other. Grounded in attachment theory, the child or family is met moment-to-moment as therapeutic needs are assessed. The framework of seven therapeutic treatment goals serves as the umbrella under which clinicians have freedom to employ a variety of interventions. A subset of goals related to enhancing the role of Parents as Partners expands clinicians' finesse in integrating parents into trauma treatment. The best-practice, evidence-informed treatment goals provide the scaffolding for dozens of clinically-sound creative and engaging play-based interventions that offer developmentally sensitive vehicles for therapeutic growth. Harnessing the rich heritage of play therapy and offering pathways for both non-directive and directive approaches to be integrated, TraumaPlay offers a clinically nuanced, child-focused, need driven approach to helping children and families heal from trauma (Goodyear-Brown, 2010; 2019; 2021).

Grounded in an integrative paradigm, this model translates evidence informed trauma treatment with children into a sequence of play-based component modules. Each component represents an important dimension of trauma treatment and articulates both a specific treatment goal and accompanying interventions. Components include:

- Enhancing safety and security
- Assessing current coping and augmenting adaptive coping
- Soothing the physiology
- Enhancing self-regulation
- Parents as Partners
- Increasing emotional literacy
- Play-based gradual exposure: post-traumatic play (the continuum of disclosure and experiential mastery play)

DOI: 10.4324/9781003166498-5

- Building a coherent trauma narrative that integrates somatosensory details, as well as thoughts, feelings, and relational impacts
- Addressing the thought life (shifting cognitive distortions, dealing with false attributions, and offering positive self-talk to counter negative self-talk)
- Making positive meaning of the post-trauma self

TraumaPlay therapists are always looking to harness the therapeutic powers of play to build on resiliencies and titrate the child's approach to trauma content through a myriad of mitigators. These are codified in the play therapist's palette (Goodyear-Brown, 2019) and offer pathways for creating competency surges and enhancing the neuroception of safety for children and teens as they approach hard things. These mitigators are all grounded in the attachment relationship and include kinesthetic involvement, need meeting, metaphor, touch, humor, nature, novelty, and containment. One core TraumaPlay concept is summed up as the Cascade of Care and involves the therapist embodying three primary roles in the therapeutic process: Safe Boss, Nurturer, and Storykeeper.

Translation of TraumaPlay Components to Telemental Health

Assessing for Current Coping and Augmenting Adaptive Coping

One of the best practice standards in trauma work is assessing for the client's current coping repertoire prior to approaching any difficult content. *The Coping Tree* intervention is a bedrock of TraumaPlay and is easily translated through the screen. This play-based assessment grew out of a collaboration between the National Child Traumatic Stress Network (NCTSN) and a task force with the Association for Play Therapy, to help clients exhaust their list of both adaptive and maladaptive coping strategies. The therapist can begin by reading Apple Farmer Annie (Wellington, 2004) through the virtual portal. We then explore what happens to apples that fall from the tree and are left on the ground, in the weather (they rot, bugs eat them, etc.) and those that ripen on the tree and get turned into a multitude of yummy foods. We then use this rubric to contrast adaptive and maladaptive coping strategies by asking the question, "When you think about the scary thing that happened, what do you do?" If there is not one discrete traumatic memory that is accessible, the prompt is rephrased to, "When you are feeling really stressed, what do you do?" The clinician can share their preferred whiteboard tool through the screen, draw a tree, and then facilitate a conversation that helps clients identify their full range of coping strategies. Figure 5.1 is an example of a collective coping tree completed by a group of professionals during an online webinar. *The Coping Tree* is appropriate for use with individual children/teens or with full family systems and the playful curiosity of this intervention is preserved through the screen.

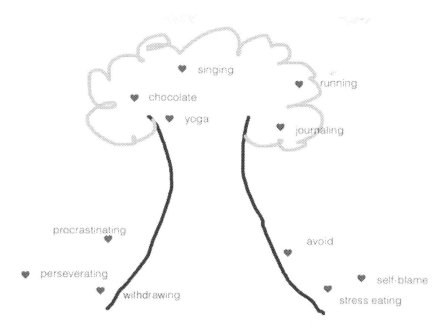

Figure 5.1 A Group Coping Tree.

Soothing the Physiology

The *Sensory Soothing Menu* is easily adaptable for telehealth sessions. In this intervention, the child chooses various sensory items that are paired with different menu items. Children enjoy using the TraumaPlay *Sensory Soothing Menu* worksheet (Goodyear-Brown, 2021) to create their own menu items which also increases their sense of ownership during the activity. The menu options include a taste, smell, touch, sound, and a visual image "that help you feel good or safe on the inside". During telemental health sessions, counselors can frame the activity as a scavenger hunt which allows clients the chance to find and show the counselor their treasures. Clients enjoy showing their therapist a special blanket they may choose for soothing touch or the sound machine in their room for a soothing sound. If a child and guardian cannot think of an item for their menu, the therapist can enhance their soothing tools by problem solving with the dyad. Through this intervention, parents sometimes realize their child has a favorite essential oil or stuffed animal that is helpful to use in moments of distress.

Through the use of household items, therapists can teach clients and their parents the needs of the triune brain through the virtual portal. Therapists can also meet sensory needs virtually by joining the client in making slime or Oobleq using basic supplies found in most houses (baking soda, eye contact solution, and glue). Children can also use household items to make musical instruments that are useful in regulation work. TraumaPlay therapists view the child's spontaneous use of musical instruments as one way in which children work externally to regulate their internal state. The video clip shown in the TedxTalk, Trauma and Play Therapy: Holding the Hard Stories (Goodyear-Brown, 2018), captures the process by which a child who has just experienced a traumatic event creates a song that gives voice to what is going on in her body. Prior to finding the words (neocortex/thinking brain) she spent time moving cyclically between frenetic strumming of all the guitar strings at once (which resulted in a cacophonous, jangled, off putting sound) and a melodic, organized strumming. It was remarkable to watch this little girl externalize the internal modulation of her arousal systems. In early virtual TraumaPlay sessions, the therapist might invite the client to make an instrument with household objects, such as an empty can filled with dried beans, while the therapist does the same. The therapist and client take turns setting and matching each other's rhythms. This facilitates the joining process, supports attunement, and becomes an anchoring transitional object/process that can be used at the beginning or end of each subsequent session as a reassuring ritualized connector.

The ability to share what is on the therapist's screen or the family's screen exists in most virtual platforms. To this end, the therapist can continue providing novelty in interventions that soothe the physiology, demonstrating a new breathing technique with background visuals from mobile apps such as Calm or Headspace. The core value of titration in approach to difficult content, paired with the recognition that relaxation is a difficult process for hypervigilant clients, therapist and client can use a shared focal point of pre-designed yoga routines (available on YouTube or elsewhere) while both engaging in this full body movement and stretching. Therapists must remain cognizant at all times of the potentially inappropriate content that can show up, pop up, or even be running down the side of a screen with previews of other videos. Due to how seriously we take the gatekeeping role of Safe Boss in TraumaPlay, our therapists abide by a content safety check during which they vet all parts of the website pages, ads, etc. on any site prior to sharing the screen. For example, in searching for short yoga routines/videos, highly suggestive poses/clothing/background music can pop up. Many of the families we serve at Nurture House have sexually traumatized children and are often easily triggered by trauma reminders or stimulating content. We are frequently helping them with boundary development and body safety curriculum. The Tackling Touchy Subjects curriculum is now digitized, and children can play boundary games through the screen with the therapist and color/write on the reproducible handouts in real time (Goodyear-Brown, 2013). Another short video, titled Consent for Kids, shown frequently in telemental health, translates an understanding of consent into developmentally appropriate language and drawn images for children (Blue Seat Studios, 2016).

A multitude of online versions of bibliotherapy resources such as Hey Warrior, Mindful Monkey, Happy Panda, and Sit Like a Frog are available through multiple websites and set the stage for practice of cycles of upregulating and downregulating. There is a simple video explanation of the Window of Tolerance (WOT) that we find is particularly helpful for some clients (Farrell, 2018). Titled, The Window of Life and the Tale of Two Lands, a panda floats along a river (the optimal arousal zone) and is introduced to the Land of Fire which you escape from by taking deep breaths and the Land of Ice which you escape from by moving your body. This is a nice, captivating introduction to the WOT virtually. Engaging in a collaborative process with the client of choosing an upbeat piece of music, like ABC by the Jackson Five, and have a dance party through the screen while moving our bodies to the point of exertion, can be very powerful. Therapists can then choose a heart rate app, measure their own and the client's heart rate, engage in a mindfulness exercise, and then take it again. When meeting virtually, the lens of the phone can act as an oximeter. Clients, as they watch the number of beats per minute drop, are usually surprised to find they can exert such control over their own physiology.

Increasing Emotional Literacy

A child's emotional literacy is comprised of their vocabulary of feelings, their ability to identify and accurately communicate a feeling, and their understanding of how feelings are impacted by self and environment (Goodyear-Brown, 2010). Through various TraumaPlay interventions, children can increase their emotional literacy which provides the child with coping and regulation skills (Goodyear-Brown, 2010). The color-your-heart and feelings rainbow are examples of assessments/interventions that work well on a shared virtual whiteboard (Goodyear-Brown, 2002; 2005). With each intervention, the therapist can create a template on the whiteboard of a heart or rainbow. Some children, though, may request to figure out the whiteboard and create their own templates. In other words, these clients are attempting to gain a sense of mastery over the technology which leads to dopamine release in their body. Additionally, the witness of mastery from the therapist causes an oxytocin release. Though telemental health likely changes the course of play therapy as it limits physical contact, it can offer similar avenues for the neurochemical work that occurs in person (Goodyear-Brown, 2019; Porges, 2009).

One of the Nurture House clinicians, Patrick Smith, created an emotional literacy intervention for telemental health sessions which works well with any telehealth platform. In this intervention, the counselor assists the child in making an emotion chart with characters from their favorite show, movie, or video game. Though clinicians often have multiple emotion charts at their disposal, the creation of a personalized emotion chart enables the child to become an active participant in identifying and labeling emotions. Furthermore, the discussion of the child's favorite show and identification of different characters offers the clinician a window into the child's world and primary influences.

A colleague currently working through TraumaPlay certification, Kristie Cain, has two sets of Todd Parr feeling cards displayed in the waiting room of her group practice. When the pandemic erupted, she took a picture of this wall and shared it with the TraumaPlay Institute which is now a favorite for virtual sessions. The image is shared through the screen, and various coloring/annotating tools are used to play Tic-Tac-Toe or Connect Four virtually. Another bibliotherapy aid, discovered by Nurture House clinicians at the height of the pandemic, is called Foodie Faces (Wurtzel & Wurtzel, 2020). While reading the book in real time through the screen, a six-year-old client became curious about the faces that lined the front and back covers of the book. This little girl problem-solved with the therapist on how to take a picture of the inside cover, share it through the screen, and annotate it with feeling words. The faces in this resource are constructed with everything from over-easy eggs to pinto bean eyes, to red pepper mouths. The whimsical nature of the book, combined with the challenge to create feeling faces out of the foods that a family has in their kitchen, led to many laughs as both the therapist and the parent/child dyad create feeling faces from the ingredients they found in their kitchens. Another bibliotherapy resource that encourages children to play with their food, Foods with Moods (Freymann & Elffers, 2018) offers an augmentation of the above intervention. The combination of emotional exploration and food invited foundational need meeting to occur while enhancing connection through the screen.

Parents as Partners

Parents need more support than ever during the pandemic. Lock downs, intermittent quarantines, and online schooling result in intensified stress (both the parent's and the child's). In 2020, our microcosms have constricted from our larger communities. The role these relational spaces and the people within them play in the rhythms of the days, weeks, and months cannot be overstated. Parents and children mitigate the build-up of relational tensions with one another through doses of time apart and changes of scenery, peer group, focal point, etc. Our exteroception, defined as the internalized feeling of the environment outside our bodies, can largely impact our sense of well-being. In TraumaPlay we are often discerning what bigness or smallness of space is most helpful in creating maximum focus and a sense of being "just right" (Goodyear-Brown, 2010). The pandemic has constrained us all to smallness and continual sameness of space, and particularly for children who need big body engagement, this constriction is problematic. Families are tethered to their homes and are constantly negotiating space and needs with one another. For parents who are dealing with non-compliance, aggression, or intense dysregulation, the constriction of the physical space makes the big behaviors seem even bigger. One practical help we provide during telemental health sessions is going room to room with the parent and creatively examining the space for ways to provide more novelty or variety. Something as simple as creating a fort/tent out of old sheets can create an ability to exterocept differently. We help parents as a matter of course to design Nurture Nooks in their home environments and equip them with Delighting-In activities that encourage daily doses of connected nurturing time. The use of Virtual Reality (VR), defined here is a three-dimensional graphic system that allows for the child to feel immersed in an interactive 360-degree environment (Ihemedu-Steinke et al., 2017), offers a way to offer expansive environments (such as beautiful wooded areas, mountain ranges, open fields, and spaces as small as a tunnel or cave). VR offers bigness and smallness in space as children work on regulation, problem solving, and social skills development, etc. (Lamb et al., 2019).

TraumaPlay's strong focus on strengthening the role of Parents as Partners lends itself beautifully to continued help for families through the screen. As we embody the roles or Safe Boss, Nurturer, and Storykeeper, we offer new experiences of holding to our caregivers so that they can offer them to the hurt children in their care. To this end, psychoeducation for parents, as well as skills development and practice of emerging skills, are balanced with giving parents cross-hemispheric play-based experiences that help parents expand their reflective capacity while becoming more soothing partners. The new TraumaPlay resource, *Parents as Partners in Child Therapy: A Clinician's Guide*, includes 45 new handouts usable via telehealth (Goodyear-Brown, 2021). These handouts and their accompanying exercises support the following treatment goals: helping caregivers turn parenting shame into paradigm shift, re-open their compassion wells for children with big behaviors, and employ discipline procedures that follow the child's need while maintaining connection and positive presence, co-regulate the child while regulating themselves, and helping them expand their WOT for holding hard stories while delighting in their children. Reading stories to children through the screen is comforting to them and provides its own form of nurture to both parents and children.

Trauma Narrative

Post-traumatic play as a form of gradual exposure (Goodyear-Brown, 2019) offers three mechanisms that can further integration of trauma content, including thoughts, feelings, and sensory impressions. The first is the Continuum of Disclosure. This process references the glimpses and snapshots of the trauma that children gift us with during the child-led play process. The second mechanism is Experiential Mastery Play (EMP) and can involve harnessing the competency surge that emerges when a child achieves something new (struggling up to the next rung of the monkey bars or building a tower) and mitigates the approach to trauma content. Through the screen, platforms such as Minecraft are options for ways to construct or co-construct environments, encourage the sense of "I can do it" and the accompanying competency surge (oxytocin and dopamine release), mitigating the child's approach to harder content that may be covered in the same session. Another game that we have honed through telemental health, "Who's Got the Power?" involves making wands and turning each other into various creatures through the screen. The therapist introduces a magic wand from the therapist's own collection and invites the client to find or make their own wand. Some children become very engaged in the wand-making process. The client may take the session outside, carrying the phone or iPad to the front or back yard while hunting for a special stick. The stick is then painted or decorated using whatever materials the client has in their home. Other clients may just pick up a pen or a pipe cleaner and pretend it is a wand. The child says, "Abracadabra, I turn you into a...frog!". If the clinician is in their fully equipped playroom, they can disappear below the screen and introduce a miniature frog-pretending they have been abruptly changed. The play therapist can also embody the change, by jump around the room while going ribbit. Either way, children tend to giggle gleefully, feels immensely powerful, and share a connected moment through the screen. In one recent dyadic session, dad and child were turned into monkeys together. Much laughter ensued as they scratched under their arms while making monkey noises. They then conspired together to turn the clinician into a clown fish...and laughed more deeply as they watched the therapist wriggle about in an imaginary ocean. Their experience of shared decision-making, and the delight engendered between them through the play enhance the attachment bond.

The third mechanism for play-based gradual exposure provides offering more structure to trauma narrative prompts when a child needs more support to approach hard content. The hallmark of this approach is the titration of the dose of exposure offered through various mediums. Puppets, sand tray work, visual storytelling, and play scene creations were TraumaPlay tools for narrative work prior to COVID and each of these have virtual translations (Goodyear-Brown & Gott, 2019). Therapists can use the Puppet Pals app for phones and iPads to co-create digital puppet stories. Recently, a client chose a "boxing squirrel" to represent herself when she is having aggression triggered by a trauma reminder and chose the "fairy godmother" to represent the role the therapist played in helping her learn to use her words instead of her fists to ask for what she needs when she is feeling anxious.

Clients can use the Virtual Sandtray App®© (Stone, 2015) to create powerful and beautiful sandtray worlds during telemental health sessions. The StoryBird website offers clients multiple ways to generate titrations of written and visual storytelling content ranging from word art poetry, to comic books, to picture books, to long story prose templates. For example, an adopted client with Fetal Alcohol Syndrome who has limited verbal and cognitive skills, struggled with depression and anxiety, and was actively cutting, was able to engage well with StoryBird. While this client was not able to write an elaborative story regarding her internal distress, she could approach the topic and engage in some reflection on her self-injurious behavior through choosing first a visual image and then generating several words and phrases to create the art pictured here. This titrated dose of exposure to "the hard thing" is a hallmark of TraumaPlay and can be creatively supported during telehealth sessions.

Transition to Telemental Health and Ethical Issues

Nurture House, like many agencies and practices, found ourselves transitioning fully to telemental health for the first time in the Spring of 2020. As play therapists, our team primarily relied on in person sessions before this point and the move to telemental health seemed daunting, yet necessary to ensure safety. Though telemental health may not be the historical norm when working with children and adolescents, results from various studies show that telemental health is an effective option. Parent training, parent-child interaction therapy, and trauma focused cognitive behavioral therapy are a few examples of modalities that have proven successful via telemental health (Funderburk et al., 2008; Lerman et al., 2020; Stewart et al., 2020). As shown throughout this chapter, the TraumaPlay model is also adaptable to telemental health. The following section contains ethical issues we encountered while adapting to telemental health and potential solutions that you may find helpful in your practice.

As most Nurture House clinicians did not have previous experience with telemental health, our leadership team coordinated a thorough telemental health training to ensure safety and ethical practice. Additionally, our team began weekly group supervision meetings to provide extra opportunities to staff cases as we made the transition. We also created guidelines to ensure the safety of the clinicians and clients and ethical practice. For example, our counselors confirmed the client's address before each session in case of emergency and to ensure that sessions were taking place within state lines. When guardians were not in the same room during sessions it was also essential to have correct contact information in case of emergencies. Practicing telehealth involves intentional effort to ensure ethical practice, but there are also theoretical aspects of the TraumaPlay model that required adjustment when practiced virtually.

The therapeutic use of self, therapist as Storykeeper, Nurturer, and Safe Boss, is fundamental to conceptualizing treatment in TraumaPlay. Though all three roles are essential to the model, the role of therapist as Safe Boss is challenging, at times, to employ in telehealth sessions. As we explain to our families, safe bosses are safe adults who keep children safe through healthy structure. At Nurture House, we work to keep our families emotionally and physically safe through didactic teaching, setting boundaries, modeling, nurturing, and encouragement (Goodyear-Brown, 2019). In person, modeling safe boss behavior in sessions is often seamless and simple, but as our staff moved to virtual sessions, we quickly realized that our presence as safe bosses needed adjustment. Our staff created new safe boss guidelines to keep our clients safe and to avoid ethical issues.

In order to create physical and felt safety in sessions, Nurture House clinicians remain within a few feet of their client at all times. Our proximity also works to show clients that we are engaged and focused on them during their session. As we transitioned to telemental health, our primary concern was the physical safety of each child during sessions while also ensuring that a private space was available, if needed. Though each child is different, our team decided that, generally, children seven years and younger needed a parent within line of sight during sessions. Due to the number of clients we see who have experienced complex trauma, our team realized that some older children also needed adult supervision during sessions and made these decisions on a case by case basis. A child's ability to regulate, their attentional abilities, and relational capacity are often impacted by trauma and are, thus, essential aspects of determining a child's capacity for telehealth without a parent present (D'Andrea et al., 2012). When a child requests one on one time with the therapist but needs a parent present, many solutions exist such as having the parent or child wear headphones. Privacy was also often essential for our adolescents who at the age of 16 are legally able to consent to their own mental health treatment in Tennessee (Kerwin et al., 2015). Though we emphasize family work at Nurture House, we made sure to create the same sense of privacy that a client would receive during in person sessions.

Obtaining privacy and confidentiality was difficult for some families with multiple children at home. Additionally, many of the parents were juggling working from home while also helping their children manage virtual school and other appointments. In these situations, it was often helpful for the counselor to problem solve with parents to ensure that the child was receiving the care they needed but in a way that was manageable for the family system. In some cases, clinicians shifted toward family work with siblings and/or parents involved. Often, these family sessions led to beautiful work that may not have been possible in person due to scheduling issues. For other families who were struggling to provide supervision during the session, the sessions shifted to the kitchen table where mom or dad could cook dinner while supervising the client. In other cases, it was helpful for counselors to problem solve with parents to encourage a successful session. For example, shifting the time of the appointment so the child is not being pulled away from a high-reward activity or offering the child a high-reward activity when the session is complete might be worthwhile (Rattan & Wrightington, 2021; Premack, 1965).

Conclusion

The COVID-19 pandemic created an unprecedented push toward telemental health services in the mental health community. Clinicians and agencies who never would have attempted virtual services found themselves offering telemental health within a matter of days when states across the country mandated shelter-in-place orders. This experience allowed many practitioners to realize the various benefits of telemental health which will likely become a permanent aspect of mental health services for the foreseeable future. Though COVID-19 is still unfortunately present at the time of this publication, it is incredible to see TraumaPlay practitioners and the wider play therapy community come together to offer support and virtual interventions to one another. The move to telemental health was not without its challenges, but virtual sessions offered an intimate look into the home life of the families we serve and in a way that is not possible through in person sessions. In many cases, beautiful individual work was facilitated because the screen served as a titration to hard content. For others, family work became a viable option for those whose schedules would not permit these meetings in person. The wider incorporation of telemental health into play therapy will provide needed services in a more flexible manner.

References

Blue Seat Studios. (2016, October 4). *Consent for kids* [Video]. YouTube. https://www.youtube.com/watch?v=h3nhM9UlJjc

D'Andrea, W. D., Ford, J., Stolboach, B., Spinazzola, J., & van der Kolk, B. A. (2012). Understanding interpersonal trauma in children: Why we need a developmentally appropriate trauma diagnosis. *American Journal of Orthopsychiatry, 82*, 187–200.

Dye, H. (2018). The impact and long-term effects of childhood trauma. *Journal of human behavior in the social environment, 28*, 381–392.

Farrell, T. (2018, July 6). The window of tolerance reimagined. https://fb.watch/5FfhPECZb-/

Freymann, S., & Elffers, J. (2018). *Foods with moods: A first book of feelings*. Arthur A. Levine Books.

Funderburk, B. W., Ware, L. M., Altshuler, E., & Chaffin, M. (2008). Use and feasibility of telemedicine technology in the dissemination of parent-child interaction therapy. *Child Maltreatment, 13*, 377–382.

Goodyear-Brown, P. (2002). *Digging for buried treasure: 52 prop-based play therapy interventions for treating the problems of childhood*. Paris Goodyear-Brown.

Goodyear-Brown, P. (2005). *Digging for buried treasure 2 (52 more prop-based play therapy interventions for treating the problems of childhood)*. Paris Goodyear-Brown.

Goodyear-Brown, P. (2010). *Play therapy with traumatized children: A prescriptive approach*. John Wiley & Sons.

Goodyear-Brown, P. (2013). *Tackling touchy subjects*. Goodyear-Brown.

Goodyear-Brown, P. (2018, March 17). Trauma and play therapy: Holding hard stories [Video]. YouTube. https://www.youtube.com/watch?v=SbeS5iezIDA&t=579s

Goodyear-Brown, P. (2019). *Trauma and play therapy: Helping children heal*. Routledge.

Goodyear-Brown, P. (2021). *Parents as partners in child therapy: A clinician's guide*. Guilford.

Goodyear-Brown, P. & Gott, E. (2019). Tech, trauma work and the power of titration. In J. Stone (Ed.), *Integrating technology into modern therapies: A clinician's guide to developments and interventions* (pp. 109–123). Routledge.

Ihemedu-Steinke, Q. C., Erbach, R., Halady, P., Meixner, G., & Weber, M. (2017). Virtual reality driving simulator based on head-mounted displays. In G. Meixner & C. Müller (Eds.), *Automotive user interfaces* (pp. 401–428). Springer International.

Kerwin, M. E., Kirby, K. C., Speziali, D., Duggan, M., Mellitz, C., Versek, B., & McNamara, A. (2015). What can parents do? A review of state laws regarding decision making for adolescent drug abuse and mental health treatment. *Journal of Child and Adolescent Substance Abuse*, 24, 166–176.

Lamb, R., Etopio, E., & Lamb, R. E. (2019). *Virtual reality play therapy* [Unpublished manuscript]. University at Buffalo. https://www.researchgate.net/profile/Richard_Lamb2/publication/323557382_Therapeutc_use_of_virtual_reality_to_overcome_real world_problems/links/5a9d62b70f7e9be37968b759/Therapeutic-use-of-virtual-reality-to overcome-real-world-problems.pdf

Lerman, C. D., O'Brien, J. M., Neely, L., Call, A. N., Tsami, L., Scheiltz, M. K., Berg, K. W., Graber, J., Huang, P., Kopelman, T., Cooper-Brown, J. L. (2020). *Remote coaching of caregivers via telehealth: Challenges and potential solutions. Journal of Behavioral Education*, 29, 195–221.

Perry, B. D., & Azad, I. (1999). Posttraumatic stress disorders in children and adolescents. *Current Opinion in Pediatrics*, 11, 310–316.

Porges, S. W. (2009). The polyvagal theory: New insights into adaptive reactions of the autonomic nervous system. *Cleveland Clinic Journal of Medicine*, 76 (Suppl 2), S86–S90. https://doi.org/10.3949/ccjm.76.s2.17

Premack, D. (1965). Reinforcement theory. In D. Levine (Ed.), *Nebraska symposium on motivation* (pp. 123–180). Nebraska Press.

Rattan, S., & Wrightington, M. (2021). Premack's principle and visual schedules. In M. I. Axelrod, M. Coolong-Chaffin, & R. O. Hawkins (Eds.), *School-based behavioral intervention case studies: Effective problem solving for school psychologists*. Routledge.

Siegel, J. D., & Bryson, P. T. (2011). *The whole-brain child: Twelve revolutionary strategies to nurture your child's developing mind*. Bantam Books.

Siegel, J. D., & Bryson, P. T. (2020). *The power of showing up: How parental presence shapes who our kids become and how their brains get wired*. Ballantine Books.

Stewart, W. R., Orengo-Aguayo, R., Young, J., Wallace, M. M., Cohen, A. J., Mannarino, P. A., & de Arrellano, A. M. (2020). Feasibility and effectiveness of a telehealth service delivery model for treating childhood posttraumatic stress: A community-based, open pilot trial of trauma-focused cognitive-behavioral therapy. *Journal of Psychotherapy Integration*, 30, 274–289.

Stone, J. (2015). The virtual sandtray app. www.sandtrayplay.com/Press/VitrualSandtrayArticle01.pdf

Wellington, M. (2004). *Apple farmer Annie*. Puffin Books.

Wurtzel, B., & Wurtzel, C. (2020). *Foodie faces*. Hachette Book Group.

6 The Power of Attachment in Telemental Health

Clair Mellenthin

Attachment is the foundation to our lives and relationships. It is through the relationship with the parent and/or caregiver a child develops their internal working model of self. When raised within a healthy, secure attachment, this relationship forms the child's inherent belief structure of "*I am loved and loveable and worthy of belonging. The world is a predictable and positive place*". A child who is raised with an insecure or ambivalent style of attachment may form a different internal working model and question their worth and belonging, as their world consistently is shown to be unpredictable and untrustworthy (Bowlby, 1982).

Attachment theory was initially developed by John Bowlby following the World Wars in Europe. He was one of the first psychoanalysts working with children and families who had been separated by war, hospitalizations, asylum, and distance. Bowlby (1988) described attachment as a lasting psychological connectedness between human beings. His theory developed as "an attempt to explain both the attachment behavior, with its episodic appearance and disappearance, and also the enduring attachments that children and other individuals make to particular others" (p. 29). Attachment behaviors are the "seeking out of others for the comfort of security" (Mellenthin, 2019, p.4) as well as maintaining proximity to one who is better able to cope with the world or offer protection from the world (Bowlby, 1988). These behaviors may manifest in adaptive manners as cooing, crying, seeking out eye contact, reaching out to be held, following a parent, or sitting close to a person. Parental sensitivity to these behaviors and an appropriate nurturing response is critical in shaping the child's internal working model of self as well as healthy coping responses.

It is through the development of a secure attachment between parent and child whereby optimal growth occurs in the child's physical, neurological, emotional, and mental development. Parrigon et al. (2015) state, "The attachment relationship between parents and children is a key mechanism by which children learn emotion skills, including emotion understanding, coping strategies, and how to manage different affective experiences" (p. 27). In times of stress or trauma, these attachment seeking behaviors are triggered, and depending on the nature of the attachment system, is either

DOI: 10.4324/9781003166498-6

met with a responsive, nurturing attachment figure or a parent who may match the distressful effect of the child, rendering both to a sense of helplessness and fear.

In the complex, modern world, families are being faced with challenging a global pandemic, the closure of schools and daycare centers, remote, online learning, and having to socially distance themselves from friends, family members, and teachers. Humans are responding with creativity, flexibility, and the use of technology to restore and maintain connections to their attachment figures and support systems. In this chapter, the impact of these events on attachment will be discussed, as well as how play therapists can harness the power of play and the therapeutic relationship to strengthen and maintain connections in telemental health.

Research

Neuroscience has confirmed what Bowlby postulated in the early 20th century. We are literally wired for connection from our earliest beginnings in utero throughout the lifespan (Schore & Schore, 2012). Modern attachment theory recognizes the impact of secure attachment on the neurological development of the right brain and being able to regulate affect and emotion (2012). It is through the attachment patterns developed between parent and child that a child learns how to respond to stress, trauma, fear, (Bowlby, 1988) as well as joy, delight, and connection (Mellenthin, 2019).

Byng-Hall (1995) stated, "Attachments lie at the heart of family life. They create bonds that can provide care and protection across the life cycle, and can evoke the most intense emotions - joy in the making, anguish in the breaking - or create problems if they become insecure" (p.45). A child needs their primary attachment figure, most often the parent, as well as multiple caring adults in their lifetime to become different attachment figures that fulfill different attachment needs. Teachers, coaches, mentors, tutors, members of the clergy, neighbors, and kin/extended family often fill these roles. Through a systemic perspective of attachment, and recognizing the need for and importance of developing these bonds, it is also important to recognize how the attachment system is activated by threats, disruptions, and separations (Shapiro, 2010), including that changes in the world that warranted the shift to telemental health in play therapy.

Transition to Telemental Health

For many therapists, the transition from in-person psychotherapy to telemental health has been challenging and a new frontier in their play therapy practice. However, telemental health has been in existence for several years and practiced successfully with children and adolescents (Domoff et al., 2019). Prior to the global COVID-19 pandemic, there was significant resistance in the field of play therapy to utilizing technology in the play room and engaging in telemental health services with children. Critics feared that it was detrimental to the therapeutic relationship (Lilly, 2018) or potentially could threaten the secure attachment between parent and child (Courtney & Nowakowski, 2018) to fear of the effects on the brain to increasing social isolation (Domoff et al., 2019).

For children and adolescents however, the transition to telemental health has been much more natural and simplistic, as many have never known life without technology and some type of virtual relational experience (Stone, 2018), from FaceTiming with grandparents who live far away to TikToking with their friends as a way to be socially engaged and connected. Many have already experienced virtual proximity maintenance (Mellenthin, 2019) with their loved ones and view telemental health no differently. McNary et al. (2018) offered poignant advice as they stated, "It is important for adults to understand that children, as digital natives who have never known life without devices like laptops, tablets, and mobile phones, and who have always had easy access to the Internet, may view technology differently than adults do" (p. 5).

For the adults in the virtual play room, specifically the therapists, understanding how to create and maintain the therapeutic relationship via virtual means is critical in being successful at helping the client to feel safe, seen, and secure within the therapeutic relationship. Geller (2020) believes that the therapeutic presence is necessary for creating safety, building stronger therapeutic alliances, and increasing therapeutic effectiveness. She writes, "Presence strengthens the working relationship between therapists and clients, through the mechanism of evoking psychological and emotional safety … and helps the client to 'feel felt' (Siegel, 2010), met, and understood" (p. 2). Therapeutic presence is a way of *being with* a client that involves the therapist bringing their whole self to the session. This helps the therapist attune to the attachment-related needs of their clients, while being "grounded in one's self" and aware and responsive to the client's verbal and nonverbal experiences (Gellar, 2020).

In the virtual experience of telemental health, being attuned to the attachment seeking behaviors of the client is critical, as is being fully present in the play therapy session. Children are adept at reading adult's nonverbal communication and may be highly sensitive toward a lack of engagement or fear that *the therapist* is not enjoying their time together, is flustered and/or frustrated by the technological experience, as well as fearful that the therapist may not enjoy *being with* them. Children may also internalize these moments to be connected to their own sense of worth and acceptance, playing into their already negative internal working model of self. This can cause a therapeutic rupture between client and therapist. Eubanks et al. (2019) defined a therapeutic rupture as, "tension or disagreement between patient and therapist on the goals of treatment, failure to collaborate on the tasks of treatment, or a strain in the emotional bond between them" (Dolev-Amit et al., 2020, p. 2).

Without the therapist being attuned to their client's experience in telemental health, they may miss these moments of misattunement and potential ruptures, leaving confusion and hurt in the therapeutic relationship. It is critical to not only identify ruptures, but to repair and resolve them as they occur (Safran & Muran, 2000). Attachment ruptures may unintentionally occur throughout the telemental health experience, as technological glitches occur, or a connection is lost, at just the moment a client begins to allow for vulnerability and emotional intimacy to be shared. The therapist may lose audio during a conflictual family therapy session and not fully understand what was communicated verbally, although can see the shifts in the nonverbal communication between family members. The therapist themselves may feel disconnected emotionally from their clients due to the remote experience and may confuse their feelings for an attachment rupture with their client (Dolev-Amit et al., 2020).

It is important to address these ruptures as they occur, when they occur within the therapeutic relationship. Even very young children can experience a moment of or sense of disconnection from their play therapist. During the transition to telemental health, a client may feel hurt or wounded by the therapist's actions, such as not being able to continue face-to-face, in-person play therapy sessions (Dolev-Amit et al., 2020). It is important for the therapist to talk about this and the potential for hurt feelings to occur openly and directly, as well as allow for their client to be able to process their own feelings in a safe space with their therapist. Identifying and giving language to the rupture is also critical, even when uncomfortable for the play therapist. By addressing and identifying the attachment rupture, and resolving these together, this can become a positive opportunity for therapeutic growth (Safran & Muran, 2000). These moments of repair help to create a new constructive interpersonal experience that has the potential to change or modify a maladaptive schema or belief about themselves and their self-worth.

Interventions

It is critical for the play therapist to remain grounded in what makes play therapy work - harnessing the therapeutic powers of play (Schaefer & Drewes, 2014) and especially developing the therapeutic relationship. Play therapy has always been centered in attachment and relationship, as the play therapist enters the world of the child's inner imaginations and experiences. Giving permission to yourself to be your authentic self in the online playroom is just as important as in the traditional playroom. Landreth (2002) wrote, "The most significant resource the therapist brings to the play therapy relationship is the dimension of self. Skills and techniques are useful tools but therapists' use of their own personalities is their greatest asset" (p. 104-105). Timeless interventions such as guided imagery, sand tray, expressive arts, and child centered play therapy can work well in telemental health.

My Worry-Free World (Mellenthin, 2020) is an Attachment Centered Play Therapy (ACPT) technique that combines guided imagery with expressive arts. This intervention is designed for use with parent and child, although it can be modified for use in individual, family, or group therapy. This is an interactive guided imagery process, whereby the child can verbalize their experience along the fantasy journey. It was developed following the global COVID-19 pandemic and resulting socioeconomic shutdown that occurred. During the transition to telemental health, school closures, and increasing isolation, many child and adolescent clients struggled with fear, anxiety, and loneliness. This guided imagery works well for telemental health, with clients being directed to gather their desired art supplies prior to beginning the guided imagery script.

Close your eyes and begin listening to your breathing. Can you hear the sound of your breath moving in and out of your body? Now put both feet on the ground with your legs uncrossed. Can you feel the floor under your feet? Imagine your chest is like a great big hot air balloon. With this next breath in, we are going to fill up the entire balloon with the air it needs to float off the ground. Ready? Take a long, deep, slow breath and fill up your balloon with air. Exhale and blow all of your worries away with a big whoosh of a breath. Let's fill up the balloon a little bit more to help it begin to float in the sky. With your exhale, think of one more worry you would like to blow away and whoosh it away with your breath. Is your hot air balloon floating yet? We can take as many deep slow breaths as you need for it to float in the sky. (Once the child determines they are ready with their hot air balloon the therapist will move to this next part of the script).

Now I want you to imagine climbing into your hot air balloon. Hold the basket steady so you can feel safe to climb in. We are going to float away to a magical place where there are no stressors, no bad feelings, and no worries at all. Imagine we are floating up into the sky and moving towards your special worry-free place. Can you begin to see this magical place? Is in an inside place or an outside place? What colors do you see in this special worry-free place? Are there any people, animals, or things around you? Or are you alone? Notice what is around you as you begin to explore this magical place. What does it feel like to be in this worry-free place?

Once you have explored this magical place, invite the child and parent to create their worry-free worlds using any of the expressive arts materials they have gathered. They can create one world together, with the child's directives or can create side-by-side worlds to share together. Ask them to be as quiet as possible while they are working on their creations. When they are finished, the therapist may want to ask the following processing questions:

- What did you like most about your worry-free world?
- Who would you like to bring to your worry-free world?
- What are your biggest worries you have in your real world?
- Who can help you in your real world when you feel worried or scared?

It can be useful to practice "anchoring" so the child can visit their worry-free world when they need to over the week. This is a Neuro-Linguistic Programming (NLP) technique that is useful to regenerate a resourceful emotion. Anchoring creates an association with the emotion and the chosen physical action (Paras, 2020). It is helpful to practice this together in session, where the client chooses a physical action such as clasping their hands together and imagines going back into their special worry-free world. Once they can find this place in their mind, invite them to breathe in the good feelings and fill up their body with their magical space. Once they feel "full", ask them to open their eyes and come back into the therapy room. Unclasp the hands or whatever physical movement they have decided to a neutral body posture. Do this three times together, with the same physical movement each time. Invite the parent and child to practice going to their magical world throughout the week in order to strengthen the resource.

Stop, Collaborate, and Listen (Mellenthin, 2020) is another very playful intervention to harness the power of narrative therapy, play therapy, and technology using an app called AutoRap by Smule. This app has been available for the last several years and has been a fun addition to attachment-orientated work with children and families. Clients can speak into a smartphone or tablet and the app will generate what they said into rap music. This has been a powerful way to make music together, share difficult or painful stories, as well as empower families to work together to write and share *their* story. Often, it can be a very tender experience to write the family story together, particularly following trauma, transition, and grief. When the family can play back their story and hear their story in the form of a rap song, they often will start giggling and soon, belly-laughing together. These shared moments together work to strengthen the core attachment system, as the family grieves together, creates together, and then can laugh and dance together.

Ethics

There are many things to consider when implementing family-based teleplay services. The therapist needs to assess for safety issues within the family system, including physical, sexual, and emotional safety prior to beginning parent–child attachment work. Without the physical presence of the therapist to maintain boundaries and therapeutic safety, the therapist needs to be especially mindful and skilled in de-escalating conflict. Research has found that in times of crisis and school closure, the rates of child abuse and domestic violence have increased (Cluver et al., 2020). During stressful or traumatic times, challenging behaviors, disrupted attachments, and disorganized interpersonal relationships are among the most common reactions of children (DePierro et al., 2019; Gurwitch et al., 2020). These behaviors, in combination with parental stress and distress have been positively correlated with increase in mental health concerns of children and adolescents (Gurwitch et al., 2020).

Another area of ethical concern is the family's access to technological resources. The family's technological literacy, facility, trust, and capacity – as well as the therapist's – need to be taken into consideration (Gurwitch et al., 2020). This has been an area that has been challenging in the face of the COVID-19 pandemic, as the technological divide has been shown to run deeper in marginalized and underserved communities. Being mindful of the family's access to resources, including play therapy materials, is also highly important. Inviting the family to create a play therapy kit using toys or art supplies from the family home may be a way to help mitigate the pressure to have "the right things". The therapist can also create an inexpensive play therapy kit and drop off at the client's home with the needed supplies to be successful in telemental health services.

The last area of ethical concern to be addressed in this chapter is the importance of the therapist to be trained in providing telemental health services appropriately and effectively to their clientele. With the onset of the global COVID-19 pandemic, many therapists were thrust into a foreign world of providing therapeutic services online, with little training or knowledge on how to most effectively provide clinical services to their clients. The American Telemedicine Association (ATA) has created practice guidelines for telemental health with children and adolescents (Myers et al., 2017), along with the governing boards of the main mental health disciplines, including the Association for Play Therapy, in creating ethical statements of the use of telemental health. Each practitioner has an ethical duty to follow their mental health discipline's directives.

Case Example

Jamal was referred for telemental health therapy services in the spring of 2020 for escalating anxiety symptoms following the state shut down order due to the COVID-19 global pandemic. His parents report that he has always been an anxious child, is prone to emotional outbursts, and has struggled significantly with tantrums. He had recently begun refusing to attend school after this was moved to an online platform. Jamal is the middle child with two older sisters and two younger brothers, who resides in an affluent gated community. During the virtual parent intake, both parents were present and appeared very comfortable with one another. They sat close together on a loveseat, in order for the camera to be able to view both of them and appeared to take turns discussing their concerns and frustrations with their child's behaviors. Jamal's father reports that he has been working from a home office prior to the shutdown, as he manages a hedge fund and can easily work remotely. Mother reports she is "the home executive" and is the full-time caretaker for the children. When reviewing the mental health history of both parents, Jamal's mother reports that she is adopted and had spent most of her childhood and adolescence bouncing around the foster care system. Her adoptive parents placed her back into the foster care system when she was an adolescent. She has no known biological family history, as she was never given access to her biological family information. She reports her husband "saved me from a life full of heartache and pain". Jamal's father reports his mother and sisters experienced anxiety. He grew up in an intact nuclear family, and reports he is in contact regularly via FaceTime with his parents and siblings. He currently provides significant financial support to his aging parents. Both parents expressed feelings of loss that they were not able to be physically close with his family due to the COVID-19 pandemic.

In the initial teleplay assessment, Jamal presented as shy but curious. His parents had been invited to attend but had declined the therapist's invitation. Jamal initially hid his face in his hands but would peek out to ask a question to the therapist. They began to engage in a spontaneous playful peek-a-boo question and answer game together. As she answered his questions, his eye contact began to be more frequent and by the end of the telemental health play therapy session, he was sitting upright and fully engaged with the therapist. Establishing rapport with Jamal was relatively easy, however, building a therapeutic trust and alliance with him and his parents took several weeks to establish.

In the first few sessions, Jamal tended to present as shy and needed help warming up. The therapist learned that he usually sat in his bedroom for the virtual play therapy sessions. She encouraged him to find things that would help him feel cozy and comfortable, as well as items he enjoyed playing with to bring to their session. This began an opening ritual in the virtual play therapy sessions of Jamal introducing one of his favorite toys and using this as both a prop and resource throughout the session. Jamal shared that his favorite stuffed animal was also his best friend, because he didn't have any friends at school or in the neighborhood. He was able to explore his loneliness and desire for friends as well as his feelings of sadness and inadequacy that "no one would ever choose me". In a subsequent parent consultation, his mother confirmed that he lacked outside friends and she discouraged him from playing with children in the neighborhood because she felt more comfortable if he played at home with his younger siblings. The pandemic had also given a wonderful excuse to not venture into the neighborhood or try to arrange – and say no to – playdates.

At week six, the therapist invited the parents to begin meeting with her regularly to address some of the underlying attachment issues present in their parenting practices as well helping them to understand how Jamal's underlying insecure attachment style was contributing to the undesirable behaviors that had warranted the therapeutic referral. Jamal's father declined to participate, stating he was too busy with work to engage. His mother however, regularly attended weekly meetings and was able to begin to recognize how her past attachment ruptures and relationship experiences were contributing to some of the unintended messaging that had taken place with her child. She began attending virtual parent–child play therapy sessions with her young son and engaging in play therapy with him. As their relationship grew, so did their attachment in a positive, healthy manner.

In time, Jamal was able to verbally invite his father to attend therapy with him. His father readily agreed, as this invitation came from his child. Jamal had decided he wanted to make *Feeling Monsters* (Mellenthin, 2018) with his father and took charge in directing his father how to decorate the monster as well as instructing him about the emotions "everybody in the whole world feels". Together, they decided to make two monsters representing happiness and anger. Jamal's father was very responsive to his son and easily engaged with him. They laughed together as they created "the ugliest monster in the universe" representing anger and engaged in silly creativity. As they shared in this creativity together, Jamal spontaneously began sharing how his mad feelings were really sad and lonely feelings. They were able to explore this as well as how Jamal's father can be a support to his child when these feelings come. Jamal asked his father to "put your work away and play with me better". This caused his father's eyes to well with tears as he began to understand his child's inner world in a new way, as well as how he misunderstood his son's attachment seeking behaviors in the past.

Jamal and his parents engaged in virtual play therapy sessions for the next several weeks together. As they were able to repair and build a more secure attachment together, Jamal's anxiety and aggressiveness decreased significantly. He was able to join the neighborhood swim team and began to make friends in his neighborhood. His mother allowed outdoor playdates to occur where social distancing could still be in place. As termination occurred, Jamal told the therapist he finally felt happy inside and believed he was "awesome like everyone else". His internal working model of *self* had shifted to believing he was loved and loveable and worthy of love and belonging.

Conclusion

As the old adage says, you are 'the best toy' in the playroom. Cochran et al. (2010) state, "It is the therapeutic relationship with her that matters more than any toy or technique, and that if she [the therapist] is "broken" and unable to relate to the core conditions of deep empathy, genuineness, and unconditional positive regard, that therapy will not happen" (p. xii). Time and technology have not changed the importance of this statement. Maintaining, rebuilding, repairing, and creating secure attachments in the families we work with, in the therapeutic relationship, and through the powers of play is the most important work we can do as play therapists. Telemental health has not changed this, it has just brought the next frontier to the forefront of our clinical work.

References

Bowlby, J. (1982). *Attachment and loss*. Basic Books.

Bowlby, J. (1988). *A secure base. Parent-child attachment and healthy human development*. Routledge.

Byng-Hall, J. (1995). Creating a more secure family base: Some implications of attachment theory for family therapy. *Family Process, 34*, 45–58.

Cluver, L., Lachman, J. M., Sherr, L., Wessels, I., Krug, E., Rakotomalala, S., Blight, S., Hillis, S., Bachman, G., Green, O., Butchart, A., Tomlinson, M., Ward, C. L., Doubt, J., & McDonald, K. (2020). Parenting in a time COVID-19. *The Lancet, 395*, e64. https://dx.doi.org/10.1016/S0140-6736(20)30736-4

Cochran, N. H., Nordling, W. J., &Cochran, J. L. (2010). *Child-centered play therapy: A practical guide to developing therapeutic relationships with children*. Wiley.

Courtney, J. A. & Nowakowski, E. (2018, September). Technology and the threat to secure attachments: What play therapists need to consider. *Play Therapy, 3*(13), 10–14.

DePierro, J., D'Andrea, W., Spinazzola, J., Stafford, E., van Der Kolk, B., Saxe, G., Stolbach, B., McKernan, S., & Ford, J. D. (2019). Beyond PTSD: Client presentations of developmental trauma disorder from a national survey of clinicians. *Psychological Trauma: Theory, Research, Practice, and Policy*. Advance online publication. https://doi.org/10.1037/tra0000532

Dolev-Amit, T., Leibovich, L., & Zilcha-Mano, S. (2020). Repairing alliance ruptures using supportive techniques in telepsychotherapy during the COVID-19 pandemic. *Counselling Psychology Quarterly*, quarterly, 1–14. doi: 10.1080/09515070.2020.1777089

Domoff, S. E., Harrison, K., Gearhardt, A. N., Gentile, D. A., Lumeng, J. C., & Miller, A. L. (2019). Development and validation of the problematic media use measure: A parent report measure of screen media "addiction" in children. *Psychology of Popular Media Culture, 8*(1), 2–11. doi: 10.1037/ppm0000163

Eubanks, C. F., Lubitz, J., Muran, J. C., & Safran, J. D. (2019). Rupture Resolution Rating System (3RS): Development and validation. *Psychotherapy Research, 29*(3), 306–319

Geller, S. (2020). Cultivating online therapeutic presence: strengthening therapeutic relationships in teletherapy sessions. *Counselling Psychology Quarterly*, 1–17. doi: 10.1080/09515070.2020.1787348

Gurwitch, R. H., Salem, H., Nelson, M. M., & Comer, J. S. (2020). Leveraging parent-child interaction therapy and telehealth capacities to address the unique needs of young children during the COVID-19 public health crisis. *Psychological Trauma: Theory, Research, Practice, and Policy, 1*(12), S82–S84

Landreth, G. L. (2002). *Play therapy: The art of the relationship* (2nd ed.) Brunner-Routledge.

Lilly, J. P. (2018, September). Leave technology out: A conscious choice for promoting unconscious play. *Play Therapy, 3*(13), 17.

McNary, T., Mason, E., & Tobin, G. (2018). The unexpected purpose of technology in the playroom: catharsis. *Play Therapy, 13*(3), 4–7.

Mellenthin, C. (2018). *Play therapy: Engaging and powerful techniques for the treatment of childhood disorders*. Pesi Publishing.

Mellenthin, C. (2019). *Attachment centered play therapy*. Routledge.

Mellenthin, C. (2020, April). Play therapy in the age of telehealth [webinar.] Presentation for Kentucky Play Therapy Association.

Myers, K., Nelson, E., Rabinowitz, T., Hilty, D., Baker, D., Barnwell, S. S., Boyce, G., Bufka, L. F., Cain, S., Chui, L., Comer, J. S., Cradock, C., Goldstein, F., Johnston, B., Krupiniski, E., Lo, K., Nelson, E., Cain, S., & Sharp, S. (2017). Considerations for conducting telemental health with children and adolescents. *Child and Adolescent Psychiatric Clinics of North America, 26*(1), 77–91. https://doi.org/10.1016/j.chc.2016.07.008

Paras, S. (2020, January 15). 5 NLP techniques that benefit the coaching journey. Coacharya. https://coacharya.com/blog/neuro-linguistic-programming-nlp-techniques-benefit-coaching/

Parrigon, K. S., Kerns, K. A., Abtahi, M. M., & Koehn, A. (2015). Attachment and emotion in middle childhood and adolescence. *Psychological Topics, 1*(24), 27–50.

Safran, J. D. & Muran, J. C. (2000). *Negotiating the therapeutic alliance: A relational treatment guide.* Guildford Press.

Schaefer, C. E. & Drewes, A. A. (2014). *The therapeutic powers of play* (2nd ed.). Wiley.

Schore, A. N. & Shore, J. R. (2012). Modern attachment theory: The central role of affect regulation in development and treatment. In A. N. Schore (Ed.), *The science of the art of psychotherapy* (pp. 27–51). Norton.

Siegel, D. J. (2010). *The mindful therapist: A clinician's guide to mindsight and neural integration (Norton Series on Interpersonal Neurobiology).* W.W. Norton & Company.

Shapiro, J. (2010). Attachment in the family context: Insights from development and clinical work. In Bennett, S. & Nelson, J. K. (Eds.) *Adult attachment in clinical social work.* Essential clinical social work series (pp. 147–172). Springer. doi: 10.1007/978-1-4419-6241-6_9

Stone, J. (2018, September). Play therapy needs the baby and the bathwater. *Play Therapy, 3*(13), 16.

7 Virtual EMDR and Telemental Health Play Therapy

Jackie Flynn

This chapter offers a brief glimpse into a robust treatment approach to help children and teens heal from trauma and other distressing events through the virtual delivery of Eye Movement Desensitization and Reprocessing (EMDR) and play therapies. Written for child and teen therapists interested in providing trauma treatment virtually, this chapter focuses on interventions with child and teen clients in the field of psychotherapy. The information presented here is not a suitable substitute for formal training in EMDR or play therapies. For safe and ethical practice, seek accredited training, qualified supervision, and EMDR specific consultation focused on child therapy from respective professional governing associations such as Eye Movement Desensitization International Association (EMDRIA) and the Association for Play Therapy (APT).

The integration of these two therapies delivered virtually is a powerful combination for remote work with children and adolescents. For the purposes of this writing, telemental health play therapy will be used to represent the virtual delivery of play therapy. Similar to in-person sessions, the integration of virtual EMDR and telemental health play therapy isn't guaranteed to be an appropriate or effective treatment for all clients however. Clinical considerations are presented throughout this chapter to assist clinicians with a determination of the appropriateness prior to the beginning of treatment. It's important to note, standards and protocols change over time, therefore some of the information presented in this chapter may be obsolete and replaced at the time of reading. Advanced training in Virtual EMDR and telemental health play therapy is highly recommended for practitioners as part of ethical professional development.

Growth from a Pandemic

At the time of this writing, the world is adjusting to ongoing changes brought on by the global pandemic, COVID-19, coronavirus disease 2019. Change can be difficult. Coronavirus has changed our therapeutic practices, perhaps forever. Not all of the changes have been negative though. This pandemic demanded that clinicians learn new skills, think about things differently, and venture out into the unknown in areas such remote therapy.

DOI: 10.4324/9781003166498-7

Child and teen therapists, along with many other healthcare professionals around the world, have been tasked with continuing to provide quality mental health services virtually. This isn't taken lightly. For many clinicians, this proved to be a substantial change from their routine daily operations of meeting with their child and teen clients in person. The transition from meeting clients in the play therapy rooms to the use of HIPAA compliant platforms to provide telemental health services to clients is now considered a new normal.

Understanding Childhood Trauma

Working with children and teen requires a specialized set of skills with applicable knowledge of development. The developing brain is magnificent. Our ability to bounce back quickly, regardless of age, from adverse life experiences is supported by our capacity to draw on helpful information stored from our learned life experiences to support the healing process. In the world of EMDR, this is known as *Adaptive Information*. The old adage "what doesn't kill you will make you stronger" may hold true for some but doesn't come without a cost. Often our clients begin treatment due to presentation of maladaptive behaviors created from distressing or disturbing events in their lives, what we refer to as *trauma*. Unprocessed childhood trauma can lead to seemingly unrelated health problems and a life filled with confusion and struggle (Nakazawa, 2015). Mental health treatment can reap lifelong benefits.

The aftermath of trauma can have a substantial impact on one's life. The sooner one can attain therapeutic support, the better. Time lengthens the memory networks and can generalize the erroneous cognitions, beliefs about oneself, that may metastasize following trauma as time goes on. In other words, the longer a cognition such as "I'm not safe". is present, the more work may need to be done. Trauma can leave people feeling a neuroception of danger, even in neutral situations (Dion, 2018). The fullness of life can seemingly deflate over time without timely treatment. Self-beliefs, also known as cognitions, can be healthy and supportive of a quality life. Except when they are not. When trauma creates erroneous beliefs, such as "I'm not safe", "I am shameful", "I am powerless" leaving people, especially children and adolescents with limited life experiences, feeling emotionally stuck.

Since our emotional memories actually begin in the womb, long before the development of linguistic and cognitive functions, we can't rely on talk therapy alone for deep emotional healing (Shapiro, 2018). This is where EMDR and play therapies show up on the scene as an effective treatment approach to use with children as it honors the developing brain and surpasses the limitations of words. Neither one of these therapies rely on words, insights, or compliance. They go deep and have great healing potential, even when delivered remotely to clients. Virtual EMDR and telemental health play therapy, can provide life-changing healing experiences. In many cases, EMDR trained clinicians focus on attachment through play-based interventions quite heavily during the preparation phase. When delivered correctly, interventions have great potentiality in a telemental health play therapy setting.

Virtual Therapy

Virtual services are quickly becoming the new normal for many. The transition to remote therapeutic work with clients has been an adjustment. Working with children and adolescents remotely can seem intimidating for some at first, but often levels out as clinicians strengthen their capacity to use technological devices, increase preparedness through training, and, most importantly, focus on the therapeutic relationship. The transition from in-person to virtual therapy has pleasantly surprised many clients and clinicians.

EMDR and Telemental Health Play Therapy

Neuroception

EMDR and telemental health play therapy aim to regulate the nervous system through desensitization of key issues, also known as *targets*. The social engagement system is a key part of the process. When working with clients online, special attention is given to facial expressions, proximity to the screen, sound, movement, and lighting. As human beings, our nervous system is wired early on to respond to sensations in the body and the environment (Dion, 2018). Much of our communication is beyond words. When working with children and adolescents virtually, clinicians can greatly strengthen the precious therapeutic relationship through creating a neuroception of safety early on. This is especially important in remote work, as the physical separation may cause some to feel disconnected. Neuroception, a term coined from by Dr. Porges (the author of the Polyvagal Theory) describes a continuum of the inner felt sense from safety to danger (Porges, 2017). The felt sense of emotions influences how we respond to the world around us (Siegel & Bryson, 2019). Telemental health play therapy can nurture the felt sense of emotions in a developmentally appropriate way. Basically, it is "getting the vibes" from another person. This neuroception is part of our clinical sessions, whether virtual or in-person. Being able fully attune to clients virtually is a common concern among clinicians newly venturing into the virtual therapy realm. The COVID-19 pandemic, however demanded telehealth options for clients, which revealed the wonderful reality that deep connection and attunement can be attained in a virtual environment, even with young children.

Trauma

When trauma occurs, the trajectory of life can change for some. Images are frozen in time. Erroneous beliefs sometimes override rational beliefs. Body sensations can hi-jack our ability to "show-up" and "be present" in life. When children experience trauma, images and felt sensations can get locked in at the developmental stage that it occurred (Shapiro, 2018). For example, we may be working with a 47-year-old client that presents as a five-year-old in session as they reprocess child abuse. Comments like "I know it's not right, but I still feel that way". can explain how trauma can remain isolated from learned knowledge until helpful treatment occurs. Throughout the EMDR process, images, cognitions, and body sensations are focused on with the goal of reducing (ideally eliminating) the emotional charge from left from the trauma. When working with clients online, clinicians can easily access images, videos, and other supportive media from the internet as it applies. Songs can greatly assist with treatment goals as part of the session. A common website used by child therapists for EMDR therapy to assist with the bilateral stimulation of virtual EMDR, emotional equilibrium, and resourcing is https://app.gonoodle.com. The GoNoodle site is an ideal support for EMDR clinicians working with children as it is engaging and offers a playful approach to movement and bilateral stimulation.

Stress

For the most part, the human race is resilient to stress. Stress is functional. It can help keep us safe and in action mode. Sustained distress or disturbing events can certainly leave their marks on some. Not everyone experiences trauma in the same way; not everyone that experiences trauma needs therapy. Some people experience seemingly unthinkable events with minimal impact on their lives, while others experience what seems to be less traumatic with greater negative consequences. The concept of "big T" and "little t" traumas is often used to describe the intensity for the person, which can vary. This distinction isn't without controversy, as some belief that labeling one's trauma as a "little t" minimizes and disregards the person's pain and suffering. For this reason, it's important for clinicians to be mindful not to rate the client's trauma, but to allow the client to determine their level of distress.

Trauma stores itself in the body and the brain. Images, erroneous beliefs, and body sensations can change our capacity to live our lives as usual (van der Kolk, 2014). When clinicians work with child and teen clients virtually, it's helpful to create an environment that allows for movement. For example, most of my younger clients continually move throughout the sessions. Movement is greatly supportive of releasing somatically stored material in the body. Trauma is often a result of immobilization, so mobilizing can work it through the body and provide relief. I ask parents or caregivers of my clients under seven to place the electronic device (laptop, computer, tablet, etc.) in a space that allows me to view them as they move around and play during the sessions. In *The Body Keeps the Score*, Dr. van der Kolk explores how movement supports trauma treatment (2014).

Shifts

The clinical treatment of trauma in children, especially when delivered virtually, often requires a paradigm shift. Children are not miniature adults. Their brains are still developing (Siegel & Bryson, 2019). Offering treatment in the same way as we do adults not only limits their healing, but it can in some cases make matters worse. Understanding the neuroscience of trauma and honoring the developing brain throughout treatment is essential, especially when working with traumatized children online.

One of the hallmarks of therapy is the magnificent value of "being with" our clients (Landreth, 2012). Sharing energy. Not being alone in the pain. Being in the same room with a client, especially our child and teen clients, seemed like the only option for quality therapy for many. As you may imagine, the shift to virtual delivery of therapeutic services isn't without resistance and skepticism. The shift into virtual therapy happened quickly. The play therapy and EMDR communities stepped up to the plate by quickly adapting current therapeutic practices virtually while training others along the way. Interestingly enough, some leaders in the field were already looking at the benefits and delivery of online work with children and teens long before COVID-19. Change agents such as Dr. Jessica Stone, creator of the Virtual Sandtray®© App and Digital Play Therapy™, and Dr. Rachel Altvater, a researcher of the trends and transitions to implementing technology in play therapy practice, are lifelines.

The transition from in-person has been truly inspiring. Many have decided to continue working online with children and teens after the pandemic once they experienced the therapeutic values. It has been a pleasant surprise to realize that strong therapeutic relationships can be established and nurtured remotely. Safety can be established online. A growing number of child therapists around the globe are closing their brick and mortar locations, and have chosen to work from their home offices online with their clients exclusively.

As a Registered Play Therapist and an EMDRIA Approved Consultant passionate about sharing the healing power of integrated EMDR and play therapy, this author has had the honor of teaching countless others how to work with children and teens online. On a side note, remote learning options are growing exponentially as well during this pandemic. Fortunately, both of these therapies, EMDR and play therapy, fit quite nicely into the virtual realm for experiential learning and for delivery of services. During a recent training session, *eight Phases of EMDR with Children and Adolescents Integrating Play Therapy Techniques,* many of the students declared that they preferred working with clients remotely offering Virtual EMDR and telemental health play therapy, over in-person sessions.

Telemental Health Play Therapy

EMDR Integrated with Play Therapy

Before we get into the specifics of virtual delivery of EMDR integrated with play therapy, it is necessary to explore the foundation of each. Let us begin with play therapy. The continuum from non-directive to directive play therapy can be successfully integrated throughout the EMDR therapy phases: History Taking, Preparation, Assessment, Desensitization, Installation, Body Scan, Closure, and Re-evaluation (Shapiro, 2018). It's important to know that there are several theoretical play therapy approaches, as delineated in the first section of this book. Clinicians pondering an appropriate path to become an EMDR trained therapist integrating play therapy with clients, whether in-person or remotely, may benefit greatly by seeking accredited play therapy training *prior* to the EMDR basic training. Obtaining play therapy training first offers a deep understanding of child development and the therapeutic use of play helps clinicians envision integration early on. EMDR is a highly structured type of therapy that integrates well with other therapies, especially play therapy.

Play and Play Therapy

A common assumption is that play therapy is used to help the child talk about what is troubling them. The truth is that the therapeutic value is actually through the *play itself*. By nature, play requires expression, flexibility, openness, and vulnerability. The therapeutic value of shared play in the clinical setting, regardless of whether it is in-person or remote, is immeasurable. For more specific information on the clinical capacity for change, read the *The Therapeutic Powers of Play: 20 Core Agents of Change* (Schaefer & Drewes, 2014). In Beyond Behaviors, Dr. Mona Delahooke describes play as one of the most therapeutic things that we can do with children as it supports integration and use of bottom-up (responsible for reflexes and automatic survival responses) and top-down (responsible for higher level thinking and cognitive awareness) functioning in real time (Delahooke, 2019). Essentially, hemispherical integration of the brain occurs through play which supports social and emotional growth and healing.

Play is a powerful approach to healing. Play therapy is more of a developmentally appropriate treatment approach for children compared to talk therapy (Stewart et al., 2016). Communicating through words alone relies a great deal on the left hemisphere of the brain, which is still in the developmental stages for children. The human brain isn't fully developed until around the mid-twenties. This is one reason why play therapy is an ideal approach as it doesn't depend on a fully developed brain. Play therapy employs more of the right hemisphere of the brain that supports emotional healing. Telemental health play therapy offers all of these benefits in a virtual realm when delivered appropriately.

Safety and Regulation

Effective outcomes for trauma treatment in children involve specific attention to relational safety with use of developmentally appropriate techniques to reprocess whatever it was that happened to them. Play therapy and telemental health play therapy naturally nurtures a neuroception of safety. The establishment of safety may take longer when working with some clients virtually. It is important to not rush the process. Take time to cultivate relationships and become comfortable in the online setting. Mindfully creating a setting that communicates calmness, confidentiality, and playfulness can help. This is especially true for our traumatized children and adolescents in EMDR treatment. It is important to keep in mind: relational safety must be cultivated clearly online. In virtual therapy, clients are not confined to our offices where we can run after them or comfort them through our presence. Direct communication with parents and caregivers to bring young children back when the therapist isn't physically present with the client is vital. Relational safety also supports therapeutic goals, especially with EMDR Therapy treatment, involving movement toward increased flexibility and greater resiliency to stressful situations. Deep emotional healing and growth occurs in remote settings when there is a safe and secure emotional connection between the therapist and child, such as what is cultivated virtual play (Delahooke, 2019). Opening a session with a puppet in the foreground of the camera shot, or with a silly hat or outfit when working with younger clients can support a neuroception of safety and support a strong therapeutic relationship. The puppets often offer an opportunity for projection, which can be extremely helpful in EMDR sessions. Playful distancing to work through the EMDR targets. For some teen clients, clinicians may find that opening the virtual EMDR and telehealth sessions with a song that is shared during the intake process can build up the therapeutic relationship.

A strong therapeutic connection is essential for effective therapy to occur (Landreth, 2012), especially when working remotely with clients. For the most part, this alliance occurs when clinicians focus on co-regulation with their clients by responding in a connected way to reactions outside of their client's window of tolerance. Telemental health play therapy can be extremely fatiguing to therapists throughout the days, so it's important that clinicians regulate themselves regularly. In April of 2020, shortly after the migration to online therapy for clinicians in the United States, a free training, *Regulation for Clinicians with Lisa Dion and Jackie Flynn*, provided a source of regulation techniques for clinicians around the world. In this training, specific regulation breathing and movement techniques for clinicians are described and demonstrated. In her book, Aggression in Play Therapy, clinicians can learn practical ways to co-regulate with clients during session (Dion, 2018).

Learning how to recognize cues of dysregulation through the screen through the lens of play therapy over electronic devices such as tablets and computers, can prevent hypo-arousal in the clinician and clients as it supports the cultivation of deeply attuned relationships necessary for complex trauma work even when meeting online. To learn more about play therapy, please visit the Association for Play Therapy at www.a4pt.org.

Virtual EMDR Therapy

As stated, Eye Movement Desensitization Reprocessing (EMDR) Therapy integrates well with play therapy virtually and in-person. They both access and provide more healing potential than talk therapy alone. EMDR is internationally recognized and evidenced based. As presented earlier in this chapter, the eight phases of EMDR are as follows: history taking, preparation, assessment, reprocessing, installation, body scan, closure, and re-evaluation. EMDR was originally created by Francine Shapiro in the early 1980s as a treatment for PTSD, Post-Traumatic Stress Disorder. Since then, it has been found to be an effective treatment for many issues for all ages over the years. One of the hallmarks of EMDR Therapy is the Adaptive Information Processing Model (AIP). Which speaks about the inclusion of positive experiences and useful information stored in the brain and body. The AIP model provides the framework throughout the eight phases of EMDR with attention to what Shapiro identified as the three prongs, Past, Present, and Future (Shapiro, 2018). Experienced virtual EMDR trained therapists reading this may already notice that the virtual process looks extremely similar to in-person delivery. Telemental health play therapy can be used to build up children and adolescent clients' adaptive information that is often in deficient due to limited life experiences.

Some of the early pioneers who laid the groundwork for EMDR as an effective trauma treatment for children include Ana Gomez, Carolyn Settle, and Robbie Adler-Tapia. With thanks to these clinicians, we have a solid base to further our capacity to heal trauma in children and adolescents. Their contributions are highly valued. Since their early work, a growing number of EMDRIA approved consultants and child therapists, many of which are Registered Play Therapists credentialed through the Association for Play Therapy, build the knowledge base of how to deliver EMDR with kids through the development of advanced training. This solid foundation greatly supports our changing shift into the realm of virtual EMDR and telemental health play therapy. An emphasis on the need for formal EMDR basic training, followed by consultation, is required for clinicians to offer it in clinical practice is vital. Remote complex trauma work alone can lead to burnout and result in ineffective, and in some cases, harmful treatment. These overviews in this chapter is not adequate training to deliver virtual EMDR and/or telemental health play therapy. For more information about EMDR and training opportunities, visit www.emdria.org.

Benefits and Challenges

In-person EMDR and play therapy isn't by any means obsolete at this point. It has undeniably changed though. Social distancing and facial masks are often included. These changes can feel somewhat disconnecting. In some cases, clinicians and clients differ on their opinions regarding whether or not social distancing and mask wearing is necessary, so safety concerns can arise. The fear of contracting the virus can initiate a fear response in clients and clinicians resulting in relationship ruptures that impede the therapeutic process. Safety concerns are why many clinicians are closing their office doors and opening up their virtual therapy space. While the COVID-19 crisis has clearly shown us that quality therapy can be attained well when apart, it's important to keep in mind that many clinicians and clients still want to meet for sessions in-person.

Prior to the pandemic, EMDRIA published a report titled, *Guidelines for Virtual EMDR Therapy at* https://www.emdria.org. At the time of its composition, virtual EMDR therapy was already being considered to increase the accessibility of therapy through remote delivery. It served as our clinical compass during the early days of the pandemic of how to proceed with EMDR therapy considering the risks. The report outlined the following areas of concerns with a disclaimer that many of the initial concerns were later reduced through investigation, preparation, training, experience, and actual practice. Specifically, the main areas of concerns included in their report are the following: safety, relationship and attunement, bilateral stimulation options, dual awareness, prevention and management of abreactions, potentiality for technological challenges, management of dissociation, issues surrounding ethics/liability/license, limited research and the efficacy of treatment and actual training, possibility for distractions, payment, access and development of resources, and assessment.

The Association for Play Therapy also provided beneficial information to the play therapy community regarding the pandemic and telehealth. Information regarding the Coronavirus Disease 2019, guidelines for returning to the playroom, supportive information for play therapists from experts in the field, and several telehealth resources in the form of documents and videos are all available at www.a4pt.org.

The following sections will cover specific, actionable procedures necessary during virtual EMDR therapy. EMDRIA's definition of EMDR clearly states what needs to happen throughout each phase, as well as the Therapeutic Powers of Play (Schaefer and Drewes, 2014). Both of these resources, along with countless others consumed during this author's career, have greatly influenced the development of techniques presented here. Ideally, trained EMDR therapists reading this will use these techniques as designed and as a spark to create their own therapeutic creativity to maximize healing opportunities for child and teen trauma treatment.

Practical Application

The following is a list of each phase with necessary procedures based on EMDRIA's definition of EMDR. For access to the definition of EMDR, refer to https://www.emdrhap.org/content/wp-content/uploads/2020/02/EMDRIA-Definition-of-EMDR.pdf. Implementation flexibility is allowed, such as using it with children remotely integrated with telemental health play therapy, as long as respective broad goals for each phase are performed (Table 7.1).

Oliver's Experience with Virtual EMDR Therapy and Telemental Health Play Therapy

Oliver began therapy in 2018, six months prior to COVID-19 global pandemic. At that time, he presented with an inability to control urination with frequent bathroom accidents at school, constant worrying about the well-being of others, and intense emotional outbursts in the mornings before school. He would perseverate on occurrences of his school teacher disciplining other children through the use of a color chart. Oliver is the oldest of two, with a younger sister, both living at home with both parents married and supportive of his needs. After four sessions, in-person EMDR and play therapy sessions, Oliver's symptoms resolved and successfully completed therapy at that time.

Oliver returned to therapy in April of 2020 as anxious symptoms resurfaced seemingly from the onset of the pandemic. He returned to therapy after expressing intense safety related worries accompanied by sleep disturbance, irritability that frequently resulted in family conflict, and emotional outbursts. He presented with intense distress that he and his family may die. Both parents expressed a sense of despair and desperation as they felt powerless to support a sense of safety for him.

In the initial Virtual EMDR and telemental health play therapy session upon return back to therapy, Oliver presented as chaotic and playful. His parents prepared a space in their home with toys, art supplies, and Nemo, their family dog.

Since he previously EMDR therapy, Phase 1: History Taking and Phase 2: Preparation were not necessary. Phases 3–8 of EMDR began shortly after a few play based breaths and resourcing activities. When directed to "play out" what was going on, he reached for nearby stuffed animals and proceeded to project a scene of death and destruction upon contact with the virus. His face turned red and his voice became shaky and loud. When

120 *Jackie Flynn*

Table 7.1 Practical Application of Virtual EMDR and TelePlay adapted from EMDRIA's Definition of EMDR (EMDRIA, 2012). A table with eight rows and three columns depicting the eight EMDR phases, procedures, and directives. The necessary procedures include components for the therapist to include in the therapeutic interactions. The directives explain a number of interventions and wording for the therapist to use within each phase

EMDR Phases	Necessary Procedures	Teleplay Directives
Phase 1: History Taking Goals	• Use professional judgement to determine if EMDR is suitable for your client. • Determine if it is good timing for therapy. • Explore potential targets from negative events. • Prepare a treatment plan to include past, present, & future issues. • Identify positive & adaptive aspects of the client's life utilizing play. • Assess if the client has adequate affect regulation skills & resources to remain stable. • Explore any secondary gain issues.	• Look at these pages to find a few of the words to describe _____ (child's name). When you think about _____ (descriptive word chosen, such as creative) and _____ (child's name), what comes to mind? This activity is based on Tammi Van Hollander's Greatness Sticks (Van Hollander, 2016), which can quickly be located through a Google search. For virtual delivery create a document to share with the client and parent(s) through the screen. The intent is to identify strengths and positive aspects of the child's life. • *Show Me Your World in the Virtual Sandtray*®© *App* This directive is intended to gather client's perception of significant elements of their life. For this directive, clinicians will need to purchase the Virtual Sandtray App. It's important to know that the client version of the application is free of charge.
Phase 2: Preparation Goals	• Discuss the framework of EMDR for informed consent with parents (and the client if appropriate). • Ensure the therapeutic relationship is sufficient for client's emotional safety. Use play therapy to strengthen client's	• *Draw an Image of a Peaceful Place where you are the only one in the picture."* This art therapy directive provides visual representation of what is often referred to as the calm place. Clinicians can strengthen its value by asking the client to describe sensory elements of the image. For example, "What sights,

(Continued)

Table 7.1 (Continued)

EMDR Phases	Necessary Procedures	Teleplay Directives
	neuroception of safety within the relationship. • Assess and support the client's ability to engage in self-soothing and affect regulation through playful means. • Assess and support adequate adaptive resources through play. • Assess and support adequate affect regulation skills for development of positive and adaptive memory networks to expand the client's window of tolerance and development of capacity for relationship utilizing play.	sounds, things to touch, and tastes. and smells are a part of your peaceful place? To reduce the risk of contamination, an image that triggers distress, the client is directed to be the only person in the image. Being alone can be triggering for some, especially younger children, so use clinical judgement regarding its appropriateness. Playful breathing techniques can be substituted for this when necessary. • *Create a Craft Container* This expressive art directive requires the client to have access to paper, glue, and other common art supplies. This tangible approach to a container creation is grounding and provides a deeper level of understanding for children struggling with implantation of its use. • *Let's listen to the Freeze Dance song.* When the music stops, we both freeze. This activity supports attunement and relational safety. While Freeze Dance songs are easily found on YouTube, clinicians may wish to use a song of the client's choice to strengthen the client's perception of significance in the relationship. • *Look around the room for something that is helpful for you in some way. For example, if I look around me, I see my blanket. It feels soft and helps to keep me cozy.*

(Continued)

Table 7.1 (Continued)

EMDR Phases	Necessary Procedures	Teleplay Directives
Phase 3: Assessment Goals	• Identify the components of the target/issue and establish a baseline response using play-based methods and expressive arts. • Direct the client to select, express or create an image (or other sensory experience) to represent it. • Identify the negative cognition associated with the identified target issue using clinical discretion with young children. • Identify the positive cognition, through playful methods when appropriate, associated with the identified target issue, then ask the client to rate it on the 0–7 validity of cognition scale. • Support the client with identifying, locating, and naming associated emotions. • Ask the client to pair the image and the negative belief (use discretion with use a negative cognition with younger clients), then rate the level	This directive provides opportunities for the client to use their chosen object as a resource in-between sessions. In my experience, I have found it helpful to provide an example for the client such as, "When I look around me, I see my shoes. They help me move around and keep my feet safe. What do you see around you that helps you?" • *Fold your paper into 8 squares, like this (place an example of the folds within the client's view of the camera.) Then, draw out the story of what happened from beginning to the end. In the first box, show me with a picture of what happened first* After the client draws in the first part, then move forward with each block prompting the client with a "Then, what happened next?" questions.: this directive supports development of the narrative, points of disturbance, cognitions, emotions, and levels of disturbance, which is supportive of target development. • *Hardest Part Charades* This playful activity allows for expression of pain in a playful way. It's important to note that it's not appropriate with all clients. Use clinical discretion.

(Continued)

Table 7.1 (Continued)

EMDR Phases	Necessary Procedures	Teleplay Directives
Phase 4: Desensitization Goals	of disturbance while locating the physical location of disturbance in their body. Activate the memory/issue. • Ask the client to notice his/her experiences while alternating bilateral stimulation. • Instruct the client to report or express observations through play or art: new insights, associations, information, and emotional, sensory, somatic, or behavioral shifts. • Use specific procedures and interweaves if processing is blocked. (only when needed, don't overuse cognitions). • Continue until the SUD level is reduced to 0 (or an "ecologically valid" rating). • Assist the individual in maintaining an appropriate level of arousal and affect tolerance. Use play-based grounding methods to support movement back into the window of tolerance.	• *Notice whatever comes up in your mind. When we stop moving, I'll ask you 'What's coming up now?' At that time, just tell me whatever you're thinking about or what you are feeling in your body. Something random may come up and that's okay. Just let me know each time we stop.* This metaphor can be used in seemingly endless applications involving Teleplay. • *Let's do the Stomping Feet and Bubble Popping* (Wunderlich, 2010) • *Let's be mirroring mimes* This directive strengthens attunement and allows the clinician to control the length and pace of the bilateral stimulation. Exploration of the term mime may be necessary for some children if they aren't familiar with the word. • *Let's tap that down with a butterfly hug* This directive provides a hemispherical integration of the body, while providing movement. This is my preferred method of bilateral stimulation with clients in my Virtual EMDR and Teleplay sessions.
Phase 5: Reprocessing Goals	• Check for a potential new positive belief related to the target memory. • Support the client in selecting a new belief or	• *Pick out the positive thought that you wish were true right now and pop it like this (create a popping sound with your mouth)* For this directive, clinicians will need a

(*Continued*)

124 *Jackie Flynn*

Table 7.1 (Continued)

EMDR Phases	Necessary Procedures	Teleplay Directives
	accessing the previously established positive cognition. • Direct the client to hold the positive cognition in mind, along with the target memory (not the original target image), and to rate the selected positive belief on the VOC scale of 1–7.	list of child appropriate cognitions placed in bubbles. The child's familiarity with the positive cognitions beforehand can increase its usefulness. • *Draw an image of it (target) looks like now* This art therapy directive provides visual representation of the reprocessed target memory/even and can strengthen the adaptive shift considerably.
Phase 6: Body Scan Goals	• Direct the client to think of the target event and the positive belief (cognition) at the same time, then scan their body for any tight, tense, or any unusual sensation. Use child-friendly somatic supports with visual representations. • If the client reports a body sensation, continue BLS (bilateral stimulation) until the client reports only neutral or positive sensations.	• *Color the body outline to represent how you feel right now at this moment – show me where you feel it in your body* This expressive art therapy directive supports somatic awareness and can then be used for more advanced techniques such as Pendulation. • *Look through the In My Body I Feel: A Book About the Felt Sense of Emotion to show me what you are noticing in your body right now* (Flynn, 2020) The visual representations in this book support the clients capacity to identify the location and name of the felt sense of emotions.
Phase 7: Closure Goals	• Use play therapy techniques to orient the client fully to the present and facilitate stability at the completion of the session and between sessions. • Inform the client and parent that processing may continue after the session. • Provide instructions and experiential practices of play therapy grounding	• *Let's mindfully breathe in and out as we trace the shape on the screen with our pointer finger with a pause at each corner 3 seconds, like this.* (Demonstrate alternating between inhales through the nose and exhale through the mouth with a pause each corner with a square This playful breathing technique can also be done in the air. It is supportive of bringing the

(Continued)

Table 7.1 (Continued)

EMDR Phases	Necessary Procedures	Teleplay Directives
	techniques for maintaining stability. • Ask the client (and parent) to observe and log significant observations or new symptoms in-between session. This can be done through journaling with words or art.	clients back into their window of tolerance. • Let's mindfully breathe deep into and out of the ground below us, a directive (Ogden & Fisher, 2015). • Look around the room. What are 5 things that you can see right now? What are 4 things that you can hear? What are 3 things that you can touch? What are 2 things that you like to smell? What is 1 thing that you like to taste? This brief activity can ground clients rather quickly after difficult processing. It can also be used to recover from an abreaction.
Phase 8: Re-evaluation Goals	• Utilizing the EMDR standard three-pronged protocol, assess the effects of previous reprocessing of targets looking for and targeting residual disturbance. • Look for new material through playful methods that may have emerged, current triggers, anticipated future challenges, and systemic issues. • If any residual or new targets are present, repeat Phases 3–8.	• *Draw a picture of what _____ (previous target) memory looks like now* This art therapy directive provides an update of previous work to assist the clinician's determination on whether to return back to the previous target to complete reprocessing or to proceed to another target. • *Create a tray of what _____ (previous target) looks like now when you think of it* This sandtray directive offers understanding of the level of resolution from previous target. This is especially useful for phase 3 if a return to the target for continuance of reprocessing is deemed appropriate based on the level of disturbance.

asked about the worst part, he played charades to act out what he later described as "corona germs" on his ice cream. The negative cognition of "I am going to die" was implicated, but not presented verbally by his therapist due to his age and presentation filled with emotional intensity. He opened his arms to full range capacity to represent his subjective unit of distress, SUD, interpreted by the therapist as a 10 on a 0–10 scale. When asked about how true the positive cognition of "I am safe". felt, he pinched fingers to represent what was interpreted by the clinician as a 2 on the 1–7, validity of cognition scale. To support awareness of somatic sensations, the client was shown a kid-friendly version of emotions with somatic re-presentations as a screen share. The same image was emailed to the parent following the session with recommendation of displaying it at home for the client to reference frequently in support of his somatic awareness. When directed to scan his body for any big feelings, he described his somatic disturbance as a "bad feeling in my tummy". At that point, the client had a complete Phase 3: Assessment with 40 minutes left in session. Then the clinician proceeded with Phase 4: Desensitization through directing Oliver to stomp out the thought of his ice-cream being infected with the virus. He stomped and stomped until the clinician directed him to pause. This mechanism of action "stomping it out" reduced the SUD quickly after only about five minutes. When he reported no disturbance, the clinician assessed the Validity of Cognition (VOC) which he danced around the room holding up his arm in an animated fashion singing, "I'm safe. I'm safe". The clinician directed him to think about his target, the virus on the ice-cream, and "I am safe." then show how true it felt. He responded with big arms open to full capacity, which was interpreted as a 7 on the 1–7 VOC scale. When directed to "freeze" and scan his body for Phase 6: Body Scan of the therapy, he described the feeling in his tummy as "gone away". With 20 minutes remaining in session, the clinician asked Oliver about his dog as an effort to mindfully close down the session. Oliver started petting and hugging his dog as the clinician asked him to mindfully pay attention to Nemo with his five senses. His body movements visibly calmed after a couple of minutes. The remainder of the session was spent engaging in child centered tele mental health play therapy.

The session online the following week, the clinician performed Phase 8: Assessment by asking the client about the ice cream and the virus. The client responded with laughter and said "That's silly. Corona can't get in my ice cream!". The clinician didn't continue reprocessing as the level of disturbance implicated was 0 on a 0–10 scale. The child and clinician engaged in child-centered telemental health play therapy for the remainder of the session to reconnect, explore potential new targets for future sessions, and strengthen the therapeutic relationship. Following the second session, a collective decision was made to pause therapy sessions as the client's symptoms resolved. Parents were advised to contact the therapists should any anxious symptoms return.

Clinical Considerations for Virtual EMDR Therapy

Regulating and responding to reactions outside of a client's window of tolerance present some challenges when working virtually with a client. Recognizing cues remotely can be achieved by paying close attention to fluctuations in client's posture, tone of voice, body movements, and facial expressions (Dion, 2018). Establishing and maintaining a deeply attuned relationship during complex trauma work is essential. While this holds true in both settings, in-person and remotely, the importance of attunement through the screen may take more effort and time for some. As many clients spend long days on the computer for e-learning at school and screen time for their entertainment to watch moves, play games, and such, they may show-up in a state of hyper/hypo-arousal more often. Complex trauma work may take more clinical preparation time to focus on attunement between the client and therapist, as it enhances the clients felt relational safety. Without deep attunement, clients may be at a greater risk for abreactions with intense emotional reactions during sessions.

Impact to others, such as family members or others in the home, is also a clinical consideration. Trauma not only affects those directly exposed to it, but others around them as well. Parent consultation, family resource building sessions, and integration sessions to discuss the experience can enhance the healing process. For child and teen clients, their friends, family members, and their communities often experience wake of trauma as it affects behaviors, relationships, and readiness to approach potential stressful situations. Consequently, it is important to provide support remotely for parents and family members through resources, consultation, and referrals when appropriate.

Technology challenges can impede the flow of sessions. Clinicians can circumvent challenges involving client's ability to connect via telehealth platform by scheduling a brief meeting with the parent beforehand to run through the process. For challenges involving stability of connections, clinicians and clients may wish to use an ethernet cable to strengthen their connection. As a general rule of thumb, an ethernet connection is utilized to increase reliability, speed, and security. Also, if electronic forms of bilateral stimulation from sites such as bilateralstimulation.io or remotEMDR are used, the client's video will turn off resulting in a visual disconnect between the client and the therapists. With some clients, this can be a safety concern. When in doubt, or if safety concerns arise, it may be prudent to choose the butterfly hug for bilateral stimulation as the mechanism of action. While these challenges with technology are important to address, it's beneficial for clinicians to recognize when resistance to engage in telehealth is present stemming from insecurities rooted in lack of knowledge and seek support from someone that can provide supervision, tutorials, and/or make any necessary repairs.

Finally, when working with clients remotely, preserving confidentiality can be a huge concern. Virtual EMDR and telemental health play therapy can sometimes get loud as emotions and experiences are reprocessed. Movement is an integral part of trauma sessions at time. Others in the home may overhear or see parts of the session. Clinicians should discuss this with parents/caregivers prior to the sessions in an effort to create an environment that optimizes confidentiality. For younger children, parents may be involved in sessions for supportive and safety reasons. The use of earbuds can also assist with confidentiality as only one side of the conversation can be overheard if that occurs.

All in all, virtual EMDR and telemental health play therapy offers effectual healing opportunity for child and teen clients via remote delivery. This opportunity requires EMDR trained therapists to seriously consider considerations the risk factors, as well as the benefits and challenges. While providing trauma therapy online with child clients brings some potential risks, it also offers hope for healing when clients need it the most. As EMDR trained child therapists around the world embrace the virtual delivery of EMDR, it's important to remember that the most important element of therapy is the therapeutic relationship which can be nurtured online.

References

Delahooke, M. (2019). *Beyond behaviors: Using brain science and compassion to solve children's behavioral challenges.* PESI Publishing & Media.

Dion, L. (2018). *Aggression in play therapy a neurobiological approach for integrating intensity.* W.W. Norton & Company.

EMDRIA (2012). *EMDRIA's definition of EMDR.* https://www.emdrhap.org/content/wp-content/uploads/2020/02/EMDRIA-Definition-of-EMDR.pdf

Flynn, J. (2020). *In my body, I Feel: A story about the felt sense of emotions.* Kindle Direct Publishing.

Landreth, G. L. (2012). *Play therapy: The art of the relationship.* Routledge.

Nakazawa, D. J. (2015). *Childhood disrupted: How your biography becomes your biology, and how you can heal.* Atria Paperback.

Ogden, P., & Fisher, J. (2015). *Sensorimotor psychotherapy: Interventions for trauma and attachment.* W.W. Norton.

Porges, S. W. (2017). *The pocket guide to polyvagal theory: The transformative power of feeling safe.* W.W Norton & Company.

Schaefer, C. E., & Drewes, A. A. (2014). *The therapeutic powers of play: 20 core agents of change.* Wiley.

Shapiro, F. (2018). *Eye movement desensitization and reprocessing (EMDR) therapy: Basic principles, protocols, and procedures.* The Guilford Press.

Siegel, D. J., & Bryson, T. P. (2019). *The yes brain: How to cultivate courage, curiosity, and resilience in your child.* Bantam.

Stewart, A. L., Field, T. A., & Echterling, L. G. (2016). Neuroscience and the magic of play therapy. *International Journal of Play Therapy, 25*(1), 4–13.

van der Kolk, B. (2014). *The body keeps the score*. Viking Penguin Group.

Van Hollander, T. (2016, November 20). The power of greatness sticks. https://www.mainlineplaytherapy.com/post/2016/11/20/the-power-of-greatness-sticks

Wunderlich, C. (2010). In stomping feet and bubble popping. In H.G. Kaduson & C.E. Schaefer (Ed.), *101 favorite play therapy techniques*. Jason Aronson.

8 AutPlay® Therapy and Telemental Health: Strategies for Children with Autism

Robert Jason Grant

Autism Spectrum Disorder (ASD) is a neurodevelopmental disorder that affects the brain in the areas of communication and social functioning. The Centers for Disease Control and Prevention (2020) estimated that 1 in 59 children have a diagnosis of ASD. Many of these children participate in clinical interventions to help address their ASD-related issues. Due to a myriad of circumstances, interventions implemented through a telehealth process have grown in popularity. Alfuraydan et al. (2020) defined telehealth as a mechanism that enables individuals to receive professional services and support at a distance. This may involve a Real-Time or Store-and-Forward method. Real-Time interaction allows clients to communicate in real time with a health care provider. Videoconferencing is viewed as a main form of Real-Time communication for telehealth programs. Store-and-Forward interaction does not depend on the concurrent presence of parties (e.g. healthcare provider and patient) such as sending emails and is less implemented in telemental health practices (Alfuraydan et al., 2020).

Telemental health for those with ASD may have advantages over traditional face-to-face approaches, including removing barriers and improving access to healthcare services especially for individuals and families living in rural and underserved areas. Telemental health approaches could decrease provider and client costs (e.g. travel time, transportation expenses, missed work). Additionally, benefits include decreasing wait times to access interventions, providing a more secure experience for children who can stay in their home setting, and research that reports that those with ASD are drawn to technology (Goldsmith & LeBlanc, 2004).

The implementation of telemental health for those with ASD is not a new concept, and the benefits continue to steadily evolve (Angjellari-Dajci et al., 2013). This does not mean that telemental health processes are perfect and without limitations. Often telehealth procedures create a certain distance which can lessen the development of therapeutic relationship and create struggles with the loss of physical presence. The therapist releases a level of control in a telemental health process that would typically be present in an in-person setting and the lack of control can create concern, especially during a crisis management situation. Some children with ASD,

DOI: 10.4324/9781003166498-8

due to social anxieties and deficits, need to practice leaving their home and interacting socially in person. The in-person process actually becomes part of the treatment experience and this can be lost when implementing telehealth. Additionally, there is a new set of skills, ethics, and procedures the therapist must obtain to be a qualified and effective telehealth provider which can take time and money to develop.

AutPlay® Therapy is a in integrative family play therapy approach designed for working with children and families affected by ASD (Grant, 2017). AutPlay Therapy was originally designed as an in-person mental health approach, but protocols have been implemented via a telemental health process to help meet the needs of those with ASD; those who require interventions but are unable to participate in person. The protocols can naturalistically transfer from an in-person setting to a telemental health setting while maintaining treatment goals and the structure of parent/family involvement. As telemental health becomes a more viable option for many with ASD, AutPlay Therapy provides a play therapy approach for mental health professionals that can be implemented through this medium while maintaining integrity and treatment outcomes.

Overview and Research

The position of telemental health in the field of ASD has grown significantly over time (Alfuraydan et al., 2020; Lindgren et al., 2016; Wacker et al., 2013; Vismara et al., 2013b; Himle et al., 2012; Boisvert, et al., 2010). Telemental health approaches have been explored as a way of supporting the delivery of a range of services for people with ASD and their families. Telemental health might also be used to improve an individual's access to behavioral intervention services. Several studies used telehealth to coach parents of children with ASD in order to conduct behavioral assessments such as functional analyses (FA), and functional communication training (FCT), via the use of videoconferencing with parents and their child located at a regional clinic, home, or school (Suess et al., 2014).

Studies have suggested that use of telemental health programs combining web-based instructional content with weekly video-conferencing coaching sessions, may support parental learning and improve a child's social communication skills (Wainer & Ingersoll, 2015). Parents have also indicated that such systems were effective, acceptable, and useable (Vismara et al., 2013a). Findings from these studies provide initial evidence for the feasibility, acceptability, and effectiveness of telemental health technologies to serve as models for delivering parental training to support conducting behavioral interventions and helping parents understand and use intervention practices in their daily interaction with their children (Alfuraydan et al., 2020).

Vismara, Young, and Rogers (2013a) proposed that telemental health can be accessed at any time of day, in any location with basic, inexpensive equipment; using interactive, personalized features to communicate and share information. Computerized software, videoconferencing, and virtual 3D interactive programs, have been used to teach various communicative, social, emotional, and academic skills to older children and adolescents with ASD. Baharav and Reiser (2010) found that online video-conferencing sessions in families' homes allowed therapists to provide live feedback and coaching to parents implementing speech and language therapy and supported the child gains that occurred in traditional therapy settings over a six-week period. Parents described the telemental health sessions at home as comparable to clinic-delivered sessions and felt comfortable using the technology to communicate with therapists.

Due to the significant increase in the use of the computer and Internet in everyday life, telemental health services could be a welcomed alternative and effective method of providing support to many families affected by ASD (Nazneen et al., 2015). This method has many advantages. First, the family can interact with a therapist directly via video, which potentially provides access to a greater range of expert therapists. Second, by providing caregivers with an opportunity to play an active role in the child's development, telemental health technology can empower caregivers. Studies of telemental health-based parent training showed that the caregivers found the training programs convenient, practical, appropriate, and helpful for increasing their knowledge about evidence-based intervention methods (Jang et al., 2012).

In addition, studies have reported positive changes in children's outcomes such as: a study of North American families with children aged <48 months who had ASD, revealed that teaching parents the Early Start Denver Model (an integrative autism approach) intervention through videoconferencing and a web tutorial increased the rates of vocalization and joint attention initiation in children (Alkhalifah & Aldhalaan, 2018). Research across professional disciplines have demonstrated benefits of implementing telemental health with those with ASD. An initial examination of the literature indicates that there has been an emergence of a body of research investigating the use of telemental health to provide provisions to individuals with ASD and the initial findings appear promising (Ferguson et al., 2019). For mental health professionals applying the therapeutic powers of play, AutPlay Therapy is a natural fit for both therapist and client, supporting many of the methods of established telehealth research for those with ASD while empowering play therapists with needed tools and protocols.

AutPlay Therapy Protocols

AutPlay Therapy protocols can adjust seamlessly to a telemental health process and thus meet the pragmatic needs of families such as distance issues, cost, and physical ability limitations to participating in person. Further, the protocols also support research outcomes for those with ASD participating in telemental health. AutPlay Therapy is an integrative family play therapy approach and implements a great deal of parent participation and training (Grant & Tuner-Bumberry, 2020). Parents are considered cochange agents and are taught how to have special play times and/or how to implement specific play therapy interventions with their children. This level of parent involvement has been supported in telemental health research for ASD in advancing skill gains. Parent training is implemented in AutPlay Therapy easily through a telemental health process with little to no difference from an in-person session.

Behavioral issues, skill deficits, and ability gains are efficiently address in AutPlay Therapy through a telemental health format. The therapist can work directly with a child leading them through a structured play intervention to address a skill issue or work with the parent, teaching the parent how to implement interventions and observe the parent and child playing the intervention together. Children with ASD who have a more limited ability often need to participate in telemental health with their parent or caregiver. The process is more family focused with the therapist training the parent and the parent leading the intervention with their child. Those children with ASD who have a more advanced ability level may participate with the therapist one on one through telemental health. Regardless of where the child manifests on the autism spectrum, AutPlay Therapy can be implemented via telemental health to address treatment needs.

Telehealth Readiness Questionnaire

Grant (2020) developed a Telehealth Readiness Questionnaire used in AutPlay® Therapy, which highlights information that should be acquired prior to beginning telehealth with a potential client. Table 8.1 describes the questionnaire which includes a ranking system for the therapist to indicate if an area is potentially problematic or not a problem. The therapist takes the potential client through a series of questions and, based on the client's responses, indicates a ranking of how problematic the response is for moving forward with telehealth sessions. The questionnaire is designed to assist the therapist is determining if the client is a good fit for a telemental health session and what areas may be potential issues that will need to be addressed before telehealth could begin.

Therapists implementing AutPlay Therapy through telemental health will need to ensure that they are fully equipped to deliver a successful session and that the client is a good fit for using telemental health. Although AutPlay Therapy has been successfully implemented for those with ASD across the spectrum, it does not mean that every child/family affected by ASD will be successful with a telemental health process. The therapist should carefully assess the potential benefits and any limitations before implementing telehealth. The therapist should also take care to ensure all best practices, ethics, and laws are being followed just as they would when delivering in person therapy. AutPlay Therapy though telemental health can be effective and pragmatically beneficial for families but should always be entered into with careful awareness and the AutPlay therapist's commitment to continually evaluating its merit.

Table 8.1 Telehealth Readiness Questionnaire. A rating scale to use to determine readiness for telehealth which includes a client's comfort, knowledge, understandings, environment, and available equipment for telehealth use

Information to Consider (questions for the therapist to ask the potential client)	Problematic Level (1–5 ranking of response) (1 = no problem, 5 = very problematic)
1) What are your communication preferences (in person, video, phone)?	1　2　3　4　5
2) What is your electronic knowledge and skill level?	1　2　3　4　5
3) What is your experience being online?	1　2　3　4　5
4) Are you comfortable with tele sessions?	1　2　3　4　5
5) Do you understand how tele sessions will work?	1　2　3　4　5
6) What type of online connection do you have at home?	1　2　3　4　5
7) What kind of technology are you using (computer, phone, tablet)?	1　2　3　4　5
8) What have been your previous treatment experiences? (in person and/or telehealth)?	1　2　3　4　5
9) Is there an ability to have a private space at home?	1　2　3　4　5
10) Any cultural considerations with a telehealth session?	1　2　3　4　5

Ethical Considerations

Barnett and Kolmes (2016) suggested that therapists implementing telemental health must understand and meet all the requirements of their professional ethical codes. They furthered that telemental health practitioners should possess the knowledge and skills needed to ensure they meet (and hopefully, exceed) the minimum expectations for the quality of professional services provided. Ethical considerations include understanding and providing acceptable technologies, creating and providing a thorough telemental health informed consent document, and being aware of and addressing any multicultural issues related to delivering a telehealth session.

Martinelli (2020) stated that mental health providers offering telemental health services must follow all the usual regulations for practicing under their license. This means they must follow HIPAA guidelines and use secure connections for online sessions. Nelson and Patton (2016) furthered that therapists are encouraged to seek ongoing training and mentorship to develop and maintain telemental health competencies, with careful consideration of clinical, technical, community engagement, and cultural competencies

The Association for Play Therapy (2020) proposed that when utilizing technology for treatment and consultation, the play therapists will provide all parties with a written telemental health informed consent, which is an adjunct to the normal informed consent document. Informed consent should be obtained as an in-person signed agreement, an electronically signed document (via a HIPAA compliant platform), or verbally obtained with: a) a plan to follow up with a written consent (i.e. returned via the postal service) and b) documentation regarding the rationale of why the document could not be signed in person, who was present, whether or not verbal consent was given, and the plan to follow up with an original signature signed document. Telemental health is not a good fit for every client. Some clients may have developmental delays that interfere with their ability to participate through telehealth. Others may not have the technology capability or resources to participate. Play therapists will evaluate before providing telemental health therapy to clients and continuously assess if working via telemental health is appropriate for the clients and their families.

Play therapists and other mental health professionals implementing telemental health practices must adhere to the ethical guidelines provided by their governing organizations. In addition, those who work with children with ASD must also consider the ethical obligations regarding using telehealth with this population. Trying to force or implement an ineffective a telehealth session for a child with ASD would be unethical. Considerations when implementing AutPlay Therapy or any play therapy approach using telemental health with children with ASD include:

- Cognitive functioning ability – The therapist must have an accurate understanding of the child's cognitive ability regarding participating in a telemental health session. Some children with ASD may have cognitive challenges, which would negate the ability to effectively participate in a telehealth session.
- Attention and attunement issues – Many children with ASD lack the attunement and engagement ability to interact in a telemental health session. They may not be able to join or be present at a level that is needed for this type of session.
- Age – The chronological age of any child is a factor when considering telemental health, but for children with ASD this also includes developmental level (age). Telemental health may not be appropriate for a young child with ASD who has an even lower developmental level presentation.
- Physical limitations – Children with ASD may have co-occurring issues that restrict their physical ability. Some physical navigation struggles may prevent them form being able to manipulate technology used in a telemental health session.

- Sensory challenges – A common feature of those with ASD is sensory processing struggles. Some children may have sensory issues with the screen/light reflected in a device used for telemental health. They may also struggle with the tone of the audio or visually how the therapist appears including the therapist's background. These sensory struggles could disrupt the effectiveness of a telemental health session.
- Crisis management plan – It is commonly understood that children with ASD are prone to dysregulation which often results in a behavioral meltdown. Therapists will need to assess if this is something that could happen during a telemental health session and is there an adequate plan in place to assist with such a behavioral meltdown. If this type of behavior is likely and there is no way to assure management of the meltdown, a telemental health session may not be appropriate.

Case Examples (Interventions)

Ryder

Ryder began AutPlay® Therapy at age nine. He was brought to therapy by his parents who were concerned with his social functioning and emotional regulation ability. Ryder lived with his biological mother and father and had one older brother. At age five he was diagnosed with autism spectrum disorder. Ryder possessed strong cognitive abilities and seemed to do well with many skills. He struggled in navigating social situations, especially those related to peer interaction. Ryder also seemed to struggle with emotional modulation ability. He would often become upset and display dysregulated meltdowns when confronted with a negative emotion. Ryder's social navigation struggles were often paired with high anxiety, which he showed limited ability to manage or cope with. Typically, the poor emotional regulation ability would trigger a behavior meltdown and most of the meltdown behaviors were occurring at home.

The school environment was a struggle for Ryder socially. He excelled academically and seemed to enjoy learning. He would become very anxious about attending school and would often perform poorly when interacting with peers. Ryder could communicate that he felt a great deal of anxiety when interacting with peers. He did not know how to talk to them, join them, or participate in play with them. Often Ryder would remain extremely quiet at school and not interact with anyone. He seemed to pursue being as withdrawn and non-noticed as possible. If Ryder was required to give a presentation or speak in class, this would be met with high anxiety and usually a behavior meltdown and refusal to attend school. Ryders parents reported feeling helpless in improving Ryder's issues. His dysregulated behavior and social anxieties seemed to be increasing. There were many meltdowns at home and his parents felt they were unable to predict or control his behavior and it was starting to negatively influence the whole family.

Ryder began AutPlay Therapy in person participating in sessions at the therapist's clinic. He presented as an extremely shy child. He was cooperative buy would speak very little, would not ask questions, and showed no assertiveness. He would typically sit on a chair in the playroom and not engage. The therapist had to lead the session time, frequently asking Ryder questions and making all suggestions for games and interventions to play. Ryder was cooperative and willing to participate, but limited in assertiveness and engagement. The therapist assessed during the AutPlay Therapy Intake and Assessment phase that much of this presentation was due to anxiety that Ryder was experiencing being around a new person/place.

Treatment goals were established to work on reducing Ryder's anxiety, learning better emotional regulation ability, and increasing social navigation success. Structured play therapy interventions were implemented by the therapist to address these treatment goals. Ryder participated in the interventions, but his engagement was limited. Ryder's parents were also learning the interventions and following AutPlay Therapy protocol by implementing the play interventions with Ryder in between session times at home. By session eight, Ryder seemed to be more comfortable and began engaging with the therapist at a higher degree. Around session eight, the COVID-19 pandemic had affected Ryder's community and he had to switch to a telehealth format for his sessions. In the switch to a telehealth format, his parents were unable to participate in the sessions and the therapist would be working only with Ryder.

Prior to the first telemental health session, the therapist conducted a readiness assessment and completed all appropriate paperwork with the parents. The first telemental health session with Ryder went well. He participated more fully with the therapist than he had in the previous in person sessions. The therapist had been implementing social engagement inventions and several of the interventions were able to transfer to the telemental health process. One intervention, the *Headbanz* game, was a favorite of Ryder's during his in-person sessions. The popular board game requires participants to ask each other questions to determine what the picture is on a card they have drawn. The therapist explained to Ryder that they could continue to play the *Headbanz* game though telemental health. Ryder had the game at home and come up with the scenario for play with each person choosing a card from their own game for the other person to guess. This was the first time Ryder had shown any initiation with play interventions.

Another intervention called *What Do I Have*, was also implemented with Ryder. In this intervention, the child is asked to go find something in their house and keep it off camera. The therapist will also find something. Once both people have found something, they take turns trying to guess what the other person has. They have twenty questions they can ask then they must make a guess. The game can be modified to ask the child to find something that is special to them or something that helps them feel calm. Ryder enjoyed this intervention and requested to play it often. This intervention and the *Headbanz* game both worked on improving Ryder's social engagement skills and were easy implemented through telemental health.

Emotional regulation goals were also worked on during telemental health sessions. One intervention implemented was called *Feelings Scavenger Hunt*. The therapist types a list of around 5–6 emotions into the chat and explains to the child they need to find something around their house that represents each feeling for them. The child should also type in a list of emotions for the therapist as well. Once both the therapist and child have found the items to represent each feeling, they both share each item they have and why it represents the feeling. The therapist should go first to model for the child. Another intervention implemented with Ryder was called *Lego Feeling*. Ryder enjoyed LEGO® bricks and the therapist had established that he had a LEGO collection at home. In *Lego Feeling*, the therapist instructs the child they are going to build something out of LEGO bricks. It can be something real or something unique they create but it must represent or describe a feeling. Typically, the therapist will give the child a feeling to create such as anger or worried. The therapist can also let the child decide what feeling they want to create with their LEGO bricks. The therapist also creates something and once they are both finished, the therapist goes first to model sharing what they created and how it describes the feeling.

Ryder seemed to progress more quickly with his treatment goals participating in telemental health sessions. His engagement ability and social interaction skills were more present and advanced. It seemed that the telehealth process had decreased his anxiety levels (which seemed to be elevated with in person sessions) and this allowed him to better concentrate on skill gains. Ryder participated in approximately five months of telehealth sessions. At this point he was able to return to in-person sessions and he also returned to in-person school which had been in a tele-process due to the COVID-19 pandemic. As Ryder returned to in-person sessions, the social and engagement skills he had gained through telemental health sessions had maintained. He continued to be fully engaged, more involved, and assertive in the return to in person sessions. Upon Ryder's return to school he completed his first in class speech with little anxiety. His parents also reported that his emotional regulation ability had improved, and his behavior meltdowns had greatly decreased. Ryder participated in an additional six more in person sessions and then graduated from therapy having accomplished his treatment goals.

Christian

Christian was five years old when he began therapy with his mother. Christian's mother contacted the therapist to inquire about telemental health sessions for her son. The family lived almost three hours away from the therapist's clinic and Christian suffered from several allergies (many things that would be present in the clinic and playroom). For these two reasons the mother was seeking telehealth sessions. Christian lived with his biological parents and two older brothers who were neurotypical. Christian had been diagnosed with autism spectrum disorder at age three and had co-occurring medical (allergy and gastrointestinal) issues. His primary autism issues included poor social navigation (especially outside of the home), limited play skills, and dysregulation challenges when lacking structure, routine, and predictability. Christian was verbal and spoke well for his age and seemed to be developmentally on task with cognitive functioning.

Christian had been mostly at home during his preschool years. He did not participate in any daycare or preschool program. He was participating in preschool activities with his parents at home and did attempt a home school co-op preschool which did not go well. At the preschool co-op Christian struggled with peer interaction; he would not play with the other children, would ignore them, and in general exhibited poor peer social skills. He often refused to listen to the adult leaders if he wanted to do something differently, and when the adult leaders would address this, Christian would have a behavior meltdown. Occasional, the parents would set a play date with another child and often Christian would ignore the other child and play by himself in isolation. The preschool co-op and play dates ended after a few unsuccessful attempts. At home, the interactions were better with his parents although Christian was still extremely rigid and demanding. He needed almost all things to go the way he wanted, or it would often lead to a behavior meltdown. Christian's behaviors at home were putting a strain on in his relationship with his brothers who were often feeling frustrated with him and were primarily avoiding all interactions.

The therapist agreed to work with family through telemental health and the parents completed a telemental health readiness assessment and all appropriate paperwork. The first three sessions followed the AutPlay® Therapy intake and assessment phase protocol adjusted for a telehealth session. Christian's mother was present and participated in the sessions with a focus on building relationship with the child and helping him feel comfortable and familiar with the therapist and the telemental health process. The parents were emailed several AutPlay® inventories to complete about Christian to better understand his strengths and deficits. The therapist spent the three session times talking with and engaging Christian. Christian was asked to take them on a tour of his room/playroom/ and favorite toys. The therapist also asked Christian to pick a favorite game he liked to play with his mother and show the therapist the game. The therapist focused on tracking, reflecting, and being present with the child and mother and learning more about Christian and how his autism affected him.

Session four was a telemental health session with the therapist and the parents to discuss the treatment goals and how the sessions would proceed. Session five through thirty focused on the directive or structured intervention phase of treatment in AutPlay Therapy. Treatment goals included improving Christians interactive/reciprocal play skills and decreasing rigidity in his preferences, schedule, and interactions with others. The therapist established a play time between Christian and his mother that would include the mother introducing structured elements during the play time to help address treatment goals. The therapist would observe the playtime and provide tracking, reflections, and feedback. The play times followed the AutPlay Therapy Follow Me Approach design which allows a child led play time with the adult integrating in directive elements to address the treatment goals. The therapist and mother had met through telehealth for two separate sessions for the therapist to teach the mother how to implement the play time.

The play times progressed slowly at first with Christian spending most of the play time in a child led process and the mother periodically interjecting a thought or preference that slightly altered the play direction. The therapist would observe and end the play time with about ten minutes left in the telehealth session to give the mother feedback. Around session 12, the mother began to introduce her preference for playing a short game together. The game would last around 5–7 minutes. Christian resisted at first but started to show flexibility with his mother introducing games and he began participating fully. The mother began to increase this choosing two separate times during a play session to introduce a 5–7-minute game that she chose. She was continuously instructed by the therapist to move progressively, but with a mindful step-shaping process. By session 20 the mother had introduced the concept of dividing the play time with half of the time doing what she wanted to do and half the time playing what Christian wanted to play. The success of this represented a huge advancement for Christian. The mother was also reporting at this time that Christian was being more flexible at home in other areas and his overall rigidness and needing things his way had decreased.

The divided play session continued, and the therapist encouraged the mother to try and generalize Christian's new ability to other areas. His mother began to include the two older brothers in a separate play time at home with Christian and set up a few play dates with other children. The results were much more positive than past attempts and the mother was encouraged to continue these efforts to strengthen Christian's skills. By the end of the telemental health sessions, Christian and his mother were having full reciprocal and interactive play sessions, play times with the whole family, play dates with other children, and Christian was participating in some one-on-one telemental health play times directed by the therapist. He had significantly increased his peer interactions and play skills and decreased his rigidness and control issues. The parents reported to the therapist that behavior meltdowns had almost completely stopped. As sessions terminated, the therapist encouraged the parents to continue with the play session skills that had been learned and to further provide Christian with opportunities to strengthen his skills.

Conclusion

Macintyre (2016) stated that understanding ASD requires careful observations; therapists must assess what is providing satisfaction and causing challenges for the individual and then select the type of modality to implement. Therapists may have to try a myriad of different strategies to discover a way to build relationship with the individual and engage them in the intervention process. Regardless of the modality/intervention selected, the therapist should always be ensuring that designated treatment goals are being addressed. Telemental health is not a new modality or intervention for the world of mental health (it has existed for decades). It is also not a new concept for working with children and their families affected by ASD.

Regardless, it may be new to many play therapists and many play therapists may be just discovering the importance of offering this method of treatment for children with ASD. As research grows, it continues show benefits and testimonial support such as the cases highlighted in this chapter illustrating that a telemental health process can be vital and, in some cases, essential for children with ASD to access mental health care. AutPlay® Therapy is an an integrative play therapy approach that has shown promise in its adaptability to a telehealth process giving play therapists needed protocol and tools to effectively implement this method for those children they serve with ASD.

References

Alkhalifah S., & Aldhalaan H. (2018). Telehealth services for children with autism spectrum disorders in rural areas of the kingdom of Saudi Arabia: Overview and recommendations. *JMIR Pediatrics and Parent, 1*(2). doi: 10.2196/11402.

Alfuraydan, M., Croxall, J., Hurt, L., Kerr, M., & Brophy, S. (2020). Use of telehealth for facilitating the diagnostic assessment of autism spectrum disorder (ASD): A scoping review. *PLoS ONE, 15*(7). doi: https://doi.org/10.1371/journal.pone.0236415.

Angjellari-Dajci, F., Lawless, W. F., Agarwal, N., Oberleitner, R., Coleman, B., & Kavoossi, M. (2013). Telehealth-based systems for diagnosis, management, and treatment of autism spectrum disorders: Challenges, opportunities, and applications. In M. M. Cruz-Cunha, I. M. Miranda, & P. Gonçalves (Ed.), *Handbook of research on ICTs and management systems for improving efficiency in healthcare and social care* (pp. 1044–1065). IGI Global. http://doi:10.4018/978-1-4666-3990-4.ch055.

Association for Play Therapy (2020). J.5 use of telemental health in play therapy. *Play Therapy Best Practices.* https://cdn.ymaws.com/www.a4pt.org/resource/resmgr/publications/apt_best_practices_-_june_20.pdf.

Baharav, E., & Reiser, C. (2010). Using telepractice in parent training in early autism. *Telemedicine and e-Health, 16*(6), 727–731.

Barnett, J. E., & Kolmes, K. (2016). Avoiding a disconnect with telemental health. *American Psychological Association, 45*(5), 53–66. https://www.apa.org/monitor/2016/05/ce-corner.

Boisvert, M., Lang, R., Andrianopoulos, M., & Boscardin, M. L. (2010). Telepractice in the assessment and treatment of individuals with autism spectrum disorders: A systematic review. *Developmental Neurorehabilitation, 13*(6), 423–432.

Centers for Disease Control and Prevention (2020). Autism spectrum disorder (ASD). https://www.cdc.gov/ncbddd/autism/index.html.

Ferguson, J., Craig, E. A., & Dounavi, K. (2019). Telehealth as a model for providing behavior analytic interventions to individuals with autism spectrum disorder: A systematic review. *Journal of Autism and Developmental Disorders, 49*(2), 582–616. https://cmps-ezproxy.mnu.edu:2299/10.1007/s10803-018-3724-5.

Goldsmith, T. R., & LeBlanc, L. A. (2004). Use of technology interventions for children with autism. *Journal of Early Intensive Behavior Interventions, 1*(2), 166–178.

Grant, R. J. (2017). *Autplay therapy for children and adolescents on the autism Spectrum: A behavioral play-based approach* (3rd ed.). Routledge.

Grant, R. J. (2020) Telehealth readiness questionnaire. https://www.autplaytherapy.com/resources/.

Grant, R. J., & Tuner-Bumberry, T. (2020). *AutPlay therapy play and social skill groups: A ten session model.* Routledge.

Himle, M. B., Freitag, M., Walther, M., Franklin, S. A., Ely, L., & Woods, D. W. (2012). A randomized pilot trial comparing videoconference versus face-to-face delivery of behavior therapy for childhood tic disorders. *Behavior Research and Therapy, 50*(9), 565–570.

Jang, J., Dixon, D. R., Tarbox, J., Granpeesheh, D., Kornack, J., & de Nocker, (2012). Randomized trial of an eLearning program for training family members of children with autism in the principles and procedures of applied behavior analysis. *Research in Autism Spectrum Disorders, 6*(2), 852–856.

Lindgren, S., Wacker, D., Suess, A., Schieltz, K., Pelzel, K., Kopelman, T., Lee, J., Romani, P., & Waldron, D. (2016). Telehealth and autism: Treating challenging behavior at lower cost. *Pediatrics, 137*(S2), e20152851O.

Macintyre, C. (2016). *Strategies to support children with autism and other complex needs.* Routledge.

Martinelli, K. (2020). Telehealth for kids: What parents need to know about remote mental health treatment. *Child Mind Institute.* https://childmind.org/article/telehealth-for-kids/.

Nazneen, N., Rozga, A., Smith, C. J., Oberleitner, R., Abowd, G. D., & Arriaga, R. I. (2015, June 17). A novel system for supporting autism diagnosis using home videos: Iterative development and evaluation of system design. *JMIR Mhealth Uhealth, 3*(2). doi: 10.2196/mhealth.4393.

Nelson, E. L., & Patton, S. (2016). Using videoconferencing to deliver individual therapy and pediatric psychology interventions with children and adolescents. *Journal of Child and Adolescent Psychopharmacology, 26*(3), 212–220. https://doi.org/10.1089/cap.2015.002.

Suess, A. N., Romani, P. W., Wacker, D. P., Dyson, S. M., Kuhle, J. K., Lee, J. F., Lindgren, S. D., Kopelman, T. G., Pelzel, K. E., & Waldron, D. B. (2014). Evaluating the treatment fidelity of parents who conduct in-home functional communication training with coaching via telehealth. *Journal of Behavioral Education, 23*, 34–59.

Vismara, L. A., Young, G. S., & Rogers, S. J. (2013a). Telehealth for expanding the reach of early autism training to parents. *Autism Research and Treatment*, Article ID 121878. doi: 10.1155/2012/121878.

Vismara L. A., McCormick, C., Young, G. S., Nadhan, A., & Monlux, K. (2013b). Preliminary findings of a telehealth approach to parent training in autism. *Journal of Autism Developmental Disorders, 43*(12), 2953–2969. https://doi.org/10.1007/s10803-0131841-8 PMID: 23677382.

Wacker, D. P., Lee, J. F., Padilla, Y. C., Kopelman, T. G., Lindgren, S. D., Kuhle, J., Pelzel, K. E., Dyson, S., Schieltz, K. M., & Waldron, D. B. (2013). Conducting functional communication training via telehealth to reduce the problem behavior of young children with autism. *Journal of Developmental and Physical Disabilities, 25*(1), 35–48.

Wainer, A. L., & Ingersoll, B. R. (2015). Increasing access to an ASD imitation intervention via a telehealth parent training program. *Journal of Autism Developmental Disorders, 45*, 3877–3890.

9 Telemental Play Therapy in Schools

Sonia Murray

One of the ethical considerations of play therapy is to always have the child's best interest at the core of any services offered. Therefore, when the COVID-19 pandemic hit in 2019, it suddenly became impossible to offer services in-person for many play therapists. It became necessary for other options and methods of delivery to be considered in order to limit the disruption to the child and their therapeutic process. Telemental health therapy, a method that has existed for many years, became an option for many play therapists. Previously only used on a limited basis, it began to be used on a significantly greater level. This chapter will explore the author's experience of setting up and providing telemental play therapy within a school setting. It will examine the ethical and legal issues of using it within this environment, plus delve into the procedures needed to provide a good basis for the play therapy to be as effective as possible. At the present time, the author has a limited number of case examples of telemental therapy within schools, but will bring together some of the lessons learned in this short amount of time.

Telemental health play therapy includes the use of compliant electronic information and communication technologies (including video and audio technology) by a registered play therapist to deliver play therapy services to an individual when they are located at a site that is different than the play therapist. The methodology that will be discussed in this chapter is a child-centered humanistic integrative approach. The emphasis will consider the complexities of undertaking telemental therapy within a school setting. In the United Kingdom (UK) during the initial national lockdown (March 2020), schools remained open to critical workers' children (children whose parents/carers' "work is critical to the coronavirus (COVID-19) response" as defined by the Department for Education (2020a), and children who were considered vulnerable, therefore this enabled telemental therapy in schools to be considered. Vulnerable children are defined by the Department for Education, (DFE) (Supporting vulnerable children and young people during the coronavirus [COVID-19] outbreak – actions for educational providers and other partners, 2020b) as

- Are assessed as being in need under section 17 of the Children Act (Legistation.gov.uk, 1989), including children and young people who have a "child in a need plan", a "child protection plan", or who is a "looked-after child"
- Have an education, health and care (EHC) plan and it is determined, following risk assessment, that their needs can be as safely or more safely met in the educational environment
- Have been assessed as otherwise vulnerable by educational providers or local authorities (including children's social care services), and who could therefore benefit from continued attendance. This might include children and young people on the edge of receiving support from children's social care services, adopted children, those at risk of becoming NEET ("not in employment, education, or training"), those living in temporary accommodation, those who are young carers, and others at the provider and local authority's discretion.

Telehealth has been around for best part of 20 years and is used to provide greater access to services for clients (American Telemedicine Association, 2009). Telehealth in schools has been facililtated since the early 2000s and was primarily to offer physical health services, but increasingly used with behavioral and mental health. Over the years it has proven to be effective (Stephan et al., 2016). However, as current technology includes improving higher definition web cams, enhanced internet speeds, and more people having access to video conferencing equipment, telehealth is becoming increasingly more popular. When the COVID-19 pandemic impacted the world, telehealth came in to its own. For many children and families it has provided an alternative way of providing play therapy. Telemental health services have allowed play therapy services to continue whereas previously, the therapy would have had to be paused until a time when the lockdown guidance changed.

To provide a context for this chapter, it is useful to briefly describe how play therapy is delivered in schools in the UK. Play therapy has been facilitated in schools in the UK since the early 1990s. It is one of the recognized forms of counseling for children and young people in schools by the Department of Education (Department for Education, 2016) and it is noted that over 60% of schools in the UK have some form of counseling (Harland et al., 2015). Presently in the UK, registered play therapists can provide play therapy in schools three different ways: 1) they are employed as a play therapist, 2) as a self-employed play therapist who is commissioned by the school to undertake specific cases or to provide play therapy to several cases, or 3) the play therapist provides play therapy to schools via an agency which is commissioned by the school. This is similar to self-employed play therapy, but the agency arranges the contracts and determines the suitability of the cases. Each role has its positives and negatives.

The one generally with the most security is being employed by the school, but there are still very few employed play therapists in schools.

As noted by Murray "delivering play therapy in schools can be perceived as a natural and safe option, but there are a number of challenges that can affect the therapeutic process". (2019, p. 165). However, with telemental therapy, there are further challenges that need to be overcome. Some of the challenges include issues around the use of technology in schools, the busy nature of schools, limited space, staff availability, and confidentiality.

For numerous children, play therapy in schools makes the services accessible to them. Due to geographic logistics, parental accessibility, and children typically being in school five days a week, undertaking play therapy in schools reduces some of the barriers to accessing treatment. Additionally, for many children, school is a known place where they may feel comfortable and this can reduce any potential stigma that may be perceived about attending therapy. From the school's perspective, providing services in school limits the disruption to the child's learning as for some children attending play therapy outside of the school may mean they are away from school for a whole morning, whereas if undertaken within the school, they are generally out for less than an hour. Sessions provided within the school also equates to less disruption to the therapeutic process due to missed appointments.

Some of the challenges of undertaking play therapy in schools include that schools are busy places, and the main emphasis is for children to achieve their learning potential. This can be sometimes be perceived in contrast to the emphasis of the therapy of being reflective rather than pedagogical. Yet fundamentally both want to help the child to reach their full potential. Other challenges include limited physical space in schools, potentially reduced confidentiality as others may see who is going to play therapy, the therapist may be perceived as a teacher, and if there are other children from the school attending play therapy, they may influence each other. We will explore these further in the chapter.

The Play Therapist in Telemental Therapy in Schools

The initial starting point with every type of play therapy is the play therapist, and this is even more relevant when everyone is living through a pandemic. One of the ethical considerations is that the play therapist needs to work within their level of competency which is "based on their education, training, supervised experience, consultation, study, or professional experience." (Joint Task Force for the Development of Telepsychology Guidelines for Psychologists, 2013, p. 793). The play therapist needs to have the foundational play therapy methodology fully embedded into their practice before considering telemental therapy. The telemental play therapist needs to possess the necessary technology and an informed knowledge and experience of using the technology so that they display confidence while engaged in telemental therapy. Additionally, they must be able to educate the parents and teaching staff about how to set up and manage the technology. Another consideration is for the play therapist to understand the potential impact of the technologies on the child.

The play therapist must have a clear understanding of working practices and procedures in schools (Murray, 2019). Each school will have their own ethos and the play therapist will need to be aware of the individual schools' culture, as this may influence how the play therapy is viewed by the school and their staff. This will be even more important if the play therapist is working remotely and may not have the impromptu opportunities to build the relationships with school staff, such as walking down the corridor or going into the staff room. The play therapist will need to factor in regular review meetings to help build the relationships with school staff.

Another complicating factor is that schools in the UK are using a variety of video conferencing platforms and may be insistent that the play therapist use the one chosen by the school. Therefore, the play therapist will need to be well versed in using several platforms, such as Zoom, Google Meet, Microsoft Teams, Blue Jeans, etc. It is acknowledged that the requirements regarding the use of telemental health platforms varies for each country. Additionally, privacy and security policies for each platform will need to be evaluated to ensure that they meet the data protection requirements for the play therapist and their country of residence. In the UK, play therapists are obliged to adhere to the European General Data Protection Regulations (GDPR) which requires that the play therapist provides information to their clients about why their data is being collected, how it will be stored and protected, how and when it will be deleted, who can request access and in what circumstances the information may be retained. This will then need to be reflected in the contract with the family and the school.

As with in-person play therapy in schools, it is essential to have clear child protection procedures. In the UK, every school needs to have a designated safeguarding lead (DSL), therefore the play therapist needs to know who the DSL is and the school's safeguarding procedures. As stated by Murray, "it is also important to communicate clearly their safeguarding role to all parties, including the child (within their level of understanding)" (2019, p. 170). If the child raises a child protection issue in the telemental therapy session, the play therapist would respond just as if they were facilitating an in-person session.

The play therapist will also need to consider the impact of school holidays on the therapeutic process. Often school buildings are closed and staff are not working, therefore the telemental therapy in the school would need to pause. A number of strategies can be implemented to maintain the therapeutic connection, including preparing the child to pause, sending postcards during the holidays or doing a small celebratory ritual like decorating biscuits (cookies) on the last session before the school holidays.

The School

Schools are busy environments with lots of changes occurring daily, particularly through the current pandemic. A number of factors need to be explored with the school before undertaking telemental play therapy in schools, similar to the considerations outlined by Murray in the chapter *Play Therapy in Schools* (2019). First, the school will need to have clear information about telemental play therapy and the services will need to be agreed to by the Head Teacher and the Governing body and/or the academy trust. In the UK, the majority of schools have a governing body which provides an independent overview of the vision, ethos, and strategic direction of the school. It holds the leadership team to account and ensures that budgets are spent appropriately. The overall aim is to raise standards and improve the quality of education delivered. One area of concern for parents, schools, and the governing body is ensuring the security of the video conferencing platform. Therefore the play therapist needs to provide information about what steps they have taken to protect the telemental play therapy sessions, such as installing a waiting room, ensuring that the session is password protected, and only sending out the session invite on the day of the session via encrypted email or text to limit the opportunity for others to access it.

Another dilemma is who will facilitate the telemental play therapy session. Staffing in schools is always at premium and often they cannot be released to support the child during the session. However, to undertake telemental play therapy, a designated member of staff will need to be allocated to the pupil to facilitate the session. Ideally, it would be preferable if it was the same person and someone who has an established positive working relationship with the child. Unfortunately, in the light of the current situation, this may not be possible, however the designated member of staff will need to know how to facilitate the technical equipment and support the pupil emotionally if required. The designated member of staff also agrees to be physically present at the location and available via phone for the duration of the session and ten minutes prior and after the scheduled session time, plus they will need to undertake a "room scan" with the laptop/tablet etc to ensure that the child is the only one present in the room. It is essential to have a practice run prior to the beginning of the child's sessions to ensure that the technology works, the school's internet security systems do not block the video conferencing platform, and the designated member of staff feels confident in facilitating the sessions. A plan is agreed upon between the play therapist, designated member of staff, and the child about what to do if the technology fails within the session.

As with in-person play therapy, consideration should be given to what needs to be in place to support the child if they become dysregulated or distressed in the telemental play therapy session. Naturally, the play therapist will use their therapeutic responding to support the dysregulation, but at times this may not be enough. This author provided play therapy services in a specialist school for children experiencing social, emotional, mental health, and behavior challenges, who often struggled to manage their emotional and behavioral responses. Therefore, a careful risk assessment was implemented for each case and this included at times having other staff members available near to the play therapy room to support the child if needed. The same consideration needs to be applied to telemental play therapy in schools. The designated member of staff must be available to join the session at any time if requested. Prior to the sessions beginning, the play therapist and the designated staff member agree to a plan and a clear script between them for what to do if they need to enter the room if the child has become dysregulated. Depending on the child's needs, it may be appropriate to ask the child to get the staff member as this may enough to regulate them. However, it may also escalate the situation as it may further their fear or shame. Therefore, it may be appropriate to ask the child to get the staff member to help by feigning that the technology is failing. Or it may be more appropriate for the play therapist to call the staff member on the phone to ask them to come in. Again, consideration would need to be given about the child's potential reactions if the play therapist is transparent regarding the reason for help being needed, or invents a difficulty with the equipment. Upon arrival into the room, the play therapist will have agreed with the staff member clear wording about what the play therapist requires the staff member to do. Such as if the child has begun to settle, then the play therapist may say, "it is ok, it seems like the equipment is working again now". Or if the child needs the adult scaffolding still, then the play therapist may ask the staff member to stay and play for a while, until the child becomes more regulated. It may be necessary to consider other procedures if the child becomes further distressed, just as you would with in-person play therapy.

As with in-person play therapy in school, an identified confidential consistent space will need to be identified, with reliable internet connection, and computer equipment. To enable the child to feel safe enough to begin exploring their issues, the space will need to be private with no interruptions and the sessions cannot be overheard. (BAPT, core competence 29) (Ayling et al., 2019, p. 290). A careful discussion and agreement will need to be had to identify the most appropriate space and what needs to be undertaken to protect the space during the child's sessions, such as providing a "do not disturb" sign for the door and/or a placing a noise machine near the door to prevent others overhearing. An issue that has arisen is that as part of schools' safeguarding and child protection policies, many schools have introduced guidance against practitioners working individually with a child in a room with the door closed. Additionally, many schools now have door with glass panels in them. This has presented a challenge around the issue of confidentiality for play therapists working in schools. To overcome this, it is agreed with the school and the parents that the glass panel will be covered except for the top remaining 20 cm. A meeting with all staff to explain the therapeutic process, the necessity of confidentiality, and the need for an interruption free space for effective play therapy is provided. Other considerations include ensuring that the space is big enough for the child to move about, that breakable items are removed from the room, and session materials needed are in the room. An additional difference between in-person play therapy and telemental play therapy in schools is that in in-person, face-to-face sessions, the play therapist brings the equipment each week, but through tele-services this is not possible. Therefore, the play therapist, in conjunction with the school, will need to provide a play kit for each child and the kit will remain in the school. This raises a number of complexities as the play therapist normally protects the play kit. Therefore the play therapist needs to educate the designated staff member of the importance of the kit being safeguarded and this is disseminated to all school staff so that elements of the kit do not get used for school lessons. Additionally, it is important to educate the designated staff member about setting up the room in the same way each week to provide the predictability that in-person play therapy would provide. Schools are clambering for space and items get stored wherever possible, thus invariably the designated play therapy space ends up with extra things in the room. As a way of trying to support this, this author provided play mats in the play kits, to define the play therapy space. It may be advisable to ask the designated staff member to take a photo of the space at the beginning to help them remember the layout.

Confidentiality is another important issue as the play therapist would normally protect any creations the child has made and tidy up the play space, but again this is not feasible during telemental health sessions. Therefore, it is important to have a discussion with the child and the designated staff member about who is going to tidy up and where the creations can be stored safely. Thankfully, the nature of the creations and the play in play therapy often provides a symbolic safety, as only the child knows what it means to them.

The Child

As with in-person play therapy, careful consideration needs to be given to each individual case and whether it is appropriate for this child right now. Therefore, it is necessary to undertake a full intake assessment at the beginning of treatment or if the child is transitioning to telemental play therapy from in-person play therapy. Consideration needs to be given to whether the child has the emotional energy at the present time to engage in the therapy process. With telemental play therapy the play therapist is not directly in the therapeutic space which leads to considerations such as: does the child have enough play skills to be able to engage in the play, does the child have a positive working relationship with a member of school staff that can help regulate the child if the child becomes dysregulated in the session, how does the child feel about viewing themselves on the screen, etc.

Many of the children that this author works with have experienced complex early interpersonal developmental trauma and therefore may not have been in a safe enough state to risk playing (Murray, 2021). Play therapy can provide the ideal environment for the child to develop their play skills by the freedom to explore within the child-centered approach, but also from observing the play therapist playing (Murray, 2021). This presents a challenge in telemental play therapy in schools as it is more difficult for the child to see the play therapist's play. In an endeavor to address this, it is suggested that the play therapist has a similar kit as the child and will mirror the play if the child requests this. The child is made aware that the play therapist has comparable equipment as it is not always possible for the child to see in the play therapist's space. It may be beneficial to have a second camera directed at the play therapist's play to replicate what a child would see during in-person play therapy. Also, it is important to gather as much information from all parties about the child's play skills before commencing to help inform the therapeutic process.

Unlike in-person play therapy, where the child can generally not see themselves, this is different in telemental play therapy. Therefore, the impact of this needs to be explored with the child prior to beginning telemental treatment. For some, viewing themselves on screen triggers uncomfortable feelings as their view of their self is poor or their face reminds them of significant others. Some platforms allow the self view to be minimized and therefore they are out of view.

The Family

As with in-person play therapy in schools, involving the parents/carers in telemental therapy in the school is essential. As noted by Murray (2019), it is vital to involve them in their child's play therapy in school as they can feel less connected due to the limited contact. Parents/carers need detailed information about telemental play therapy and how it works within the school setting to be able to make an informed decision about the appropriateness for their child. It may be helpful that the play therapist carries out a demonstration with the parent/carer to provide a clear view of how it works. It is essential to gain informed consent from the person who holds legal guardianship of the child and the play therapist's consent form needs to reflect the differences of telemental play therapy as well as the usual considerations for in-person play therapy. Due to the potential disconnected element for parents/carers, it is important to organize regular reviews with them to help them to further support their child. The author has anecodotal evidence from parents that undertaking play therapy and telemental play therapy in schools has removed the issue of finding childcare for their other children so they could bring their child to the sessions, reduced the financial implications of traveling to the session, and reduced their time away from their work place.

Research

At the present time, there is currently limited, if any research on telemental play therapy in schools. It is an area that needs researching urgently. There has been research undertaken on telehealth including a review of 70 studies of the effectiveness of Telemental Health (Hilty et al., 2013). It concluded that telemental health services are effective and for some clients it is more effective than in-person services due to the physical and psychological distance. In a review of school telemental health literature and different programs, they concluded that it greater access to services, increased efficiency and a larger capacity for more students to receive a service, including students who do not have a diagnosable disorder (Stephan et al., 2016; Carton et al., 1998). This is also supported by Carton et al. (1998) who found "96% of the students followed through with school mental health services, whereas only 13% of the students followed through with community mental health services." (p. 82). Furthermore, it is report that it was "well received by both providers and recipients of the consultation and care" (Stephan et al., 2016, p. 270). This has been the author's experience of both in-person play therapy and telemental play therapy in schools.

Case Examples

Case One

*The following case examples will illustrate the process of setting up telemental play therapy in schools. The information and the material have been changed to protect the identity of the children.

Toby was receiving in-person play therapy in the play therapist's therapy room prior to the COVID-19 national lockdown. Most of the play was physical and the overriding theme was the child's need to win. As the lockdown approached, the author explored with the school the option of transitioning to telemental play therapy in school as the family home environment did not allow confidentiality. A full discussion was held with Toby's parents and the school about telemental play therapy. Both parties were given time to consider this approach. The parents discussed it with Toby while the school sought permission from the Governing Body. The play therapist provided detailed information about what was required. In a video discussion with the school, the play therapist was shown different room options until one was agreed upon. The day before the National Lockdown, the play therapist delivered a small play kit to the school for Toby. A mat was provided to delineate the therapy space.

The child's classroom teaching assistant was identified as the person who would support the telemental play therapy. The play therapist spent time with the teaching assistant educating her about telemental play therapy and ascertaining how the technology worked. The telemental play therapy was all ready to go when the parents became concerned about Toby attending school and potentially transmitting the virus to other vulnerable family members, so they withdrew him from school. This led unfortunately to a three month pause in the play therapy.

Upon his return to school, the telemental play therapy began. Toby was so pleased to be back to having play therapy sessions. In the first session, he explored his play kit and checked if the play therapist had the same and they then compared. Additionally, he wanted to see the play therapist's space, so she moved the camera around the room, showing him the space. He also wanted to know if there were other people in the therapist's space. He also told the play therapist about his room and where it was in relation to his classroom.

It was noted that his play was less physical. This may have been due to the limited space on the mat, or he knew the school's rules about that type of physical play was being not allowed in school, or he did not need the physical release of that play at this time. However, the need to win theme emerged again, but this time in the form of making up games with playing cards and story cards. The play therapist was following the child's lead and there was no option for her to win. As the sessions progressed, Toby's creativity about inventing games developed and he wanted the play therapist to play more co-operatively. The play moved to using Rory's Story Cubes; Toby and the play therapist had a set each. Toby and the play therapist took turns using a cube to co-create stories or try to guess what the other had. They would show the cube to the camera so the other could see it. The stories became more imaginative as the weeks went by, the play became fair and Toby was not only able to tolerate losing but began laughing when he lost. Alongside this, his sense of self and belief in his capabilities increased. This began to be reflected in his schoolwork. His sessions are on-going.

Case Two

John has experienced a complex traumatic early childhood, but is now in a safe environment. He has a limited internal sense of safety and perceives threat regularly. He is hypervigilant, particularly to sound and movement. In the play therapist's therapy space, this was apparent, but it lessened as the sessions progressed. However, when he transitioned to telemental play therapy to his school, his hypervigilance rocketed. As schools are busy and noisy, he struggled to regulate in the telemental sessions and would repeatedly check out any movements or sounds outside the door. This would also lead him to then attempt to manage other children's behavior outside the room as he considered that they were not following the rules. This impacted on his ability to remain focused and engage in the therapeutic process. Following discussions with the staff member, it was agreed to consider a different time as unfortunately the initial time coincided with a class group going out to break and the telemental therapy space was near the external exit and the toilets. Additionally, the coverings over the glass panel was slightly adjusted to allow for less movement to be seen. Following these adjustments and the predictability of the sessions, he began to become used to the therapeutic space. He was able to begin to relax, trust the safety of the therapeutic space, and begin to engage in the therapeutic process.

Case Three

Telemental play therapy can provide a similar experience to in-person play therapy and for some children it is even safer that in-person play therapy. Many of the children this author works with have experienced complex interpersonal developmental trauma and significant attachment disruptions. For many of these children, a person being physically in the room with them is a potential threat. Therefore, with telemental play therapy that potential risk is reduced. This has been apparent with another child having telemental play therapy in school, Hana. During in-person play therapy, Hana's overriding need was to please the play therapist and she would do/say what she thought the play therapist wanted. She was also guarded against exploring any of her experiences either in the play or verbally. However, as school was a safe place for her and the play therapist was not directly in the room, she felt more free, thus being able to risk exploring her previous experiences of interpersonal trauma. Even within this, the play therapist was a witness to the play and the exploration of the trauma was fluid as long as the play therapist did not interject. Any reflection or discussion was still too overwhelming and would result in a play disruption. Hana would then move to art based activities to regulate herself. By the play therapist witnessing, Hana would continue the trauma play and would come to a resolution.

Conclusion

The global pandemic has pushed play therapists into looking at other ways of facilitating play therapy. With the technology available in these current times, telemental therapy has provided a platform for play therapy to continue. For some children, telemental therapy within their home environment would not be appropriate, therefore this chapter has explored how telemental play therapy can be facilitated within a school setting. It has examined some of the benefits and the complexities of undertaking it in a school setting, plus discussed some strategies for enabling it. It has been a huge learning curve, but the greatest teachers have been the children. They have shown what they have needed, been flexible, open, and willing to try. Their capacity to get what they need to develop and grow always impresses the author and reminds us to trust the therapeutic powers of play and the therapeutic relationship whatever the delivery modality method.

References

American Telemedicine Association. (2009, July). https://www.unmc.edu/bhecn/_documents/evidence-based-telemental-health-with-cover.pdf. https://www.unmc.edu/bhecn/_documents/evidence-based-telemental-health-with-cover.pdf

Ayling, P., Armstrong, H., & Gordon Clark, L. (2019). *Becoming and Being a Play Therapist*. Routledge.

Carton T., Harris V. S., Weiss B. (1998). Posttreatment results after 2 years of services in the Vanderbilt School-Based Counseling Project. In M. H. Epstein, K. Kutash, & A. Duchnowski (Eds.), *Outcomes for children and youth with emotional and behavioral disorders and their families: programs and evaluation best practices* (pp. 653–656). PRO-ED, Inc.

Department for Education (DFE) (2016). *Counselling in Schools: A blueprint for the Future – Departmental advice for schools leaders and counsellors*. DFE.

Department for Education (2020a). *Critical workers and vulnerable children who can access schools or educational settings*. https://www.gov.uk/government/publications/coronavirus-COVID-19-maintaining-educational-provision/guidance-for-schools-colleges-and-local-authorities-on-maintaining-educational-provision

Department for Education (2020b). *Supporting vulnerable children and young people during the coronavirus (COVID-19) outbreak – actions for educational providers and other partners*. https://www.gov.uk/government/publications/coronavirus-COVID-19-guidance-on-vulnerable-children-and-young-people/coronavirus-COVID-19-guidance-on-vulnerable-children-and-young-people

Harland, J., Dawson, A., Rabiasz, A., & Sims, D. (2015). *NFER teacher voice omnibus: Questions for the Department For Education – June 2015*. DfE.

Hilty, D. M., Ferrer, D. C., Burke Parish, M., Johnston, B., Callahan, E. J., & Yellowlees, P. M. (2013, June). The effectiveness of telemental health: A 2013 review. *Telemedicine Journal and E-Health*, 19(6), 444–454.

Joint Task Force for the Development of Telepsychology Guidelines for Psychologists (2013). Guidelines for the practice of telepsychology. *American Psychologist*, 68(9), 791–800.

Legistation.gov.uk (1989). *Children act 1989*. https://www.legislation.gov.uk/ukpga/1989/41/contents

Murray, S. (2019). Play therapy in schools. In P. Ayling, H. Armstrong, & L. G. Clark (Eds.), *Becoming and being a play therapist: Play therapy in practice* (pp. 165–176). Routledge.

Murray, S. (2021). Play therapy: the ideal environment for play development and the repair of play deprivation. In S. Jennings, & C. Holmwood (Eds.), *Routledge international handbook of play, therapeutic play and play therapy* (pp. 327–340). Routledge.

Stephan, S., Lever, N., Bernstein, L., Edwards, S., & Pruitt, D. (2016). Telemental health in schools. *Journal of Child and Adolescent Psychopharmacology*, 26(3), 266–272.

10 Neurodiverse Older Teens and Young Adults in Telemental Health Play

Kevin B. Hull

The COVID-19 pandemic has impacted all parts of society, particularly for older teens and young adults suffering from neurodevelopmental challenges. Many byproducts of the pandemic have added several layers of fear, frustration, and panic to coping systems which were already strained. Loss of routine, fear of death, the pressure of unpredictability, and the unknown are just a few of the obstacles that neurodiverse individuals faced during the COVID-19 pandemic. Practitioners working with neurodiverse older teens and young adults faced many obstacles and had to find innovative ways to deliver telemental health services to meet the needs of this unique population. Working with neurodiverse individuals during the pandemic emphasized the need for practitioners to be flexible, patient, and innovative, while also creating unique opportunities for therapeutic growth and stabilization in neurodiverse clientele.

The goal of this chapter will examine some of the challenges facing neurodiverse clients during the early stages of the COVID-19 pandemic and how telemental health play therapy was used with this unique population. Challenges such as loss, fear of death and illness, disruption in routine, and inability to connect with family and friends created stress for neurodiverse individuals, which caused regression in behaviors and the erosion of mental and emotional strength. Telemental play therapy was useful in releasing stress and bolstering mental and emotional strength through putting thoughts and feelings into words and through finding metaphors in anime, fan-fiction, and digital art.

Neurodiversity Factors of Older Teens and Young Adults and the COVID-19 Pandemic

The developmental challenges of neurodiverse individuals are significant and far reaching. Social problems, such as social rejection and bullying are common, as well as difficulties managing emotions and understanding perspectives of others and situations. There are many co-occurring problems like obsessive-compulsive disorder, ADHD, depression and anxiety, as well as the physical manifestation of stress-induced ailments like gastro-

DOI: 10.4324/9781003166498-10

intestinal problems or auto-immune disorders (Hull, 2017). In general, stress wreaks havoc on a system already in a state of ill-managed tension, however, COVID-19 has adversely affected neurodiverse individuals in areas of emotional regulation, cognition, socially, and the self.

Emotional Regulation Challenges

Neurodiverse individuals struggle with emotional regulation (Siegel, 2006), leaving the individual in states of being that are "inflexible, maladaptive, incoherent, deflated, and unstable" (p. 250). From an early age, the overactivation of the autonomic nervous system (ANS) creates a cascade of effects resulting in reactive behaviors, lack of autobiographical memory, and disrupted relationships with peers and caregivers (Panju et al., 2015). The ANS activation creates an overload effect on other parts of the brain, and there are not enough resources to handle the demands. The parts of the brain that are responsible for applying the vagal braking system (Porges, 2011) are delayed and do not engage when necessary (Bal et al., 2010). Thus, reactive, impulsive behaviors are exhibited, and sometimes the individual can appear to be in a state of awkwardness and seem "frozen". In order to create a sense of equilibrium, the neurodiverse individual strives to maintain a sense of control of the environment. The need for predictable routines and schedules, as well as developing repetitive, specific interests constitutes a sense of "sameness" that helps the individual cope with the unexpected.

Neurodiverse older teens and young adults represent a segment of the population with neurodevelopmental challenges that do not receive much attention in the literature or in the general area of services provided (Hull, 2020). However, individuals in this demographic range are dealing with perhaps one of the hardest transition points in life, such as coming to terms with a sense of self, learning to be independent, and making career/education choices that will define their adult life. While the challenges mentioned above continue to create difficulties in everyday life, many older teens and young adults struggle with a sense of self. The sense of self, comprised of self-understanding and elements of self-worth and self-confidence, tend to develop later for neurodiverse individuals. Lind (2010) discusses how the activation of the sympathetic nervous system creates a lack of autobiographical memory, a key ingredient in the forming a sense of self. Since the later teen and young adult years are comprised of new challenges requiring a strong sense of self, this time period tends to be challenging from an emotional health point of view. Neurodiverse older teens and young adults tend to suffer from anxiety and depression, general feelings of despair, and self-loathing that is turned inward, often with beliefs that they are flawed and damaged (Lei & Ventola, 2018; Han et al., 2019).

Cognitive Challenges

The cognitive challenges of neurodiverse older teens and young adults are many. Cognitive distortions are common, as a result of the emotional upheaval and the disruption of memory from ANS activation. Thoughts such as "I'm worthless", "I don't matter", or "I can't" dominate the thinking landscape, and these thoughts are directed negatively toward the self. Many neurodiverse young adult clients shared that they wake up with a sense of dread, and "that I wake up each day at zero" which is a reference to having little or no sense of self-value or competence at the beginning of the day. These feelings align with findings regarding the lack of a sense of self that accompanies delays and disruptions of autobiographical memory throughout the developmental years (Hull, 2020; Lind, 2010).

By the time neurodiverse individuals reach early adulthood, much of their experiences tend to be dominated by a sense of failure. Social struggles, which often include bullying and rejection, along with academic challenges, often leaves the individual with a pessimistic viewpoint about themselves or the future. Often lacking an internal locus of control, the thinking process of neurodiverse individuals tends to be dominated by negative thinking, particularly when thinking of the future, and is driven by feelings of fear. This tends to reinforce rigid and resistant behaviors, with the individual clinging to familiar places and routines, terrified to branch out and take chances. Many neurodiverse individuals struggle with "episodic future thinking" (Lind, 2010, p. 437), leaving them unable to "envision one's self in a future state or situation" (Hull, 2020, p. 90). This leads to avoidant behaviors and procrastination regarding tasks connected to preparing for their future such as filling out job applications, applying for technical college/university, or taking on adult-like responsibilities.

Social and Self Challenges

As evident in the above sections, emotional dysregulation is linked to cognitive distortions, often leaving the neurodiverse individual with a incongruent sense of self and living in a fear-based, reactive approach to life. Social rejection that begins in childhood is common, as neurodiverse children can appear odd and clumsy, often resulting in "shunning" by peers (Carter, 2009, p. 153). A lack of perspective-taking makes it difficult to connect with peers, and the neurodiverse child often appears selfish and without empathy. Without the ability to pick up on social cues, social learning is delayed and the neurodiverse individual often avoids social situations, retreating into a solitary world that is much safer. Over time, people and crowds are sensed as unpredictable and scary, and a pattern of avoidance and escapism occurs. Neurodiverse older teens and young adults face extra pressure from society and caregivers to step into new roles and often are asked to do so alone. Starting new educational or vocational programs, getting a job for the first time, and navigating banking, paying bills, and asking for help are all new and terrifying experiences. Even with parents and caregivers to help, many neurodiverse older teens and young adults feel like they are alone in a strange, and potentially dangerous world.

The Impact of COVID-19 on Neurodiverse Individuals

One does not have to be immersed in the world of neurodiverse individuals long to realize that anything new or unpredictable is usually met with resistance and emotional dysregulation (Siegel, 2006). The COVID-19 pandemic produced a sense of uncertainty, unpredictability, danger, death, and illness. For neurodiverse older teens and young adults, what seemingly little solid grounding they felt at a new and challenging stage of life was washed away as the COVID-19 pandemic caused worldwide panic and forced change. Some of the individuals with whom I work made statements such as, "I feel like life will never be the same", as well as "I didn't realize how good things really were until this", and finally, "What is the point of doing anything? Nothing seems to matter or make a difference".

Overcoming Shutdowns and Inaccessibility to Mental Health Care

A wider, more impactful part of the COVID-19 pandemic was the shutdown of mental health offices and limited access to providers of mental health services. In many areas, offices and clinics were forced to close, and many providers shifted to online platforms to deliver their services. Online platforms proved to be essential, and presented some limitations as well as opportunities. Sometimes technology broke down which caused frustration, and for some clients it took time to adjust to seeing their therapist in a new medium. Some clients mentioned that the ritual of coming to the office and being face-to-face with this writer was very important to them, as well as the familiarity of the space. For many, particularly young adults in transition that are homebound due to feeling "stuck" (no job, no schooling/vocational training, etc.), coming to this writer's office is one of the few times they leave the house.

However, despite the barriers, online sessions created some unique opportunities. One opportunity was the chance to model overcoming challenges and adapting to change through shifting sessions to an online format. Hull (2020) discusses the role of the "Coach" (p. 90) in working with the neurodiverse population, which is described as helping clients learn to adjust to changes in their environment instead of shutting down. Another important opportunity of telemental health was getting a glimpse into the home environment of the client, which provided a chance to view a broader dimension of self by allowing the client to share personal items and personal space with their therapist, which is not possible in traditional formats where clients come to an office to receive services.

Creating a New Sense of Connection

Many mental health professionals experienced a disruption in relationship and connection with clients that created feelings of hopelessness and fear, in addition to a personal "psychological suffering" (Neto et al., 2020, p. 1). Vulcan (2016) discusses how the body becomes a "translating" (Vulcan, 2016, p. 332) tool in working with the neurodiverse population, and how a practitioner's physical presence is a foundation for change and growth. The pandemic disrupted this process and many practitioners who work with the neurodiverse were left feeling unsure of how a connection would materialize in a digital format. However, telemental health sessions, and teleplay sessions in particular, proved that co-regulation was possible despite being physically distant. Gradually, clients became comfortable and while some were resistant, most stated that they found the telemental health sessions to be enjoyable. When asked about the biggest challenge with telemental play sessions, one older teen stated, "I suppose it took some getting used to, I mean, once I focused on the fact that you (the therapist) were still you, and we're talking like we always have, I calmed down and it felt better".

Overcoming and Connecting: Teleplay with Neurodiverse Older Teens and Young Adults

Anime: Finding Normal in the Chaos of the Pandemic

Japanese anime has grown in popularity in the general population (Allison, 2009), and is very popular amongst neurodiverse individuals (Rozema, 2015). Due to the significant amount of challenges that neurodiverse individuals face during development, it is no wonder why anime is an inviting escape from the often chaotic world in which these individuals must live. One assumption about why anime is attractive to the neurodiverse population is that many find comfort in "escapism" (Sosso, 2017, para. 3), which is related to the need for control in order to feel safe. Anime is a very useful tool in psychotherapy (Hull, 2020) and can easily be adapted for teleplay sessions. First, clips of shows can be shared through the online platform, and these clips can be paused so that discussion can take place. Second, information about a certain anime can be easily accessed and shared between therapist and client. For example, a web site such as *animanga.fandom.com* can be accessed by client and therapist simultaneously so that characters, plots, and summaries can be explored. Table 10.1 contains examples of anime and the themes contained therein.

Table 10.1 Examples of Anime and Fan-Fiction with Themes. A table with three rows and 4 columns depicting anime and fan-fiction and associated themes. Anime shows include Naruto, re: Zero, and Avatar the Last Airbender. Fan-fiction includes Wings of the Phoenix, Phantom's Keep, and Different Kind of Knight. Themes are described for each

Anime	Themes	Fan-Fiction	Themes
Naruto (Pierrot Production Studio, 2007)	Overcoming challenges, orphan, family of origin issues, abandonment/rejection, self-development, emotional and impulse control, self-understanding/acceptance.	**Wings of the Phoenix** (Tamashi, 2013) (Fantasy/Adventure)	Attachment, dealing with change, developmental challenges, friendship, family, self-acceptance.
Re: Zero (Watanabe & Yokotani, 2016)	Starting over, dealing with the unknown, building/sustaining friendships, self-acceptance, self-understanding, dealing with negative emotions.	**Phantom's Keep** (Diamondbeast, 2012) (Humor/Adventure)	Family dysfunction, managing several family roles and expectations, self-awareness and self-understanding, self-development, being different.
Avatar the Last Airbender (DiMartino et al., 2006)	Friendship, forgiveness, self-development/self-acceptance/self-understanding, overcoming challenges, trusting others, asking for help, resilience.	**Different Kind of Knight** (Maigrlchloe, 2012) (Romance/Adventure)	Love, rejection, friendship, choices and consequences, self-development.

Themes and Metaphors in Anime that Mirror Real Life

There are several elements that make anime useful in working with neurodiverse older teens and young adults. The first element is the themes similar to challenges found in real life, from which metaphors may be drawn to help the young person better understand their own challenges and find ways to overcome those challenges. Themes such as death and dying, love, friendships, and overcoming hardships are common, as well as the experiencing of emotions such as sadness, fear, and despair can be found. There are also representations of positive life experiences such as personal strength, the joy of friendships, humor, and using imagination and creativity to cope with life's challenges. The therapist can pull metaphors from these themes and help apply them to the young person's real-life challenges, and in doing so increase coping, as well as creating a guide for the young person encouraging them and bringing comfort (Hull, 2020). For example, Roger, a 17-year-old high school student was extremely frustrated by the pandemic due to the loss of connection to his friends at school. The transition to online learning was a challenge for Roger, and he initially refused to log on to his virtual classroom. Roger stated, "I want to be with my friends, it makes school easier and I'm sad that I can't see them". During a session, Roger told his therapist about his favorite anime. The therapist noted the theme of transition and change in the story, and the two explored the themes surrounding Roger's situation. The therapist guided Roger to identify the coping skills in the characters in the anime as the characters faced the unknown of unfamiliar situations. By seeing how his favorite characters adapted to change and exploring the grief that comes with losing familiarity, Roger was able to gradually accept a new normal and finally engaged in online learning.

Self-Development and Self-Representation

A second element which makes anime useful with neurodiverse older teens and young adults is in regard to self-development and self-representation. Many young people identify with a character or characters in their favorite anime and examining these characters can reveal similarities as well as provide a template for exploring personal characteristics. As discussed previously, neurodiverse older teens and young adults struggle with self-understanding and self-knowledge, as it is hampered by disruptions in memory (Lind, 2010). Identifying with a character in anime can increase self-awareness and self-knowledge through seeing the character as a guide, both in imagining possessing the characteristics of the character and examining the self to see similarities in the application of those characteristics (Halovic, 2020; Ting & Lim, 2012). Anime presents many characters who are social outcasts, struggling with acceptance from society at large, and feeling the pressure to change to societal expectation (Rubin, 2008). Many ASD individuals identify with these themes and find it comforting to see and hear a story of someone who struggles with the same problem, in order to "maintain a sense of belonging" (Ting & Lim, 2012, p. 51).

For example, Erika, a 19-year-old, was in her first semester of college when the pandemic hit. Identifying as a "college student" increased her self-worth, but as her classes were moved to online, she regressed. Like many neurodiverse individuals, a sudden change triggered a sense of shock, which was translated into a sense of self-loathing, resulting in her withdrawing from the world and isolating herself in order to feel safe. Her grades dropped as she began to miss classes and assignments. "It just isn't the same, this isn't real college", she remarked. During sessions she shared her favorite anime show, along with some of the characters in the show. Her therapist noted a theme in one of the characters, which was a sense of strength and self-value that resulted from the character suffering as a result of a challenging situation. This was an important metaphor to present to Erika, which helped her see herself in a new way in light of being "in lockdown". "I'm still a college student", she remarked, "And this is just temporary". Identification with an anime character helped her see herself in a new way, and brought a sense of strength and control despite being in a situation that was unpleasant.

A Pathway to Increased Perspective-Taking

A third element making anime useful is that it is a tool for increasing perspective-taking. As previously discussed, a major challenge for individuals with ASD is the ability to see situations and others from a different perspective. However, narrative approaches have been found to be useful in broadening perspective and improving social skills, as well as reducing social anxiety. Through identification with anime characters and examining themes that emerge from the interactions throughout the story, the neurodiverse older teen and young adult is able to visualize from a different vantage point. For example, Stephen, a neurodiverse young adult, began experiencing depression as a result of forced changes that came with the pandemic. Stephen revealed to his therapist that he had not realized how fragile life could be and that he felt afraid to face the future because "what if this happens again". A theme in one of the anime that Stephen liked was a constantly changing world in which the main characters had to adapt in order to survive. Through reflections and observations, Stephen's therapist helped him see the similarities found in the anime and the real-life situation of the pandemic. As a result, Stephen and the therapist talked about ways in which Stephen could adapt to the changes, and identified coping skills that would be useful in his adaptation. Stephen's sense of depression lifted as he was able to see a broader perspective of the future through realizing that he could adapt no matter what the future might bring.

Fan-Fiction: Creating Narrative and Self-Representation

It is well known in the literature that narrative therapy is an effective approach with neurodiverse individuals (Cashin, 2008; Black et al., 2019). In addition, older teens and young adults tend to be drawn to concepts of story, particularly in the realm of a repetitive or specific interest. One area that has increased in popularity in recent years is a genre of online literature known as fan-fiction. Fan-fiction is the idea of taking a personally beloved character such as Naruto or Harry Potter, and freely exploring different creative avenues of the character and the world in which they inhabit, but with no limits and with the freedom to incorporate imagination. For example, a version of the fan-fiction of Harry Potter may have Harry in the gender of a female, yet all the other parts of the story (Hogwart's, Hagrid, Ron, and Hermione) all stay the same. In this manner, the author explores the similarities and differences of Harry being female, and other "fans" of Harry Potter can read the story and offer constructive criticism through reviews. Websites such as *fan-fiction.net* have seemingly endless categories and genres of stories and characters for curious and interested readers. Table 10.1 contains some examples of fan-fiction along with themes contained therein.

Fan-fiction as a repetitive, specific interest can be a satisfying hobby both to write and to read for neurodiverse older teens and young adults. Themes of overcoming challenges, death and loss, as well as social relationships and love can be explored and read about, or written about. From an internal locus of control perspective, tapping into the creativity of the client through mastery of both the character development as well as the outcome of a story is helpful for many reasons. First, it can help the neurodiverse individual make sense out of the often chaotic outer world through an exercise of expressing their inner world. This theme may be why fan-fiction tends to be so popular with adolescents and young adults in the general population, not just in the neurodiverse community. A second reason for the power of story writing is the opportunity for self-representation, which is important for neurodiverse older teens and young adults who are often less emotionally mature than peers and who struggle with self-understanding and self-confidence (Cashin, 2008; Hull, 2017). Story writing is a chance to "play" with real life situations and challenges, and to provide plot twists as well as creating character's qualities and abilities like the superpower of flying or supreme intelligence.

As applied to telemental health play therapy, the use of fan-fiction with older teens and young adults has many benefits. First, the ability to share a screen makes it possible for both therapist and client to see the same material. The client can be in charge, taking the therapist to the fan-fiction website and pulling up the specific genre and stories that are meaningful. A second benefit is that together, therapist and client can explore the content of the story, while the therapist highlights themes and metaphors that can be used in perspective-taking, as well as reflections of the self. Metaphors relating to daily living can be identified, such as overcoming challenges, relationship struggles, and developing intentionality and overcoming fears. One powerful theme found in a particular fan-fiction (to be discussed in the case study) was the theme of unexpected change, which matched perfectly with the theme of unexpected change related to the COVID-19 pandemic. Therapists can be aware of the themes going on in the client's world and look for those embedded in the stories and bring them to the client's awareness. A third benefit was less resistance from the client because it was something the client enjoyed and felt in the "expert" role, which translated to feeling in control.

Digital Art: Expressing Emotions through Creativity

As previously mentioned, the COVID-19 pandemic created behavioral, emotional, and cognitive setbacks in many neurodiverse older teens and young adults due to increased levels of stress. Digital art as a teleplay technique is an effective way for therapists to create relationship and connection, in addition to providing a release for stress and emotional expression. Many neurodiverse individuals struggle with putting emotions into words and often feel confused by emotions. Art techniques allow the creative side of the brain to awaken, and create a pathway for an activity where words are not necessary. Art therapy techniques have been found to be useful with neurodiverse individuals in building upon strengths and increasing relationship with family members (Wright et al., 2011), in addition to increasing one's self-image and communication skills (Schweizer et al., 2014). Malchiodi (2018) states that digital art in particular helps neurodiverse individuals who may find "the manual process of drawing frustrating" (p. 30). The use of digital art, whether it be using the "White Board" on Zoom, WebEx, etc. or looking at images through screen sharing, provides a dynamic and engaging quality to telemental health work and an interactive element necessary to play therapy.

Three overall benefits were discovered through the use of digital art during telemental health sessions. One was the ability of the neurodiverse young person to express thoughts and emotions through a visual medium. This "thinking in pictures" theme is useful for many neurodiverse young people (Rozema, 2015) as many struggle with putting thoughts and feelings into words. Pictures that helped represent feelings and memes that expressed thoughts, expanded the neurodiverse young person's expressive ability to talk about fears, and even put a humorous emphasis on things like the COVID-19 pandemic. Another benefit of using digital art was the distancing effect and shift in perspective that visual representations provide. Play therapy in general helps put difficult topics and scenarios into a less scary context because of the ability of the client to manipulate the outcomes (Hull, 2017), and digital art is a way for the neurodiverse young person to generate a chosen conclusion. Digital art adds a component of narrative therapy by creating a story effect in which the outcome could be manipulated as well as adding coping skills through the exploration of other possibilities. Since many neurodiverse individuals have memory deficits, particularly in the area of autobiographical memory, this application of digital art provided a narrative on which to draw when fears and worries surfaced, as well as improving self-worth and self-acceptance through the creative process.

Case Study

Jason is 20 years old and was diagnosed with ASD at age 13. Jason lives with his disabled mother and his maternal grandparents, who have many health concerns as well. Jason and I have worked together since he was about 17 years old. Jason faced many developmental challenges in his later teen years that include anxiety, gastrointestinal problems, self-rejection, and severe social anxiety as a result of online bullying. Jason struggled in traditional education settings and finished his high school degree through a hospital home-bound program. After high school, Jason went through a period of tremendous emotional and cognitive growth, and prior to COVID-19 Jason was working a part time job, learning to drive, and was volunteering at a local charity. Once COVID-19 hit, Jason's place of employment and the charity closed, and the progress that Jason made was completely lost. Terrified as a result of compulsively watching the news, Jason was convinced that his mother and grandparents would die, leaving him "all alone in this world". He stopped driving, refused to leave the house, and obsessively thought about his own death and dying. He referred to himself as a "Professional Hermit" and said he would never go anywhere ever again.

I experienced feelings of helplessness and despair after two telemental health sessions. I was afraid that I would "lose" him; that the fear and sudden change would make him completely regress and he would not even want to meet with me. His caregivers were frustrated with him and telling him "Get back out there; you can do it!", which only activated his autonomic nervous and resulted in withdrawing and isolating behaviors. Since high school, Jason became interested in Japanese anime and also fan-fiction surrounding his favorite anime. He told me, "Anime helps me make sense of the world"; and "Anime helps me understand myself".

Using principles from Child-Centered Play Therapy, I told him that our sessions would simply consist of him showing me clips from anime and reading story excerpts from the fan-fiction that he liked, with the only "rule" being that a certain amount of time during the session would be to process what we had watched. He was thrilled, and instead of dreading our sessions, he looked forward to them and had clips and story excerpts ready for me to see and read.

Some of the major themes that were evident in the anime and fan-fiction was overcoming challenges like fear, testing oneself in difficult situations, believing in oneself, and delayed gratification while working toward a goal. For example, one particular anime *Re:Zero: Starting Life in Another World* (Watanabe & Yokotani, 2016) dealt with the theme of a main character who is transported to a world with which he is not familiar, and who is filled with self-loathing and shame. *Re:Zero* carries the message that people can change the outcome of their life but they will have to work to get rid emotional barriers like fear, and learn to love and accept who they are. In the processing stage of our sessions, Jason and I applied metaphors from *Re:Zero* such as dealing with a world that is unfamiliar (COVID-19 pandemic), learning to accept himself as "good enough" and valuable, using resources and friends to get help and asking for help when needed, and overcoming fears by making choices that put Jason in control. Adding to this last theme and tapping into his love of fan-fiction, I encouraged Jason to write and create his own stories using himself as the main character along with the characters from other anime shows that he liked.

Ultimately, Jason improved and the metaphors from anime were useful in helping him overcome fears of death and his loved ones dying, as well as learning to accept himself in this new phase of life and in a very different looking world. The themes and metaphors from his favorite anime shows helped to shift his perspective and gradually he was able to overcome the fears of death and dying, as well as being abandoned. He drew a sense of inner strength through relating to the anime characters, which increased his sense of self-understanding and self-value. He began to venture back into society and resumed his part time job, and made some new friends. The creativity process through Jason writing fan-fiction was helpful in reducing anxiety, in addition to giving him an increased sense of control that translated to him pushing himself to overcome fear and resume his activities that he was doing prior to the pandemic.

Conclusion

The COVID-19 pandemic was challenging for many neurodiverse older teens and young adults due to social, emotional, and cognitive challenges. Telemental health play therapy provided a pathway for connection between therapists and clients. Anime, fan-fiction, and digital art was useful in processing fear and loss, expressing thoughts and feelings, and to adapt to a changing world in order to meet goals. The metaphors and themes found in anime and fan-fiction help neurodiverse older teens and young adults expand perspective of self and others, and helps increase self-understanding and self-development. Identifying with the characteristics of characters in the stories create inner strength resulting in growth and self-confidence, self-understanding, and self-acceptance. Digital art during telemental play makes sessions with older teens and young adults engaging and fun, in addition to allowing for the expression of thoughts and feelings and using images to serve as a representation of self.

References

Allison, A. (2009). The cool brand, affective activism, and Japanese youth. *Theory, Culture, and Society*, 26, 89–111.

Bal, E., Harden, E., Lamb, D., Van Hecke, A. V., Denver, J. W., & Porges, S. W. (2010). Emotion recognition in children with autism spectrum disorders: Relations to eye gaze and autonomic state. *Journal of Autism and Developmental Disorders*, 40(3), 358–370.

Black, R., Alexander, J., Chen, V., & Duarte, J. (2019). Representations of autism in online harry potter fanfiction. *Journal of Literacy Research*, 51(1), 30–51.

Carter, S. (2009). Bullying of students with asperger syndrome. *Issues in Comprehensive Pediatric Nursing*, 32(3), 145–154.

Cashin, A. (2008). Narrative therapy: A psychotherapeutic approach in the treatment of adolescents with Asperger's Disorder. *Journal of Child and Adolescent Psychiatric Nursing, 21*(1), 48–56.

Diamondbeast (2012, April). *Phantom's keep*. Fan-fiction. https://www.fanfiction.net/s/7979887/1/Phantom-s-Keep

DiMartino, M. D., Konietzko, B., & Ehasz, A. (2006). *Avatar: The last airbender. [Television series]*. Burbank, CA: Nickelodeon Animation Studios.

Halovic, S. (2020). Using the manga/anime Naruto as graphic medicine to engage clients in conversational model therapy. *Psychotherapy and Counselling Journal of Australia, 8*(1). https://pacja.org.au/2020/08/using-the-manga-anime-naruto-as-graphic-medicine-to-engage-clients-in-conversational-model-therapy/

Han, G., Tomarken, A., & Gotham, K. (2019). Social and nonsocial reward moderate the relation between autism symptoms and loneliness in adults with ASD, depression, and controls. *Autism Research, 12*(6), 884–896.

Hull, K. (2017). Play therapy with children with ASD and chronic illness. In L. Rubin (Ed.), *Handbook of medical play therapy and child life: Clinical interventions for children and adolescents* (pp. 69–87). New York: Routledge/Taylor & Francis.

Hull, K. (2020). Creating space for therapeutic change: Boundary expansions with autism spectrum clients. *Journal of Infant, Child, and Adolescent Psychotherapy, 19* (1), 86–97.

Lei, J., & Ventola, P. (2018). Characterising the relationship between theory of mind and anxiety in children with Autism Spectrum Disorder and typically developing children. *Research in Autism Spectrum Disorders, 49*, 1–12.

Lind, S. E. (2010). Memory and the self in autism: A review and theoretical framework. *Autism, 14*(5), 430–456.

Maigrlchloe. (2012, April). *Different kind of knight*. Fan-fiction. https://www.fanfiction.net/s/7508729/1/Different-Kind-Of-Knight

Malchiodi, C. A. (2018). Introduction to art therapy and digital technology. In C. A. Malchiodi (Ed.), *The handbook of art and digital technology* (pp. 21–41). London: Jessica Kingsley Publishers.

Neto, M. L. R., Almeida, H. G., Esmeraldo, J. D. A., Nobre, C. B., Pinheiro, W. R., de Oliveira, C. R. T., Sousa, I. C., Lima, O. O. M. L., Lima, N. N. R., Moreira, M. M., Lima, C. K. T., Junior, J. G., & da Silva, C. G. L. (2020). When health professionals look death in the eye: the mental health of professionals who deal daily with the 2019 coronavirus outbreak. *Psychiatry Research, 288*, Art. no. 112972.

Panju, S., Brian, J., Dupuis, A., Anagnostou, E., & Kushki, A. (2015). Atypical sympathetic arousal in children with autism spectrum disorder and its association with anxiety symptomatology. *Molecular Autism, 6*, 64.

Pierrot (Production Studio) (2007-2017). *Naruto Shippuuden*. Tokyo, Japan: Pierrot Studio.

Porges, S. W. (2011). *The polyvagal theory: Neurophysiological foundations of emotions, attachment, communication, and self-regulation* (1st ed.). New York: W. W. Norton.

Rozema, R. (2015). Manga and the autistic mind. *English Journal, 105*(1), 60–68.

Rubin, L. C. (2008). Big heroes on the small screen: Naruto and the struggle within. In L. C., Rubin (Ed.), *Popular culture in counseling, psychotherapy, and play-based interventions* (pp. 227–242). New York: Springer Publishing Company.

Schweizer, C., Knorth, E. J., & Spreen, M. (2014). Art therapy with children with autism spectrum disorders: A review of clinical case descriptions on 'what works'. *The Arts in Psychotherapy, 41*(5), 577–593.

Siegel, D. J., M.D. (2006). An interpersonal neurobiology approach to psychotherapy. *Psychiatric Annals, 36*(4), 248–256.

Sosso, G. (2017, July 5). *Autism and anime connection.* CARD-USF. https://cardusf.wordpress.com/2017/07/05/autism-anime-connection.

Tamashi, D. (2013, October). *Wings of the phoenix.* Fan-fiction. https://www.fanfiction.net/s/9743524/1/Wings-of-the-Phoenix.

Ting, D. H., & Lim, W. M. (2012). Identity formation and self-esteem through anime consumption. In *International Conference on Contemporary Marketing Issues (ICCMI).* 48–54.

Vulcan, M. (2016). "I'm a translating body": Therapists' experiences working with children diagnosed with autism spectrum disorder. *Journal of Psychotherapy Integration, 26*(3), 326–337.

Watanabe, M., & Yokotani, M. (2016). *Re:Zero: Starting life in another world.* White Fox Studios.

Wright, C., Diener, M. L., Dunn, L., Wright, S. D., Linnell, L., Newbold, K., D'Astous, V., & Rafferty, D. (2011). SketchUp™: A technology tool to facilitate intergenerational family relationships for children with autism spectrum disorders (ASD). *Family and Consumer Sciences Research Journal, 40*(2), 135–149.

Section III
Special Interventions

11 Using the Virtual Sandtray®© App: A Boy's Journey to Healing

Heidi Gerard Kaduson

During the COVID-19 pandemic, play therapy was shifted from in-person to telemental health as a means of reaching children who were in the need of psychotherapy. Many therapists found this transition to be difficult, especially with trying to engage the children who had only known in-person play therapy. One of the major goals of telemedicine is to develop next-generation telehealth tools to enhance healthcare delivery (Ackerman et al., 2010). The Virtual Sandtray®© App (VSA) (Stone, 2015), which had been a valuable tool in the in-person playroom, easily transitioned to telemental health for continuity of care and for sandtray therapy to be used as a viable treatment through this new medium. Since treatment is best when prescribed to meet an individual's needs in play therapy (Kaduson et al., 2020), use of the VSA became a powerful tool to help many of the children during this difficult time.

Prescriptive Play Therapy

Play has the power not only to facilitate normal child development but also to alleviate abnormal behavior. Play therapy is defined as *"the systematic use of a theoretical model to establish an interpersonal process wherein trained play therapists use the therapeutic powers of play to help clients prevent or resolve psychosocial difficulties and achieve optimal growth and development,"* (Association for Play Therapy, 1997). Play therapy has been the major form of child psychotherapy since the 1950s, and it has evolved from model specific treatments to more integrated and prescriptive models (Drewes et al., 2011; Schaefer & Drewes, 2014). Instead of strictly adhering to one particular school of thought, eclectic therapists employ elements from a range of theories and/or techniques with the aim of establishing an intervention tailored to a particular child. (Kaduson et al., 1997; 2020). Prescriptive play therapy is a therapeutic approach that incorporates a variety of theories and techniques in order to customize play intervention to meet the specific and diverse needs of individual children. The focus is to resolve a specific problem or problems that brought the child into therapy. Through this approach, it serves us well to know the history of play therapy so that it can deepen our understanding

DOI: 10.4324/9781003166498-11

of the theoretical roots of the models and techniques we might use when we treat different types of disorders and different types of children (Johnson, 2016). The field of play therapy has had tremendous growth since the 1950s, and with the increased use of the prescriptive (eclectic, integrative, evidence-informed) approach, it will continue to evolve to meet the specific needs of children (Kaduson et al., 2020).

The prescriptive play therapy model was first described by Heidi Gerard Kaduson et al. (1997) in their book *The Playing Cure: Individualized Play Therapy for Specific Childhood Disorders*. The book detailed the application of the therapeutic powers of play (Schaefer, 1993) to the common psychological disorders of youth. The popularity of prescriptive play therapy has mushroomed over the past two decades, and it is likely to continue to expand in the years ahead. Prescriptive play therapy is founded on a set of principles that serve as fundamental cornerstones of the approach and guide its practice (Kaduson et al., 2020). These principles include

1. Differential Therapeutics: some interventions are more effective than others for certain disorders; a child who does poorly with one type of play therapy may do well with another (Beutler & Clarkin, 1990)
2. Eclecticism: the more remedies you have in your repertoire, coupled with the knowledge about how to apply them differentially, the more effective one would be in meeting a specific child's needs
3. Integrative Psychotherapy: being able to combine different theories and/or techniques to strengthen or broaden the scope of the interventions
4. Prescriptive Matching: seek to match the most effective play intervention to each specific disorder or presenting problem (Norcross, 1991)
5. Individualized Treatment: tailor the intervention to meet the needs of a specific child.

Within this prescriptive play therapy approach, sandtray is an important technique used to help children work through psychological difficulties. The therapist's playroom allows children to be in a safe place and pick what type of play they are interested in doing and the prescriptive approach support this process. Many children choose sandtray to explore and illustrate their world with miniatures.

Sandtray Therapy

The therapeutic use of sand and miniatures dates back to the early 1900s when Margaret Lowenfeld used sandtray as a nonverbal alternative to assist clients in communicating and resolving internal and external conflicts and experiences. She called her approach the "World Technique" (Lowenfeld, 1979). Dora Maria Kalff, a student of Lowenfeld's and a Jungian therapist, applied Jungian concepts to the World Technique and developed

"Sandplay". Although Lowenfeld and Kalff equally valued the use of sand therapy as a nonverbal approach to therapy, their views of process and outcomes differed. For Kalff, the important aspect of sandplay was healing at the unconscious level. Her approach was to sit quietly and observe as the client created the sandtray and then interpret the symbols provided by the child's sandtray creation. On the other hand, Lowenfeld saw sandtray work as a type of dialogue for children who had difficulty expressing themselves; therefore, she actively engaged with clients, asked questions, and refrained from interpreting symbolism. Instead, she let the child identify the sandtray's meaning (Hutton, 2004).

The use of sand and miniatures in therapy have been viewed through the eyes of different therapeutic approaches – Gestalt therapy (Oaklander, 2000), Adlerian therapy (Bainum et al., 2006), Jungian therapy (sandplay) (Peery, 2003), and constructivist therapies (Freeman et al., 1997; Spooner & Lyddon, 2007), including Solution Focused therapy (Homeyer & Sweeney, 2017; Nims, 2007; Sweeney, 2011; Taylor, 2009). Just as the philosophy behind each of these theories differ, so does their application to sandtray, including the therapy goals, therapist roles, client directives, and whether or not to use interpretation.

The play therapy use of sandtray components in a therapeutic setting is practiced widely with a variety of clients in various settings, and for a wide spectrum of clinical issues. Sandtray therapy provides mental health professionals with an expressive, experiential technique to use in an intentional, purposeful manner to move therapy forward. The definition of sandtray therapy reflects this contention that it is a cross-theoretical approach. As such, it does not include theory-specific language. Homeyer and Sweeney (2017) offer the following definition: "Sandtray therapy is an expressive and projective mode of psychotherapy involving the unfolding and processing of intra- and inter-personal issues through the use of specific sandtray materials as a nonverbal medium of communication, led by the client or therapist and facilitated by a trained therapist" (p. 6). But for one to use this approach in the in-person, traditional way, a certain amount of material is needed to properly offer sandtray experience to clients. At a minimum a tray of sand and a set of miniatures are necessary.

Sweeney (2020) delineated the therapeutic benefits of sandtray therapy as they relate to the therapeutic powers of play (Schaefer & Drewes, 2014).

Please refer to Table 11.1.

Due to the playful nature of sandtray therapy, children freely express what may have been difficult to express verbally due to shame, guilt, or fear. Instead, they creatively merge fantasy and reality and expand on possibilities, often surprising even themselves (Mook, 2003). Yet the sandtray provides structure and safety due to the sandtray's concrete boundaries which can be particularly helpful with those who have aggressive and impulsive tendencies (Sweeney & Homeyer, 2009).

Table 11.1 The Therapeutic Benefits of Sandtray Therapy (adapted from Sweeney, 2020). A table with ten rows describing the therapeutic benefits of sandtray therapy as adapted from D. Sweeney (2020). The table includes descriptions of ten key elements of therapeutic sandtray work including expression, kinesthetics, therapeutic distance, safe space, use for trauma, overcoming resistance, communication medium, removes defenses, processing transference challenges, and access deep issues

1. It inherently gives expression to nonverbalized emotional issues. Like other expressive and projective therapies, sandtray provides a *language* for clients unable or unwilling to verbalize.
2. It naturally has a unique kinesthetic quality. There is an innate and unique sensory and kinesthetic experience in sandtray therapy, which serves as an extension of foundational attachment needs.
3. It serves to create an indispensable therapeutic distance for all-aged clients, so that they can speak through the play rather than verbally. Children who are experiencing difficulties do not express themselves through verbalization. They do, however, have the ability to express their difficulties through a projective medium (such as sandtray), which allows them to access their unconscious.
4. It creates a safe place for abreaction to occur. Children that have experienced trauma need a therapeutic setting in which to abreact in order to relive their traumatic experience and assimilate pieces of it slowly as they repetitively play it out. Sandtray gives the therapeutic distance needed so that unexpressed issues can emerge.
5. It is an effective intervention for traumatized clients. When considering the neurobiological effects of trauma (Badenoch & Kestly, 2015; De Bellis & Zisk, 2014; Gaskill & Perry, 2014; van der Kolk, 2014), provision of an expressive intervention is crucial.
6. It is effective in overcoming a child's resistance. The inherently engaging and nonthreatening nature of sandtray therapy often captivates the reticent child who fears the verbal engagement they perceive psychotherapy to be. Through sandtray, the therapeutic connection can easily occur.
7. It provides an effective communication medium for the client with poor verbal skills. Combining the always essential element of providing developmentally appropriate therapeutic interventions for children, therapists also encounter children who have poor verbal skills [e.g. stuttering]. Sandtray therapy helps children who experience language deficits or delays, physiological challenges, or social difficulties.
8. It also cuts through verbalization used as a defense. For children who may be verbally astute or may use verbalization as a means to resist or manipulate, sandtray therapy provides a means of legitimate or undefended communication.
9. The potential challenge of transference can be effectively addressed and processed through sandtray therapy.
10. It has the ability to access deeper intra-personal and inter-personal issues more thoroughly and more rapidly. Children feel safe working in the sandtray and, therefore, can present complex issues that may be underlying behaviors that others can see.

Empirical Research

Traditional Sandtray

Outcome research in the use of sandtray therapy is extremely limited. Although there is a large body of work comprised of published case studies, theoretical articles, and general practice literature, well designed outcome efficacy studies are few. As a technique, sandtray therapy can easily fit into many different theories that are empirically supported treatments. Therapists who use cognitive-behavioral therapy can integrate sandtray therapy as a technique to assist clients in working through the various phases of the treatment protocol. Recently, sandplay therapy was used in a case study to assess its effect in clinical symptoms and neurophysiological change with a subject diagnosed with generalized anxiety disorder (Foo et al., 2020). There are two well-designed outcome studies regarding group sandtray therapy (Flahive, 2005; Shen, 2006). While the number of participants in the study was very small, there was slight improvement in treatment group, but the control group displayed worsening behavior. Certainly, additional research is critical to assure that interventions have empirical research to support them.

Virtual Sandtray App

The Virtual Sandtray App has been involved in a few studies to date. Judi Parson and Bronwyn Cole, affiliated with Deakin University in Australia, conducted a study with local Child Life Specialists using the VSA. This pilot study included 15 pediatric patients aged 5–17 who used the VSA for an average of 24 minutes while in the hospital. Excerpts include: "What you liked about the VSA: How you could show what you wanted to make. You could make anything. What you didn't like about the VSA: Loved it, nothing bad". (Stone & Parson, 2017, slide 26). Staci Born and Christen Carotta of South Dakota State University conducted a pilot study investigating how children would use the VSA as a school counselling intervention (Born & Carotta, 2019). School counselors and students reported positive results, including "They liked being on it and creating their world. It was a great tool for me to build relationships with them without having to have them talk a lot". (slide 24) and "It made me feel like I could do anything because there was endless limits" (slide 17). Current research includes a psychosocial and medical procedure distraction study through the University of Alabama with pediatric burn patients (J. Stone, personal communication, December 8, 2020).

Telemental Health Sandtray Use

Many play therapists have a sandtray and miniature collections in their traditional playrooms. However, since the pandemic began, children were no longer treated in person. Play therapy treatment was provided via telemental health and traditional sandtray work could not be done with the children. The struggle and challenges many play therapists had were increasing as the pandemic continued. Difficulty engaging children over telemental health was a major problem at first, and then with modifications, several techniques were created to help provide play therapy treatment for children via telemental health. However, it became evident that children were more resistant to this type of treatment. Therefore, some play therapists were not able to provide the therapeutic care that they had been able to do within a playroom setting. Certainly, there was tremendous difficulty providing actual sandtrays for play therapy treatment over telemental health.

Before telemental health was mandated due to the pandemic, there were a number of digital tools that had been used in the therapeutic playroom. Children would many times choose to use the digital tool due to their own interests and familiarity with it. One of those tools became an alternative to the actual sandtray in the playroom. This was the Virtual Sandtray App (VSA) (Stone, 2015).

The Virtual Sandtray App

The Virtual Sandtray (VSA) is an app that fundamentally respects "Sandtray Therapy", as delineated by Homeyer and Sweeney (2017) and allows children to create a tray using tools for digging, painting, placing, and manipulating models, but in addition, the tray can be saved, loaded again, shared (encrypted), photographed, and videoed as the tray is being created. The VSA can meet the traditional needs of sandtray therapy and expand its use in new ways that were previously impossible (Stone, 2015). In prior years, when children were to create their world in sand, some had difficulty doing so due to sensory issues, such as not being able to tolerate touching the sand or manipulating the sand. Therefore, the VSA was a viable avenue for those children who needed to work with a sandtray. For many children, this was more exciting than traditional sandtray due to the fact that it was on an iPad, and children are frequently experts in working with apps and video games on various platforms. The digital aspects of the VSA offered much more complex actions than the traditional. While in traditional sandtray, one can dig in the sand and reach the blue below (which could represent water). With the VSA, children can dig in the sand, reach the water, and change the liquid level from various types of water to lava, poison, and more. The categories of models or miniatures that are used in traditional sandtray are mostly available through the VSA and children can place different quantities of the miniature (i.e. an entire group of one animal or more), change the size and position, as well as animate many miniatures to reflect more of what they were seeking to depict and explore. In addition to those features, there are many more graphic models that enhance the creation of the sandtray as well as possibly facilitating children's exploration into more unconscious material. One of the interesting aspects of the VSA is that one can rotate the tray, move it in different directions and zoom in and out to allow children to see different aspects of the tray that is created. At the time of this writing, the VSA has over 7,000 3-D models to choose from; each can be duplicated, animated, sized as needed, and changed at any time to meet the individual child's needs. The VSA also has many environments to choose from, which becomes the backdrop of the sandtray, thereby broadening the psychological experience and emphasizing the mood of the tray that is desired.

While all of the history and research about the use of play therapy has been increasing, no one could have predicted how treatment would have to change when the world was afflicted with the pandemic COVID-19. Play therapy has typically been in a playroom with a trained play therapist and child using the therapeutic powers of play (Schaefer & Drewes, 2014). Then, without warning, therapists were no longer able to see children in person and had to develop different methods to work with them over telemental health via Zoom or other platforms. Therapists needed to recreate play therapy through different mediums. Having a prescriptive integrative approach lead the way into the creation of "Teleplay", which was adapting play therapy for telemental health (Kaduson et al., 2020). The research on how to best accomplish this was certainly not available due to the acute onset of the pandemic. Therefore, a lot of the play therapy interventions were technique-based. Fortunately, having prior use of the VSA with children in the playroom illustrated how children accepted and enhanced their sandtrays without actually touching the sand.

Pre-COVID-19, the VSA app was downloaded on the playroom's iPad. Historically, digital tools in the playroom attracted many of the latency aged and teenaged children. In the initial days of the pandemic the VSA was not available to clients on their own iPad, however, this was soon to be resolved. The creators of the app worked quickly to add a remote version of VSA. The new addition allowed children to download a "client version" of the app at no cost at all. They were only able to use the app on their own iPad or iPhone if the therapist was also connected remotely and gave them the ID and password, thereby preserving the therapeutic interaction. This advancement allowed many children to use this intervention even though they were not permitted to come into the playroom or see others during quarantine. In fact, children who were already in play therapy treatment needed to continue their psychotherapy due to the increase in anxiety and depression brought on by the pandemic and quarantine.

Indicators for Use in Telemental Health

Sandtray therapy is appropriate for most presenting problems or diagnostic considerations, which generally refer to externalizing disorders, such as attention-deficit hyperactivity disorder, oppositional defiant disorder, or conduct disorder, and internalizing difficulties, such as anxiety and depression. In addition, it is appropriate for children with trauma backgrounds or stress problems, all of which were exacerbated by the pandemic. Children on the autistic spectrum may have had more difficulty with the sensory issues surrounding touching the sand or moving it, but when the sandtray became virtual via the VSA, it gave children on the spectrum a chance to explore and develop awareness through sandtray therapy. One must note, however, that not everyone is suited for sandtray therapy whether in the playroom or remotely. Children who are experiencing psychosis can also be overwhelmed by the sandtray process. Therefore, therapists should be very well trained and sensitive to how children respond, with regard to any psychotherapy with children.

When traditional sandtray or the VSA is used in the playroom, children had the privacy of a safe place and confidentiality as parents had to sign their consent to treatment. The fact that the sandtray work on the VSA is encrypted and password protected, allowed for even more reassurance that the children's tray work would remain in the therapeutic file and not at risk of being seen by others. When the VSA became upgraded to include a remote feature, the creators kept that as an integral part of the medium. All therapists should be cognizant of the critical nature of maintaining and sustaining confidentiality in treatment and beyond, maintaining confidential records and maintaining any and all products that may result from a therapeutic interaction. In the VSA, the children's trays can be saved, uploaded again, and shared only with the permission of the child and therapist. As indicated prior, a feeling of safety is needed before children can work through their own psychological difficulties. The VSA provides that even though the therapist and child were not in the playroom together. This opened up many of the children through play therapy and allowed for continuation of a tray the following week without hesitation because their work was saved and ready.

Ethical Considerations

The use of telemental health technologies in psychological practice has steadily increased over the last two decades and is expected to grow substantially in the years ahead (American Psychological Association, 2010a; Maheu et al, 2012). Attention to general ethical principles in the *Ethical Principles of Psychologists and Code of Conduct* (American Psychological Association, 2010b) is necessary during psychological practice whether it is conducted in person or remotely. It is also important to consider the safety of children during telemental health and to have a safety plan in place (Luxton et al., 2012). Therapists must understand the integration of various technologies into clinical services, and be aware of the ethical, legal, and clinical challenges that exist. For example, the therapist needs to examine the appropriateness of telemental health health for clients, informed consent, confidentiality, clinical, and technological competence, and emergency safeguards and procedures (Barnett & Kolmes, 2016). Ascherman and Rubin (2008) also emphasized the core ethical principles for the conduct of psychotherapy with children, including boundaries, privacy, and confidentiality in the therapeutic space, and following HIPPA guidelines to use secure connections for online sessions.

The importance of the ethical considerations is also included in the Association for Play Therapy's *Play Therapy Best Practices: Clinical, professional and ethical issues.* (2020). It strongly encourages play therapists to receive training, supervision, and educational opportunities in order to maintain high quality telemental health care. Along those lines, the Association requires that,

> When utilizing technology for treatment and consultation, the play therapists will provide all parties with a written telemental health informed consent, which is an adjunct to the normal informed consent document. Informed consent should be obtained as an in-person signed agreement. An electronically signed document (via a HIPAA compliant platform), or verbally obtained with: a) a plan to follow up with a written consent (i.e. returned via the postal service); and b) a documentation regarding the rationale of the document could not be signed in person, who was present, whether or not verbal consent was given, and the plan to follow up with an original signature signed document.
>
> (Association for Play Therapy, 2020, p. 20)

This encourages the play therapists to fully understand the potential benefits and limitations of telehealth through the use of technology and make sure that it is a good fit for every child. The limitations include technical and equipment failure and possible risks of confidentiality. Therefore, the ongoing training of the play therapist in both technology and treatment is of utmost importance.

With regard to the VSA specifically, it is imperative that the clinician discuss the use of the VSA with the parents/caregivers prior to use. The download of the free client version will often require parental consent or assistance. Discussing the fundamental and theoretical purposes of using the VSA will assist with parental comfort. Additionally, if the use of the VSA, as with traditional sand therapies, elicits emotional reactions warranting in person attention, the parents/caregivers can be available to assist.

Case Illustration

Billy, a 10-year-old boy in fifth grade, was referred for play therapy by his parents after exhibiting difficulties with anger and increasingly explosive behaviors. He was excited about being in play therapy because his older brother had been in treatment with me several years ago. However, when the pandemic COVID-19 began in March, the schools were going remote and families were required to quarantine, Billy was told he had to see me virtually. He was very appropriate with other adults and teachers, but the anger difficulties at home were becoming much more frequent. When his parents asked him what was wrong, he would respond that there was nothing wrong. He would hold in his anger when around other people and peers, and he would explode at home and be more defiant than anywhere else. His parents were very supportive, but he neither talked about what was bothering him nor would he discuss any school or social issues. Billy had a group of friends since first grade, but he hadn't seen any of them for several months.

Upon intake, which was done remotely on the Zoom platform, Billy didn't mention going to the playroom since his parents had told him it had to be remote. He asked what we could do over the internet because there wasn't a playroom to be in. We played some games that we both had in our own locations. That seemed to work at first, but it wasn't getting Billy to the issues at hand. He had trouble verbalizing any negative feelings and would fall back on saying that everything was fine. By the second session, I told him that I had arranged for his iPad to have an app for making a sandtray virtually. He was very excited to try it, and we began to use the VSA on the third session. Since Billy did not have more than one device, our sessions would begin with seeing each other through Zoom, and then when the VSA was started, we would be able to hear each other but no longer see each other (the Zoom window was behind the VSA on the tablet screen). This seemed to help Billy find enough distance so that he could produce his sandtray world and talk about every piece of the creation. I only had to explain about how we would share the tray, the environmental options, and the general workings of the app. He immediately understood before I even finished, since he was so familiar with the digital world.

Billy began by making a land of dragons in one portion of the tray. He was amazed at how many different dragons he could use. He wanted them different sizes and some of them were also moving. Their home in the tray was on a volcano that was erupting. While the VSA has volcanoes to use, he wanted to make his own because he was in need of a certain type of lava and lava flow within the volcano. This portion of his tray took an entire session, and while he was creating it, I used this metaphor to symbolize the anger within – not only volcanoes but also people. I reflected that he had a lot of protection around the volcano with all types of dragons. He told me that there only one that was the king, and it sat at the top of the volcano. The rest of the dragons were protecting that king and, of course, the volcano. He said that if they didn't, the volcano could erupt and kill every one of them. When I told Billy we had five more minutes, he asked if I could make the tray stay where it is? I explained the workings of the VSA and how it would be saved under his username if he wanted to go back to it next week. That pleased him.

The following week (session 5), Billy immediately asked for the room ID and password to get to his tray again. It was during this week that he put another section onto the tray, which was a land of domestic cats. He had one of them very large, as the leader of the group, and added identical cats but made them smaller, saying that the leader had these cats around for comfort. The cat section was on grass with a lot of vegetation in the form of trees and flowers. He did not do anything further to the dragon side of the tray but spent the entire time on the cat portion to reflect the positive nature of this section, and how the largest cat relied on others to comfort him because the dragons had been seen only by the leader cat. The others were too small to see the other side of the tray. The more Billy expanded the details of his tray, the more he began to understand some of the reasons why he was creating the different sections. He said that in the world there are bad guys like the dragons and volcano, but there were also good guys like the cats. He told the dragons don't need anything to survive so they just protect the volcano. The cats needed food and water, and they were much more peaceful. The tray was saved again because Billy was clear that he would continue it the next week.

On the sixth session, Billy added a section where there was a farm for food to be grown, and a group of homes where people lived, but you couldn't see any of the people because they were all quarantined. This description facilitated Billy putting a hospital in the tray near the homes. He also decided to put a large lake behind the hospital which was filled with moving fish. He spent a lot of time deciding which houses would work, which farm animals would be seen, and how big the hospital had to be to care for all the people who were trapped inside of it (his description of being quarantined). He talked a lot about the pandemic during this session, and although he said it didn't really bother him because no one he knew had it. He did get more anxious when he was creating the hospital and talking a lot about what he had heard regarding the nurses and doctors. At the end of this session, he asked me to make sure to save the tray, even though that is what was done every week. The anxiety of the pandemic's existence was clear.

In the next session, Billy once again asked for his tray, and this time he said he needed to get the cats some of the fish from the lake, so he created a waterfall and river to allow for the cats to access their fish. His comfort level increased enough so that he was able to go back to the dragon side and volcano to enhance some of the rocks and look for other dragons (since VSA updates regularly). He found one that he really liked, and it became the center of the dragon land. It had three heads – one was mean, one was smart, and one was kind. He admired his volcano and was very positive about how good he was at making this sandtray. I validated his feelings and used his metaphors to describe what could possibly be indicated in his tray. This was the first time he was connecting all aspects of the tray together.

On the next session, Billy created a portal by using several of the miniatures in the app and placing it between the evil side and the good side. He said that the portal was there in case someone needed it. He didn't go further into that, but he began to see the dragons as the angry side and really very explosive. Because the sandtray could reflect underneath the sand, he put items under (that could not be seen from the sand level of the tray, but those items were clearly representing to him the pressures that caused the volcano to possibly erupt without notice. He had several different types of explosives under the sand that could blow up if not cared for properly. He was beginning to understand his own anger within, and how it was fueled by the pandemic, the hospital, and the isolation that had occurred during this time. He finished his tray by putting an environment of being in space outside of the earth and floating. He added some stars above each of the sections of the tray, which he said would keep the tray safe from asteroids and also not let the cats get injured at all by the dragon side if it increased.

Billy finished with the tray two weeks later, and he was much more relaxed and less explosive at home, which was communicated by his parents. He was extremely proud of his tray and wanted me to take a picture of it and send it to him. Through his work with the VSA, Billy was able to gain insight into his own behavior, communicate his feelings better, and enjoyed the online sessions (which initially he thought would be so boring). His sandtray world helped him alleviate the pressures which were self-inflicted and create the opportunity to leave the negative feelings behind and walk through the portal to the peaceful side.

Conclusion

During a time of confusion and fear, children have had to try to understand an unprecedented time of a pandemic, quarantining, and loss of "normalcy". The use of the VSA was how Billy was able to get in touch with those feelings and resolve some of the issues that were underlying his explosive behaviors. Children need to have play therapy whenever they cannot figure out what to do. Exhibiting bad behavior allows for children to be referred, and with the proper conditions in place, therapists can align with children and help them explore their feelings through the use of many different telemental health techniques. The therapist should be open to different types of interventions and theories so that it can match the any child's needs. This is what the VSA did for Billy to explore and conquer his explosive behaviors.

References

Ackerman, M. J., Filart, R., Burgess, L. P., Lee, I., & Poropatich, R. (2010, Jan–Feb). Developing next-generation telehealth tools and technologies: Patients, systems, and data perspectives. *Telemedicine Journal and E-Health*, 16(1), 93–95.

American Psychological Association (2010a). Telepsychology is on the rise. *Monitor on Psychology*, *41*, 11.
American Psychological Association (2010b). *American Psychological Association ethical principles of psychologists and code of conduct*. http://www.apa.org/ethics/code.
Ascherman, L. I., & Rubin, S. (2008). Current ethical issues in child and adolescent psychotherapy. *Child and Adolescent Psychiatric Clinics of North America*, *17*(1), 21–35.
Association for Play Therapy (2020). J.5 Use of telemental health in play therapy. *Play Therapy Best Practices: Clinical, Professional and Ethical Issues*. https://cdn.ymaws.com/www.a4pt.org/resource/resmgr/publications/apt_best_practices_-_june_20.pdf
Association for Play Therapy (1997). A definition of play therapy. *The Association for Play Therapy Newsletter*, *16*(1), 7.
Badenoch, B., & Kestly, T. (2015). Exploring the neuroscience of healing play at every age. In D. Crenshaw, & A. Stewart (Eds.), Play therapy: A comprehensive guide to theory and practice (pp. 524–538). Guilford Press.
Bainum, C. R., Schneider, M. F., & Stone, M. H. (2006). An Adlerian model for sandtray therapy. *The Journal of Individual Psychology*, *62*(1), 36–46.
Barnett, J. E., & Kolmes, K. (2016). The practice of tele-mental health: Ethical, legal, and clinical issues for practitioners. *Practice Innovations*, *1*(1), 53–66.
Beutler, I. E., & Clarkin, J. (1990). *Systematic treatment selection: Toward targeted therapeutic interventions*. Brunner/Mazel.
Born, S., & Carotta, C. (2019, April 29). *Virtual Sandtray: Feasibility and strategies for use in counseling settings* [Conference session]. Minnesota Association for Children's Mental Health Conference, Duluth, MN.
De Bellis, M. D., & Zisk, A. (2014). The biological effects of childhood trauma. *Child and Adolescent Psychiatric Clinics of North America*, *23*(2), 185–222. https://https://doi.org/10.1016/j.chc.2014.01.002
Drewes, A. A., Bratton, S. C., & Schaefer, C. E. (2011). *Integrative play therapy*. Wiley.
Flahive, M. W. (2005). *Group sandtray therapy at school with preadolescents identified with behavioral difficulties* [Doctoral dissertation, University of North Texas]. Dissertation Abstract International, AAT 3196148.
Foo, M., Freedle, L. R., Sani, R., & Fonda, G. (2020). The effect of sandplay therapy on the thalamus in the treatment of generalized anxiety disorder: A case report. *International Journal of Play Therapy*, *29*(4), 191–200.
Freeman, J., Epston, D., & Lobovits, D. (1997). *Playful approaches to serious problems*. Norton.
Gaskill, R. L., & B. D. Perry (2014). The neurobiological power of play: Using the neurosequential model of therapeutics to guide play in the healing process. In C. A. Malchiodi, & D. A. Crenshaw (Eds.), *Creative arts and play therapy for attachment problems* (pp. 178–194). Guilford Press.
Homeyer, L., & Sweeney, D. (2017). *Sandtray therapy: A practical manual* (3rd ed.). New York: Routledge.
Hutton. D. (2004). Margaret Lowenfeld's 'World Technique.' *Clinical Child Psychology and Psychiatry*, *9*(4), 605–612.
Johnson, J. L. (2016). The history of play therapy. In K. J. Connor, C. E. Schaefer, & L. D. Braverman (Eds.), *Handbook of play therapy, second edition* (pp 17–34). Wiley.
Kaduson, H. G., Cangelosi, D., & Schaefer, C. E. (Eds.) (2020). *Prescriptive play therapy: Tailoring interventions for specific childhood problems*. Guilford.

Kaduson, H. G., Cangelosi, D., & Schaefer, C. E. (Eds.) (1997). *The playing cure: Individualized play therapy for specific childhood disorders.* Jason Aronson.

Lowenfeld, M. (1979). *Understanding children's sandplay: Lowenfeld's world technique.* Allen & Unwin.

Luxton, D. D., Kayl, R. A. & Mishkind, M. C. (2012). Mental health data security: The need for HIPPA-compliant standardization. *Telemedicine and e-Health, 18,* 284–288.

Maheu, M., Pulier, M., McMenamin, J., & Posen, L. (2012). The future of telepsychology, telehealth, and various technologies in psychological research. *Professional Psychology: Research and Practice, 43,* 613–621.

Mook, B. (2003). Phenomenological play therapy. In C. E. Schaefer (Ed.), *Foundations of play therapy* (pp. 260–280). Wiley.

Nims, D. R. (2007). Integrating play therapy techniques into solution-focused brief therapy. *International Journal of Play Therapy, 16*(1), 54–68.

Norcross, J. C. (1991) Prescriptive matching in psychotherapy: An introduction. *Psychology, 28,* 439–443.

Oaklander, V. (2000). Gestalt play therapy. In H. G. Kaduson, & C. E. Schaefer (Eds.), *Short-term play therapy for children* (pp. 28–52). The Guilford Press.

Peery, J. C. (2003). Jungian analytical play therapy. In C. E. Schaefer (Ed.), *Foundations of play therapy* (pp. 14–54). Wiley.

Schaefer, C. E. (1993). *The therapeutic powers of play.* Jason Aronson.

Schaefer, C. E., & Drewes, A. A. (2014). *The therapeutic powers of play: 20 core agents of change* (2nd ed.). Wiley.

Shen, Y. (2006). *The impact of school-based group sandtray counseling on the self-esteem of young adolescent girls* [Doctoral dissertation, Texas A & M University-Commerce]. Dissertation Abstract International, AAT 3245238.

Spooner, L. C., & Lyddon, W. J. (2007). Sandtray therapy for inpatient sexual addiction treatment: An application of constructivist change principles. *Journal of Constructivist Psychology, 20*(1), 53–85.

Stone, J. (2015). Virtual Sandtray App. https://www.sandtrayplay.com/Press/VirtualSandtrayArticle01.pdf

Stone, J., & Parson, J. (2017, August 13–15). *Introduction to the Virtual Sandtray App* [Conference session]. Australasia Pacific Play Therapy Conference, Sydney, Australia.

Sweeney, D. S. (2020). Sandtray therapy. In H. G. Kaduson, & C. E. Schaefer (Eds.) *Play therapy with children: Modalities for change* (pp. 9–24). American Psychological Association.

Sweeney, D. S. (2011). Integration of sandtray therapy and solution-focused techniques for treating noncompliant youth. In A. A. Drewes, S. C. Bratton, & C. E. Schaefer (Eds.), *Integrative play therapy* (pp. 61–73). Wiley.

Sweeney, D. S., & Homeyer, L. E. (2009). Sandtray therapy. In A. A. Drewes (Ed.), *Blending play therapy with cognitive behavioral therapy* (pp. 297–318). Wiley.

Taylor, E. R. (2009). Sandtray and solution-focused therapy. *International Journal of Play Therapy, 18,* 56–68.

van der Kolk, B.A. (2014). *The body keeps the score: Brain, mind, and body in the healing of trauma.* Viking.

12 Foundations of Virtual Playrooms

Rachel A. Altvater

The coronavirus disease 2019 (COVID-19) pandemic ominously impacted the entire world in a matter of moments. Global quarantine, stay-at-home, and social distancing orders disturbed nearly every aspect of modern human existence, including mental health care. The prevalence of adverse mental health conditions, substance use, and suicidal ideation amplified during this time (Czeisler et al., 2020; Pfefferbaum & North, 2020). A voluminous number of mental health providers instantaneously transitioned to the teletherapy platform to provide continuity of care during a medical and mental health crisis. Innovative, virtual adaptations to traditional psychotherapy practice emerged to ease the transition of therapeutic services during an alarming time.

Play therapists were confronted with a distinct experience for adjusting their play therapy practices, as tangible, therapeutic tools became inaccessible. Remote sessions introduced a novel therapeutic environment and uncertainty with employing clinical modifications and adjustments. Prior to providing traditional, in-person play therapy services, play therapists receive adequate instruction and practice to competently construct a therapeutic play space and implement relevant play therapy interventions. Little to no instruction was offered pre-COVID-19 on how to adapt this specialized form of practice to the virtual platform. Skilled play therapists in teletherapy and Digital Play Therapy® (Stone, 2020) provided guidance at the start of the pandemic for the field to sufficiently transform play therapy practice in this new era.

Following the trend of child and adolescent educators creating virtual classrooms for online learning, play therapists began to creatively construct virtual play therapy offices. The parameters of the virtual services were unclear at times for play therapists and child clients due the exorbitant amount of possibilities available online. Carefully selecting virtual tools when there was heightened uncertainty surrounding available virtual interventions and inexperience and discomfort with digital tools resulted in considerable unease. The introduction of virtual playrooms allowed play therapists to reconnect to their play space and selected therapeutic toys in this reformed environment. Their familiarity with a predetermined playroom appeared to

DOI: 10.4324/9781003166498-12

aid play therapists in feeling more competent and connected to their typical practice.

This chapter will focus on the purpose and utility of a virtual playroom. Due to the unique needs and preferences of the modern child and the recent sociocultural shift to heavier reliance on remote treatment during the coronavirus pandemic, clinically and culturally appropriate adaptations of play therapy practice to an online medium are indispensable. A discussion of how to select and apply theoretically sound interventions based on a chosen framework and basic play therapy principles will be included. The central focus of this chapter will be speaking the modern child's language, adapting practice for continuity of care during an ongoing global crisis and beyond, and broadening the choice of play therapy interventions to meet contemporary needs.

Assessing, Understanding, and Connecting with the Modern Child

A vital aspect of play therapy practice is understanding a child's internal and external reality to gain insight into their world and support them in a manner that meets their developmental needs. It is the responsibility of child mental health professionals to enter a child's zone of understanding and ways of communication. This shows the child that their helpers are attempting to comprehend their experience, thus, both they and their voices matter. Therapeutic toys are implemented in treatment to provide a suitable method to communicate a child's thoughts, feelings, experiences, needs, and desires and to facilitate their healing journey. Play is a child's natural mode of communication, and technology is the modern facilitator of that communication.

The COVID-19 pandemic drastically increased reliance on technology for most aspects of daily living. While the adjustment presented abrupt shifts in routine and normalcy, creative methods were implemented to provide some sense of predictability and consistency. Fortunately, many younger clients were already regularly immersed in this virtual network. Contemporary communication, connection, and play habitually occur through digital screens. The modern child is raised in an era that does not understand life without access to the world in the palm of their hands. Shifting to a digital platform is truly meeting a child where they are, which not only greatly abets them, it also unlocks the opportunity for a substantial amount of innovative possibilities in the therapeutic process.

To genuinely understand child clients, it is crucial to recognize where they are developmentally – cognitively, emotionally, physically, and socially. In order to provide advantageous therapeutic care, a deep understanding of these facets of their lives is fundamental. Socially, children are well versed in navigating digital and virtual platforms. Modern children are comprised of Generation Z, also known as the iGeneration or iGen for short, and a younger generation not yet officially classified by name. The iGen is comprised of individuals born between the mid-1990s and early 2010s. They were the first generation to emerge in a society with screens; they do not understand a life without smart devices, computers, the internet, and social media. Those in the iGen and succeeding generations are qualified as digital natives (Prensky, 2001; Stone, 2020).

A common concern expressed by older generations is that children are inhibited by screens. The primary fear is that they present fewer opportunities for creative, imaginative play (Altvater et al., 2017). From an outsider's perspective, children are *just staring* at their screens. From an insider's perspective, there is an entire world yet to be uncovered and constructed beyond the confines of that screen. It serves as a gateway to immeasurable possibilities. Countless genres of digital games present infinite possibilities on the screen, which provides a space for exploration, projection, processing, connecting, communicating, and much more. For a comprehensive list of game genres and information about the therapeutic powers of digital play, see Stone (2020).

There is often a disconnect between generational cultures, which leads to increased misunderstanding and subsequent issues between these opposing perspectives. Shifting perspectives to see the virtual world through a child's eyes allows play therapists to truly meet the child where they are in their modern play space. As Brené Brown eloquently states, "In order to empathize with someone's experience, you must be willing to believe them as they see it and not how you imagine their experience to be" (direct source unknown). Translating this concept to the digital platform will foster deeper consideration, cohesion, and healing. Complete immersion in this virtual space with your client affords them the opportunity to use their expertise and familiarity in this digital ecosystem. With valued and necessary guidance and support, they can navigate their path toward internal resolution in this space.

It is essential to begin here, prior to implementing a virtual playroom or other innovative, virtual methods to play therapy, as preconceived notions, discomforts, and uncertainties will ultimately dictate the direction of therapeutic work. Implementing interventions that do not align with one's comfort and understanding is likely to impede the therapeutic process (Altvater et al., 2017). Children are perceptive and generally developmentally egocentric in some regards. Play therapists' discomfort with a therapeutic tool may unintentionally translate to a sense of rejection toward the client (Altvater et al., 2017). A feeling of unease is natural for digital immigrants, those who were born and raised prior to the pervasive use of digital technologies (Prensky, 2001; Stone, 2020). Self-reflecting on and working thorough personal barriers will fortify professional directions and allow play therapists to join the modern child in their network.

Once this deeper level of competence and connection is established in the virtual platform and a child's interactions in this space, play therapists will be better able to align their theoretical framework to their choice of interventions, allowing for more expansive conceptualizations to occur. Play therapists know that play is substantially more than *just* play. This sentiment holds true for both traditional and digital and virtual methods of play as well. Society has advanced over the past several decades to a heightened reliance and preference for building virtual networks, and at increasingly greater rates since the COVID-19 pandemic. Play therapy practice must follow suit to keep up with and provide culturally responsive best practices for the population that is served.

Core Tenets of Playrooms

Therapeutic tool and intervention choice in virtual playrooms align with conventional play therapy practice. Understanding core play therapy principles is elemental in implementing clinically sound therapeutic interventions across therapeutic settings and platforms. This brief review of foundational material will serve as a basis for modification and application of play therapy practice in the virtual playroom. For more extensive information about necessary play therapy foundations, refer to the first section of this text.

Construction of a therapeutic play space, and choice of play therapy tools and interventions in that space, is dependent upon the play therapist's chosen theoretical framework. This section will serve as a general guide; however, specifications may vary depending on chosen orientation. Play therapists must align their practice with the core principles of their chosen framework to remain in line with evidence-based and research-informed practices.

Therapeutic Connection

A core agent of change in play therapy is the therapeutic relationship. When a child is provided with the conditions to be fully seen, heard, understood, and accepted, healing occurs (Stone, 2020). While selection and implementation of intervention is significant in the therapeutic process, the relationship is of utmost importance. Landreth (2012) delineates objectives of the relationship. He explains that "the objective is to become so absorbed in the relationship with the child that everything the therapist does becomes a response to the relationship" (p. 176). The following are his identified objectives of the play therapy relationship:

1. Establish an atmosphere of safety
2. Understand and accept the child's world
3. Encourage the expression of the child's emotional world
4. Establish a feeling of permissiveness
5. Facilitate decision-making

6. Provide the child with an opportunity to assume responsibility and to develop a feeling of control

The modern child primarily socializes and connects through the virtual platform. Meeting them in their familiar and preferred space supports and enhances the objectives of the relationship. To truly comprehend a child's world and foster a sense of emotional and physical safety, understanding, acceptance, permissiveness, and control, play therapists must meet them where they are. Presently, children are on the screen engaging in digital play, connecting with their friends, completing school related tasks, and much more. Stepping into a child's world to empathize with and acclimate to their culture deeply abets the connection.

Research further supports the benefit of technology-based interactions on the therapeutic relationship:

> *Initial concerns about alliance in telemental health were raised when the idea of communicating with others via computer was uncommon and there was very little research about how people maintained any type of relationship via information and communication technologies. As technology has improved, real-time communications with high levels of social presence cues have made digital communication more attractive, useful to, and ubiquitous among the general population. These methods of communication are now routine and commonplace ways to maintain and even strengthen relationships.*
> (Lopez et al., 2019, pp. 75-76)

They indicate that research often finds that clinicians experience greater concern about the impact of technology on the relationship than clients. They recommended that the therapist implement techniques to increase comfort and methods for supporting the relationship in this platform (Lopez et al., 2019).

Choice of Therapeutic Toys

Play therapists are intentional about their therapeutic play space. A key factor in choice of therapeutic tools, legendarily expressed by Landreth (2012), is that "toys and materials should be selected, not collected" (p. 156). Each toy serves a distinct purpose in the playroom to guide the child to understand, process, express, and release therapeutic material. As play is a child's natural mode of communication and serves as a distinct dialect to meet their developmental capabilities, toys and other materials are elected to represent and serve as a metaphor for their words (Landreth, 2012). Play therapists want to assure that the lexicon in the playroom provides the opportunity for the child to formulate cohesive thoughts, feelings, and actions.

Landreth (2012) distinguishes seven essentials in play therapy to consider when establishing a comprehensive compendium of playroom materials:

1. Establishment of a positive relationship with the child
2. Expression of a wide range of feelings
3. Exploration of real-life experiences
4. Reality testing of limits
5. Development of a positive self-image
6. Development of self-understanding
7. Opportunity to develop self-control

The culmination of items in the playroom generates a solid therapeutic space that grants permission for the child to safely and comfortably communicate their thoughts, feelings, and experiences. Adding digital and virtual tools in the modern playroom is invaluable for the advanced play language that digital natives speak to align with their idiolect and further meet the seven essentials in the modern era.

Another fundamental component of carefully selecting therapeutic toys is to consider the categories of toys to include to facilitate an adequate range of thematic material. Landreth (2012) identifies three broad categories of toys to include in the playroom: real-life, acting-out aggressive-release, and creative expression and emotional release. Kottman and Meany-Walen (2016) identify five general categories of toys: family-nurturing, scary, aggressive, expressive, and pretend-fantasy. A play therapist's specialization and the common presenting concerns within their client population will further determine selection of toys to represent their clients' needs. A consideration of culture and diversity in the toy selection process is also crucial (Gil & Pfeifer, 2016). For an extensive list of suggested traditional play therapy tools, see Landreth (2012; pp. 167-169) and Kottman and Meany-Walen (2016; pp. 6-13), and for comprehensive considerations with digital play therapy tools, see Stone (2020; pp. 94-124).

Establishing Playroom Parameters

Traditional, in-person playrooms have a distinct boundary, as they are typically within the confines of an office or other predetermined space. Choice of staple, traditional playroom toys also remains relatively the same. Virtual playrooms present a unique experience, as the figurative borders of the room are a bit more ambiguous. The virtual platform and internet offer a surplus of options for inclusion and further exploration, as the library of digital interventions to incorporate in virtual playrooms is ever-growing. A collective issue for play therapists constructing this novel playroom is clearly establishing and honing a distinctly delineated therapeutic space. While an abundance of options provides more opportunities to meet the complex needs of diverse concerns in the contemporary age, it also contributes to heightened uncertainty and anxiety.

When establishing parameters for virtual playrooms, play therapists must first align with the core tenets of their theoretical orientation. How does this framework conceptualize psychopathology? What is the nature of psychological change? How are symptoms reduced or relieved and psychopathology healed? What is the rationale for and choice of therapeutic techniques and interventions? What virtual therapeutic toys will support these interventions? These questions are essential to consider when carefully selecting appropriate tools and refining the virtual space.

Play therapists then work toward instituting comfort and competence with various virtual interventions. Due to the evolving catalogue of digital tools, it is inevitable that play therapists will experience unfamiliarity with available items. As soon as new technologies are introduced, the next edition or succeeding trendy item is on the horizon. Developing adequate knowledge of available software, popular games and apps, and how to navigate the digital platform is sufficient for virtual play therapy sessions.

If play therapists remain comfortable with not knowing everything but knowing enough, they will be better able to navigate unfamiliar terrain in a skilled manner. Knowing enough means having a general understanding of the core principles of digital play therapy and being acquainted with navigating smart devices/computers and apps/the internet. Play therapists are encouraged to vet items prior to implementing them in sessions when applicable and appropriate by doing research about potential interventions (e.g. watching a YouTube video of a gamer playing a particular game) and playing prior to introducing in sessions. This not only assists in understanding the tool itself, it gives the play therapist an opportunity to understand how the tool can be used and conceptualized in a therapeutic manner.

Pinpointing virtual playroom parameters is a continual process. The confines of the room are dependent on therapist comfort level and choice of therapeutic tool. As the catalogue of possibilities grows and the powers of play are recognized in digital and virtual practice, the parameters are likely to develop further. The play therapy field is in its infancy stage with using these exceptionally valuable tools in practice. The cyber world is expansive, and there are vast possibilities to advance practice and further aid clients in this space.

Virtual Playrooms

A virtual playroom is a computer-generated version of a play therapy office. Play therapists and clients are granted access to interact together in this space while physically apart. Of note, while virtual playrooms are primarily used on the teletherapy platform at this time due to continued COVID-19 social distancing restrictions, they can also be used when the therapist and client are physically present in the same location. Virtual playrooms may be preferable for some clients, and they provide a cleanlier play space, especially with the enhanced cleaning procedures during the present health crisis. This section will provide foundation and consideration for creating a virtual playroom.

Creating a Virtual Playroom

The design of the virtual play therapy space will vary depending on clinical style and choice of therapeutic tools. However, the core features of traditional playrooms, such as making it a warm, child-friendly space, fostering an inviting, therapeutically permissive environment, and including toys that are easily accessible, culturally inclusive, and developmentally and clinically appropriate, will continue to be paramount in the creation of the space. For play therapists with physical and virtual offices, maintaining consistency and predictability is recommended. Employing adaptations of physical play therapy tools in virtual playrooms and adding digital tools in traditional playrooms allows for a more unified therapeutic environment and experience.

Virtual playrooms are constructed through a presentation program, most popularly Google Slides. They are comprised of a single slide or series of slides with various pictures of objects that are linked to digital and virtual toys, games, expressive arts, websites, documents, or other created or chosen interventions. The playroom is presented to the child through screen sharing via the teletherapy platform or by sending a link to allow for them to enter and directly interact in the room from their screen.

When creating the playroom, the play therapist first chooses a background for the slide. The backdrop of the space could be a picture that the therapist uploads, such as a photograph of the physical playroom, obtains from a search engine, such as a simple wall and floor background, or creatively constructs, such as a tablet screen. Google Slides is directly connected to Google Images, which streamlines the search for and addition of items to the space. The play therapist then identifies the choice of therapeutic toys and searches for various images to serve as a representation of those toys. After adding selected items to the room, websites or other slides are linked in the presentation to the items. For example, if a play therapist wants to include dress up in their virtual playroom, they can add a picture of a piece of clothing, a wardrobe, or a mirror to the menu and add a link it to a website on the object that offers interactive, virtual dress up. The link is added by highlighting the object, and then selecting insert > link from the ribbon (options in the toolbar, such as file, edit, view, etc.) in Google Slides. Play therapists can also use the presentation program's editing tools to create interactive games directly on the slides. For visual step-by-step instructions and an example of a virtual playroom, see Altvater (2020).

Using a Virtual Playroom

At the onset of services, play therapists provide psychoeducation about the purpose of play therapy treatment. Similarly, when incorporating digital and virtual interventions, therapeutic rationale is provided to caregivers about these tools. The play therapist explains the purpose, benefits, and potential limitations. Frontloading the conversation with this information will connect caregivers to the process (Stone, 2020). Providing a tour of the virtual space is also useful; it is synonymous to inviting caregivers into an in-person playroom. This is likely to increase their understanding and comfort with the therapeutic space and treatment process. Additionally, depending on the age and developmental ability of the child, the caregivers might require further instruction on how to access various links to guide and support the child in learning how to navigate the playroom on their end.

Play therapists then decide how they would like to invite the child into their virtual playroom. They have the option to screen share the playroom, share a unique playroom link to the Google Slides presentation, or publish the playroom to the internet via a web address and share the link with a client. When screen sharing, either the play therapist maintains control of the slides or they present their slides with remote access and grant the child the ability to control the cursor in the room. Of note, if the latter is preferred, the play therapist can override access at any time. To grant remote access, download the "Remote for Slides" Google Chrome extension on the Chrome web browser. A remote access link and code will be provided when presenting the screen with the remote feature. When sharing a unique playroom link, the play therapist makes a copy of the presentation for the duration of the session, adjusts editor access to the slides to allow anyone with the link to access and edit the slides, and then sends the link to the child. With this method, both the play therapist and child are present in the space at the same time. This is a preferred method when screen sharing options are unavailable. When publishing a playroom to the internet, the child can access the playroom from the link. This method differs, as it is unable to be edited when interacting with the space in real time. Therefore, the child is unable to engage in interactive games on slides with the play therapist in the same manner that they would with the unique slideshow link. The child is able to click on the various objects in the room, which takes them to their respective links. The method of inviting the child into the space will depend on teletherapy platform capabilities and play therapist preference.

Similar to a traditional play therapy office, it is beneficial to provide the time and space for a child to explore the room to establish comfort and familiarity. Oftentimes, when a child first enters an in-person playroom, they examine the room. Thematic material might not readily present itself in the first few sessions during this stage of exploration and assessment. The same process occurs in the virtual play space. A child will only become aware of what tools are beneficial to their unique therapeutic process after a thorough examination of what is available to them.

After the child establishes comfort and familiarity within the virtual playroom, they will connect more deeply to the toys, which will facilitate the therapeutic powers of play (Schaefer & Drewes, 2014). Play therapists are encouraged to assess thematic material throughout sessions to gain greater insight into the child's internal experiences and to facilitate the healing process. Ryan and Edge (2011) explain that "[t]hemes are viewed as abstractions not only from behavior, but more importantly, represent significant, underlying, emotional issues that children then express spontaneously in their play therapy" (p. 356). They identify common subthemes, including safety or protection, comfort, nurturing, distancing or rejection, chaos, trauma and abuse with primary relationship, power, mastery, sense of completion, control/victimization, weakness or helplessness, and aggression. Assessing for these themes and others that may surface in sessions will give valuable information about where the child is in their process. When the play therapist is less familiar with the digital and virtual tools, it can be more challenging to identify relevant therapeutic content. Connecting to potential underlying reasons for use of particular therapeutic tools will increase understanding and aid the play therapist in supporting the child in a way that is comfortable, familiar, and beneficial for them. Further utilization of the virtual playroom will depend on the treatment method and choice of intervention outlined by the play therapist's theoretical framework.

Ethical Considerations

Play therapists prioritize safeguarding the child's Protected Health Information (PHI). The playroom is to be used on a privacy compliant teletherapy platform. Play therapists must refer to their state and national credentialing boards, the Association for Play Therapy (2020), and their liability insurance to receive clarification about specified teletherapy regulations. The playroom, itself, can be Health Insurance Portability and Accountability Act (HIPAA) compliant with proper configurations on paid versions of Google Workplace. HIPAA is a privacy and security compliant standard to protect PHI in the United States. A Business Associate Agreement (BAA) must be reviewed and signed by the administrator of the Google Workplace account prior to using Google related services that have PHI. It is advised to not include PHI in the virtual playroom. The privacy compliance in this space is primarily intended to keep the content of play therapy sessions as protected as possible.

There may be times where technology-based interventions do not fully comply with privacy standards. Play therapists must inform caregivers and clients of these potential limits and obtain consent and assent for use of digital and virtual mediums in treatment. Limitations that may occur when using online interventions include collection of cookies and varying website permissions. Many games and websites that children frequent do not comply with privacy standards and may require downloads or logins. The play therapist and child will obtain permission prior to downloading any apps or programs or logging into any websites if the child does not already have established login information. The play therapist and child will not converse via any game-based chats or message boards, keeping all discussions to the privacy compliant teletherapy platform, and will use non-identifying nicknames at all times when entering public and non-privacy compliant online spaces during the session.

Additional privacy considerations include parental permissions, targeted advertisements, and private browsers when venturing from the virtual playroom to other online interventions. When frontloading the conversation with caregivers about the playroom, it is advantageous to inquire about what the child is able to access and if there are any parental controls on their screen. While all that will be included in the playroom is appropriate and child-friendly, device restrictions can inhibit children from retrieving some links and entering sites. For example, some children are unable to go to YouTube, so videos that the child would access on their screen would want to be provided from alternate sites, such as YouTube Kids or VideoLink. Targeted advertisements (ads) and prepopulated search histories could inadvertently reveal some of the play therapist's personal online use and/or content from other children's sessions. It is recommended to turn on private browsing, as it blocks the device from recording browsing history. Of note, while this history will not store and display on the screen, the information is still stored on websites' servers. It is also useful to use ad blockers to decrease the volume of ads on websites. There are extensions for Google Chrome to assist with this process.

Case Example

Flora, a five-year-old bicultural child, was in play therapy services for a year prior to the transition to teletherapy due to the COVID-19 pandemic. Sessions were primarily child-centered, with occasional implementation of filial instruction and techniques to assist the family system. Flora was initially slow-to-warm in treatment, but once rapport was established, she frequently exhibited difficulty concluding sessions. Play therapy treatment focused on strengthening her self-concept due to developmental delays, establishing clarity about her school refusal, and processing pain associated with her chronic medical illness.

At the start of teletherapy services, the family was encouraged to create a private play space at home. They were instructed to include several toys that were similar to toys frequently chosen in the play therapy office and a couple of Flora's favored toys at home. The intention was to maintain consistency in the therapeutic environment to best support her during this unfamiliar and uncertain time.

Similar to the start of services, Flora was reluctant to participate in telemental health sessions. She frequently left the room, closed the laptop in the middle of session, became tearful, and informed her parents that she did not want to attend therapy. The virtual playroom was established in an effort to assist Flora in reconnecting more to her typical play therapy process. A picture of the in-person playroom was set as the initial background and virtual versions of toys present in the room were included for therapeutic familiarity and predictability. The playroom was initially screenshared with her, and she was provided with links to enter spaces that she screenshared and could join interactively.

Flora initially hesitantly entered the virtual playroom. Despite her trepidation, she was seemingly more inquisitive and engaged during the session that it was introduced. She examined the various virtual toys, similar to her initial exploration when she began play therapy services. Slowly, Flora reengaged in the process. She showed particular interest in construction and nurturance items, both in-person and virtually.

The focus of the play shifted during this time. While the change in platform initially appeared to be a primary factor for discomfort and reluctance, once Flora reengaged in the process, it was apparent that she was processing heightened levels of fear and stress. She was particularly interested in playing with an online building blocks website and an interactive, virtual dollhouse created on Google Slides. Themes of unstable and unpredictable foundations in her construction and not being allowed to leave the house, becoming sick, and requiring medical attention were readily apparent throughout her play.

Due to Flora's chronic medical illnesses, it is postulated that the start of the pandemic was exceptionally anxiety-provoking for her. She was considered high risk, and her family took additional precautions to keep her safe. Abrupt changes in routine were also challenging for her to navigate due to her age and developmental difficulties. Her schooling ceased for several weeks, with no clear indication when she or her classmates would return. Once school resumed, she attended school online, which was yet another unfamiliar experience.

Transitioning play therapy services to a new platform while navigating significant fears and a series of new experiences was understandably challenging for Flora. The virtual playroom afforded her the opportunity to reconnect to an emotionally safe and supportive space that she was accustomed to. While at this time the pandemic is still occurring and she is actively processing her concerns and challenges in online play therapy services, her anxiety symptoms have decreased, and she returned to her typical level of interaction in sessions.

Conclusion

The COVID-19 pandemic led to an innovative delivery of virtual play therapy practice to meet the modern child's needs during an unprecedented crisis. Play therapists creatively modified services to provide a sense of consistency, familiarity, connection, and support through an extremely uncertain and anxiety-provoking time. The virtual playroom, a refined, interactive, computer-generated play therapy office, was introduced during this transition. The playroom and carefully selected digital and virtual toys and interventions align with conventional play therapy practice, the play therapist's theoretical framework, and needs of the client population.

It is crucial to remain flexible and implement change in practice as generational and societal cultures shift to provide therapeutic care that meets the needs of the modern child. When these transformations occur, there is often pushback and heightened discomfort and trepidation, as change is difficult. Change is also inevitable and necessary to advance as a field and society. It is the honorable responsibility of a play therapist to lean into the child's play process, empathetically shift perspective, make necessary adjustments to provide a validating, accepting, and inclusive therapeutic environment, and become fully immersed in their world for a moment. Let them lead the way.

References

Altvater, R. A., Singer, R. R., & Gil, E. (2017). Part 1: Modern trends in the playroom – preferences and interactions with tradition and innovation. *International Journal of Play Therapy*, 26(4), 239–249. https://doi.org/10.1037/pla0000058

Altvater, R. (2020, October 14). *How to create a virtual play therapy room* [Video]. YouTube. https://www.youtube.com/watch?v=L_B2oUk9Jok

Association for Play Therapy. (2020). Play therapy best practices: Clinical, professional, & ethical issues. https://www.a4pt.org/resource/resmgr/publications/apt_best_practices_-_june_20.pdf

Czeisler, M. É., Lane, R. I., Petrosky, E., Wiley, J. F., Christensen, A., Njai, R., Weaver, M. D., Robbins, R., Facer-Childs, E. R., Barger, L. K., Czeisler, C. A., Howard, M. E., & Rajaratnam, S. M. W. (2020, August 14). *Mental health, substance use, and suicidal ideation during the covid-19 pandemic – united states, june 24-30, 2020* (Morbidity and Mortality Weekly Report Volume 69, Number 32). Centers for Disease Control and Prevention. https://www.cdc.gov/mmwr/volumes/69/wr/pdfs/mm6932a1-H.pdf

Gil, E., & Pfeifer, L. (2016). Issues of culture and diversity in play therapy. In K. J. O'Connor, C. E. Schaefer, & L. D. Braverman (Eds.), *Handbook of play therapy* (2nd ed., pp. 599–627). Wiley.

Kottman, T., & Meany-Walen, K. (2016). *Partners in play: An Adlerian approach to play therapy* (3rd ed.). American Counseling Association.

Landreth, G. (2012). *Play therapy: The art of the relationship* (3rd ed.). Routledge.

Lopez, A., Schwenk, S., Schneck, C. D., Griffin, R. J., & Mishkind, M. C. (2019). Technology-based mental health treatment and the impact on the therapeutic alliance. *Current Psychiatry Reports*, 21(76), 1–7. https://doi.org/10.1007/s11920-019-1055-7

Pfefferbaum, B. & North, C. S. (2020). Mental health and the covid-19 pandemic. *The New England Journal of Medicine*, 383, 510–512. https://doi.org/10.1056/NEJMp2008017

Prensky, M. (2001). Digital natives digital immigrants. *On the Horizon (MCB University Press)*, *9*(5), 1–6. https://www.marcprensky.com/writing/Prensky%20-%20Digital%20Natives,%20Digital%20Immigrants%20-%20Part1.pdf

Ryan, V., & Edge, R. (2011). The role of play themes in non-directive play therapy. *Clinical Child Psychology and Psychiatry*, *17*(3), 354–369. https://doi.org/10.1177/1359104511414265

Schaefer, C. E., & Drewes, A. A. (2014). *The therapeutic powers of play: 20 core agents of change* (2nd ed.). Wiley.

Stone, J. (2020). *Digital play therapy: A clinician's guide to comfort and competence*. Routledge.

13 Expressive Therapies in Telemental Play

Leslie Baker

Play is a notion of flow. Csikszentmihalyi (1990) defines flow as "...the state in which people are so involved in an activity that nothing else seems to matter; the experience is so enjoyable that people will do it even at great cost, for the sheer sake of doing it". Space and time disappear as a youth finds their way into the flow of play and all else seems to disappear. To witness flow, one only need look at a youth creating something: a drawing, a sandtray, a drama with miniature animals or dolls, a poem on their tablet, or art on their phone app. To experience flow, one must have the ability to focus attention; to concentrate without distraction. Expressive therapies create these opportunities. In all communities, children and teenagers illustrate their brilliance in expressing themselves creatively in simple and powerful ways. If you take the time to observe play, you will see what youth are communicating in their expressive creations.

Universally, play is a sacred space to create, master, explore, and find solutions for the challenges one faces in the world at large. This chapter will explore expressive therapies in telemental health play therapy, including relevant research, theories, and expressive therapy interventions used in expressive play therapy. It will look at the pros and cons of expressive therapies via telemental health and the ethics of telemental health regarding expressive therapies including not doing harm, confidentiality, and managing digital assets. It will include specific expressive play therapy interventions in assessments, art, dance, music, sandtray, and augmented reality. Lastly, a case study will illustrate the theory and practice of expressive therapies in telemental health play therapy. The case example will reflect the use of the Expressive Therapies Continuum, (Lusebrink, 1991) and *Therapeutic Powers of Play: 20 Core Agents of Change* written by Dr. Charles Schaefer & Dr. Athena Drewes in 2013 to apply the expressive therapies interventions in telemental health play therapy.

Expressive Therapy – Traditional Play to Telemental Health Play Therapy

Expressive play therapy holds a healing element, or sacred space, for the client known as the "therapeutic alliance". The therapeutic alliance is the

DOI: 10.4324/9781003166498-13

unseen "felt" place where change and growth occur in the therapy. Traditional expressive play therapy holds that change occurs when a youth meets in person with the expressive therapist to share their story and the therapist is the witness to the youth's story. Together, the youth and clinician interact around the story (externalization, sensory processing, attachment, arousal reduction, and affect regulation) (Malchiodi, 2008) and that interaction becomes the therapy. However, this long recognized traditional relationship has been evolving since the digital age found its way into telemental health (Baker, 2019). As the digital technology age continues to expand, clinicians need to be cognizant that youth are born with technology "in their hands". To them, the use of technology is more an extension of their being versus simply a tool. How we navigate with parents and youth is crucial for a successful expressive therapies experience (Baker, 2019).

Expressive therapies used in play therapy have been shown to be effective in helping youth to cope with their issues. This includes treating clients of different ages, disorders, and symptom profiles. Southwell (2016) noted widespread improvements in their program *yourtown's Expressive Therapies Intervention* (YETI) in areas of general functioning and improvements in children's self-worth as well as in attachment between the parent and child. Slayton et al. (2010) reviewed studies from 1999 to 2007 and found a small amount of quantifiable evidence to support the claim that art therapy is effective.

Traditional playrooms typically have all the expressive materials to create multiple opportunities in expressive therapies from art, drama, music, dance, poetry, and sandtray, with no worry about creating messes! The expressive materials are at one's fingertips – easy to access for both clinician and youth. The play commences and, depending on the theoretical construct of the play therapist, a youth may choose an expressive intervention or an expressive intervention may be presented to them. The work begins as the play therapist provides presence to the youth with eye contact, observation, mirroring, and reflecting on the process of the expressive intervention in which they are engaged.

There are pros and cons every expressive therapies play therapists should consider. Pros include providing youth easier ways to express themselves, more viable solutions for communication, allowing for suppressed emotions to surface, and they may aid a youth in achieving better self-awareness, and relief from stress or anxiety, learning disorders, autism, and other traumatic experiences. Some potential cons in the use of expressive therapies can be that certain expressive therapies interventions prove to be too emotionally provocative and create dysregulation. Another concern can be sensory over stimulation, many youths do not like sand, finger paints, clay, or certain pitches in music. Another concern is physical agility, and ability for movement and dance and drama.

This generation embraces technology as a way of life. In telemental health play, the face-to-face play therapy session now takes place through a camera lens. Using the youth's language, becoming interested in what you see, hear, and notice in the camera view can provide novel ways to connect with your client. For example, you may see their pet. Inquiring about the pet can be a way into the child's world. They may also want to know about your screen world as well. It is critical to be mindful of what is in your own screen view.

Play therapists must recognize and bridge a sense of distance by utilizing engagement skills that require a different level of intention and action depending on the needs of the case. Some cases may need a soft but intentional approach for youth who are challenged in using telemental health. Clinicians may offer use of the chat feature, turning away from, or turning off the camera as an easier way for the youth to talk. Other cases require a more energetic or enthusiastic approach with youth. These youth may need more energy to engage in the therapeutic process. Clinicians may shorten session times to address attention span capabilities of the youth.

In initial meetings with parents, it is crucial to have them join in the production side of telemental health play. This includes setting up a private playroom space, enlisting parents to gather expressive play supplies, and organizing these items so they are easily accessible in a box. In addition, they need to provide a phone, tablet, laptop, or desktop that can access free applications plus a table, markers, crayons, paper, glue stick, tape, scissors (age appropriate), and playdough. Clinicians can also consider providing a ready-made kit to the families and mailing it to them. In addition, clinicians can email handouts of creative interventions, and templates or put together a packet of documents made available on a shared drive. Expressive therapies are particularly effective with telemental health play because the interventions are experiential and engaging.

Another exciting option in expressive teleplay is the use of co-play. Expressive therapists can have parents/caregivers co-play with youth side by side by working on an expressive intervention at the same time as the youth. Play therapists can mirror the play of the youth on their screens if they are not screen sharing. An example of this would-be youth using a sandtray to tell a story and the clinician then mirrors their story. Another effective option is to use augmented reality applications. Augmented reality (AR) is an enhanced version of reality created using technology to overlay digital information on an image of something being viewed through a device (such as a smartphone camera). For example, apps, such as *Just a Line and Quiver*, offer expressive therapy interventions that allow for AR exploration in storytelling and creative play.

Expressive interventions and digital tools abound in this new space. Expressive modalities are essential in the play therapist's toolkit in both traditional and teletherapy modes. The Expressive Therapy Continuum (ETC) provides a model of the client's internal process, their interaction with media, and their level of expression. This is described in three levels:

- Kinesthetic/sensory level – primal, base awareness of the art media and the client. It is in balance of kinesthetic and sensory where the healing resides.
- Perceptual/affective level – the balance again between emotion and form perception. Too much emotion can hinder form and too much form can dampen emotion.
- Cognitive/symbolic level – problem solving, decision making, and other cognitive processes, metaphors, and symbols. The balance lies between the expression of personal symbols with the meaning and insight in these expressions (Malchiodi, 2006).

The ETC has developed from a hierarchical model to a model that sees these processes as inclusive and progressive. Developing an understanding of the ETC model can further assist play therapists in assessment and treatment with expressive therapies in play therapy.

Expressive Therapies Assessment Intervention

Expressive therapies interventions in telemental health play therapy are useful to assess youth and family dynamics. Burns and Kaufman (1970) developed a diagnostic tool called the Kinetic Family Drawing (KFD). This tool is used by directing a youth to draw a picture of their family, including themselves, doing something. It helps to show without direct conversation the youths' feelings about themselves and their relationships to those in their family. This can be a useful guide to the dynamics they live in and feelings they experience about themselves. Another expressive/projective assessment tool is the Family Play Genogram developed by Eliana Gil (2016). This involves drawing a family genogram; then, the family and/or youth place miniatures they choose to represent each family member into the genogram drawing. This allows for assessment of the youth's perception of the roles and relationships in the family as well as their place in the family. If the family is also playing, the family members choose their miniatures, representing themselves and others in the family. This creates multiple layers of perceptions and will help the play therapist in the assessment and focus of therapy.

Expressive Therapies Interventions for Teleplay

Sandtray Intervention

Sandtray, a nonverbal and verbal therapeutic modality, provides an external arena through which youth can express internal events. The *World Technique* approach was originally developed in the late 1920s by British pediatrician and psychoanalyst Margaret Lowenfeld (2005). This projective technique allows the youth to express their perceptions including concerns and conflicts in a safe environment, often leading to solving their inner problems. The process of sandtray allows for youth to externalize the stories and images, have a sensory processing experience, grounding, soothing, and kinesthetic experience. Sand tray includes exploring attachment in the relationships they create in the sand and in the relationship created with the clinician in the room.

More recently, the *Virtual Sandtray App*®© (VSA), developed by Jessica Stone and Chris Ewing (Stone, 2015), offers an in-person option, along with telemental health accessibility in two ways. The VSA can be shared over a telemental health platform or VSA offers a remote feature so the client can sign in from a remote location, create protected trays in their location while the therapist witnesses the creation, and allows access during the session only. Saved trays can be loaded to the client during subsequent sessions and the work can continue.

Where Do I Feel? Intervention

Observing the expressive art through the lens of ETC is useful. ETC in this activity begins with the kinesthetic/sensory level of engaging with crayons and paper. The perceptual/affective includes sensing the body as a whole and emotions within body. Lastly, in processing this intervention, the play therapist evaluates the cognitive/symbolic balance. How is this intervention perceived, do the colors symbolize the feelings accurately, and does this intervention have meaning for the youth?

Bilateral Scribbling Intervention: Neurosequential Art Approach

Starting with different color crayons, one in each hand, bilateral scribbling is the process of scribbling with a leader and a follower who mirrors the partner's scribbling. The general process is to go up and down vertically, back and forth horizontally (Bilaterally – crossing midline), straight and arching (crossing midline), up and down and back and forth while mirroring the partner. The speed and intensity are decided upon by the leader and then roles are switched (Klodony, 2021a; 2021b). The leader can also add large bilateral circles and move to smaller circles throughout the scribble (Chapman, 2014). The *Bilateral Scribbling* allows for rhythmic, repetitive motion leading to regulating and relating through mirroring. This intervention utilizes the Neurosequential Model of Therapeutics (NMT) (Perry, 2006), a bottom-up approach and the kinesthetic/sensory level of the ETC. The mirroring between the youth and play therapist and/or youth and parent activate mirror neurons which in turn build attachment, empathy and assist in downregulation (Figure 13.1).

Groove Like Me! Intervention

Groove Like Me! enlists movement and was developed in 2019 in sessions at Therapy2Thrive®. The client chooses music and demonstrates a series of movements or a dance to the play therapist and/or parent/caregiver. The therapist/parent/caregiver repeat the sequence of movements back to youth using the same music. They play back and forth, offering music and movements, mirroring and repeating. This may culminate in a dance together in which they choose to perform each person's creative movements/dance. This intervention provides another opportunity for applying ETC.

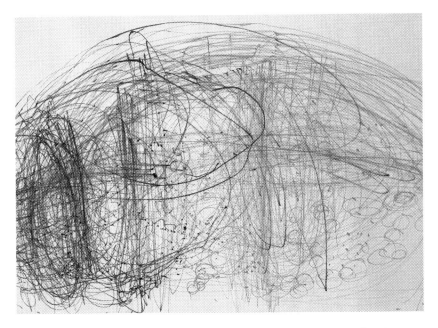

Figure 13.1 Bilateral Scribbling Intervention. Mirror neuron depiction drawing

Kinesthetic/sensory – experience of music and movements chosen and danced;

Perceptual/affective – how is the perception of balancing the expression of emotion in the moves to the music;

Cognitive/symbolic – is there awareness in the choice of music and/or movement; does it hold meaning for the youth.

Just A Line App

Just A Line, (Google, LLC, 2019) is the first collaborative Augmented Reality (AR) app that allows you to make simple drawings or create fun games like tic/tac/toe in augmented reality, then share your creation with a short video. It also has a feature that allows you to share your screen with another phone in in the same room and draw together. Touch the screen to draw, hit record and share what your created. This app is available on Apple and Google Play for iPhone and Android phones.

Quiver Masks App

QuiverVision has a mask application, available on the iPhone, that allows youth to print free coloring pages from their website (QuiverVision, n.d.). Color them, scan them and then view them on their device (phone or tablet) while interacting with the images in AR. Become a quiver character and act out your story. QuiverVision offers coloring apps as well as other apps that are available on Apple and Google Play for iPhone and Android phone.

These AR app interventions provide an opportunity for applying ETC. Kinesthetic/Sensory – experience of using coloring, paper, photos, and video; Perceptual/affective – how the perception of balancing the expression of emotion in the interaction of AR with body and visual perceptions, and Cognitive/symbolic – is there awareness of the way the AR experiences changes the way we think about reality and how that may change meaning.

These intervention examples are a just a beginning of how expressive therapies in play provide multifaceted tools that allow youth to begin the conversation in a new way. As the client manipulates the materials, they are not only symbolically and/or metaphorically communicating their story, but they also process and work through their challenges in the expressive modality.

Clients are often able to try new things, battle foes, and explore multiple options with differing outcomes without experiencing consequences in the real world. Experiencing multiple expressive modalities or using the same expressive modality in each session – the children and adolescents find new endings, develop solutions, and may find meaning to their troubles, worries, pains, and losses.

The Rich Field of Expressive Therapies

The expressive therapies field contains varied experts. Play therapists need to be informed about the variety of professionals present in the field; each with specialties and certifications in the different modalities of expressive therapies. The graphic lists essential associations by the modality and the website for more specific information. It is important to honor each of these expert modalities and the value they bring to Expressive Therapies as a valued treatment modality for clients seeking healing and hope in mental health care (Figure 13.2).

Dr. Bruce Perry (2006) developed the Neurosequential Model of Therapeutics (NMT), an innovative approach to the treatment of trauma. It is crucial for play therapists to ensure the youth is regulated first and that the relational and cognitive goals set are at the youth's developmental age. Dr. Perry noted in an interview in 2012 with Laura MacKinnon:

> *Rhythm is regulating. All cultures have some form of patterned, repetitive rhythmic activity as part of their healing and mourning rituals — dancing, drumming, and davening (swaying slightly while reciting liturgical prayers). Many interesting programs have developed around the use of pattern repetitive motor activity, drumming, rhythmic breathing (as in yoga), and a variety of other somatosensory activities as simple as walking that turn out to be effective with dysregulated children, youth and adults.*
>
> (MacKinnon, 2012, para 19-21)

This highlights the benefits of play, dance/movement, music, and drama therapies and the value they provide in the healing of trauma. In a study of children (approximately age eight) coping with hospital stays, Siegel et al. (2016) found that those children who engaged in an expressive arts activity versus those on a waitlist noted improvements in mood after the therapy sessions. A study by Hill and Lineweaver (2016) concluded that art intervention completed by individual children significantly decreased negative affect over other non-art interventions in the treatment of grief. Telemental play therapy gives the clinician the opportunity to treat youth no matter where they reside – in hospital, at a rural or distant location, or at home.

Dr. Cathy Malchiodi (2020), in using arts, imagination, and play in integrative ways, helps clients to reimagine their narratives especially trauma and loss. Trauma is a full body experience. It often needs a full body approach to work through the trauma. The ability to provide expressive therapies in play allows for curiosity to explore. Curiosity allows for risk taking. Taking risks allows one to face their fears. Expressive modalities allow one to face the

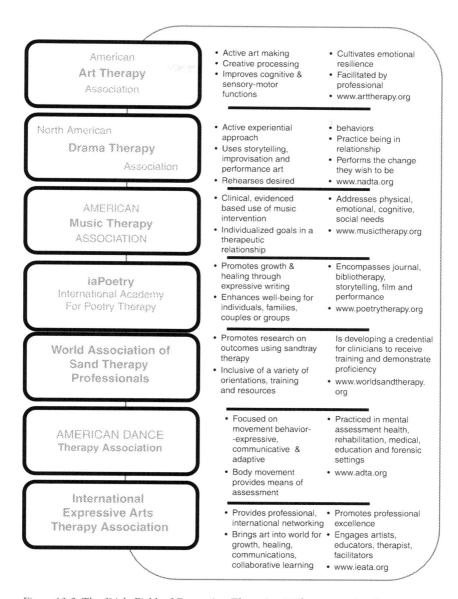

Figure 13.2 The Rich Field of Expressive Therapist. Different creative therapy organizations.

fears in multiply modalities. This ultimately creates an opportunity to trust oneself again. Restoring one's self trust develops a sense of self-efficacy and the freedom to express one's self more fully and authentically. All these expressive modalities can be experienced through teleplay.

Ethics with Expressive Therapies in Teleplay

Stoll et al. (2020) identified six ethical challenges in delivering telepsychiatry/psychotherapy. These include data security, privacy, confidentiality, clinical safety, competency, and preparedness for clinicians, legal and regulatory and financial concerns, informed consent, and social justice concerns. These are all important in telemental health/teleplay. There are some special ethical considerations when using expressive therapies play therapists should be considering.

Clinicians need to collaborate with parent/caregivers in accessing applications on devices. Downloading free or low fee applications on devices can be challenging and, in most cases, need adult permission and assistance. It's a best practice is to test run the applications before you recommend them to a family. Watch out for in-application purchase requirements, inappropriate content for youth or sharing opportunities which should be monitored so sensitive creations are not posted.

Clinicians must assess the therapist–client relationship when assessing a client for telemental health play sessions. Developing a rapport with the youth for an online relationship is as critical as the engagement of the youth in expressive therapy interventions. A child or teen who is unable to engage on the screen or to participate via telemental health play therapy will need to be reevaluated.

Difficulty in building a rapport in telemental health play therapy brings up a vital point: potential client abandonment. If a youth is unable to prosper using the telemental health platform, we are now in a therapeutic relationship and are responsible to provide continuity of care to that youth. Options to maintain this therapeutic relationship and provide the continuity of care include moving into co-play, working with the parent/guardian and youth, seeking supervision, looking at alternative treatment plans, changing approaches in play therapy assessments and goals, redefining the course of therapy, or transitioning back to face-to-face treatment. Lastly, one may need to refer out, but until the youth is connected, continuity of care is critical.

Finally, play therapists must be responsible in maintaining expressive therapy digital assets – art, poetry, photos, video recordings of play, dance, drama, sandtrays. Taking any photos or videos should only be acquired with a formal written consent. The clinician is responsible for the protection and management of digital assets that are in their possession. Use of a secure email is key and storing digital assets on secured servers like Dropbox, Google Drive, OneDrive, or other secure cloud servers is a best practice as well as uploading assets into a client's electronic record. Deleting digital assets that are not stored securely is also important. Confidentiality is a key ethical concern in managing digital assets for youth.

Applied Telemental Health Play Therapy: A Case Example

Jamal, the youngest of two siblings, is a mixed-race eight-year-old boy of African American and South Asian descent. He was referred to therapy for underperforming academically. Jamal presented with communication issues in expressive language and reading. Jamal is receiving services from resource and speech. These services were initially provided at school and are now, online via Zoom. Jamal rarely interacts with the resource teacher. Jamal's mother reports that he struggles with social aspects of being asked to read aloud and feels embarrassed to do other resource activities in the group. A quiet child, Jamal, was often by alone on the playground and lunch. Jamal would communicate with his mother, but had only limited communication with his sister, Jaszel, or his father. Since the pandemic, Jamal has withdrawn further; fearful of the virus and reluctant to leave the house.

Jamal's father is authoritarian while mother is authoritative in her approach with Jamal. Mom seems successful with soft, gentle coaxing, leading Jamal to comply with homework and, often, in leaving the house. However, his tantrums had worsened. During the telemental health intake, his mother disclosed that Jamal suffered hypoxia post-delivery and this may have resulted in a neuro-developmental trauma, Social (pragmatic) Communication Disorder (SCD).

With this potential diagnosis, we agreed to try telemental health play therapy. Jamal was functioning below the developmental level for his age. His withdrawn behavior intertwined with tantrums and the lack of communicating at school, on Zoom and at home, created challenges in his daily living. I approached the case from Prescriptive Play Therapy Approach, (Kaduson et al., 2019) integrating Child Centered Play Therapy (CCPT), Directive Play Therapy, Attachment Theory, and NMT with ETC. Our goals: to develop a therapeutic alliance, build attachment, and work to develop the treatment plan with the bottom-up approach. Further, I developed an individualized treatment for Jamal taking into consideration his specific needs, cultural needs, and personality. I focused the goals of treatment on the *Therapeutic Powers of Play: 20 Core Agents of Change*, (Schaefer & Drewes, 2013) facilitating communication with self-expression through sandtray, direct teaching and indirect teaching. I fostered emotional wellness with positive emotions and stress management and enhancing social relationships by focusing on building a positive therapeutic relationship and working on attachment with parents.

I proceeded with a multimodal approach of integrating expressive therapies, working with the ETC model observing each expressive intervention for the balance of kinesthetic/sensory, perceptual/affective, and cognitive/symbolic levels. I also included family psychoeducation, school psychoeducation, and conjoint sessions with mother and son, as well as father and son, to strengthen attachments. I designed interventions matching his specific developmental needs and continued assessing regularly to monitor progress and update the goals and the treatment.

We started with the Family Genogram assessment tool. Jamal's mom bought Minecraft figures and provided a tray of sand. Even though Jamal used few words in the initial sessions, it was fruitful. I created a family genogram with large circles and squares to have room for Jamal's figures. The form was then securely emailed to his mother for printing and given to Jamal for use with the family genogram intervention. Jamal chose the Minecraft figure *Steve* as himself. *Steve* is human and does not say anything. He is extraordinarily strong and a great jumper. He chose *Drowned* as his father. *Drowned* can attack and kill a mob. *Enderman*, who Jamal chose as his sister, is a neutral mob that can teleport and will only attack if it makes eye contact with the player. Lastly, Jamal chose *Villager* as his mother; this character is a passive mob that lives, works, and interacts in the village. (These are simplistic explanations of the characters roles and powers). I asked if any of his characters would like to share. He said, "No". In assessment, this is not unusual, especially in this case. Knowing a bit about the case, the characters and their roles gave me a potential glimpse into dynamics.

After the assessment phase, Jamal had the option to choose anything in his room including art supplies or toys he liked, for our sessions. The sandtray was available on his table with all the figures visible. He chose the Minecraft characters again. He was silent as he built his scene in the sandtray. I mirrored my sandtray to his sandtray. Mirroring my tray and miniatures to Jamal's story in the sand. This would be considered parallel play. A process by which therapist and child are playing alone, side by side, not interacting. He circled the characters facing one another, added a green dragon and beads covered by a cup. We explored the tray to see if characters in the tray wanted to share anything. "No" he said. At the end he said, "that was fun!" He decided that he wanted to meet again.

After, I set up a telemental health session with the parents. We discussed psychoeducation for them regarding developmental trauma. I provided handouts on developmental trauma, soothing tools, and approaches to tantrum behaviors. We also discussed involving the school and decided to provide handouts to the school. These meetings were all completed on a telemental health platform, consents were signed, and documents were emailed to the provider on secure emails.

The telemental play continued with sandtray play using the Minecraft characters for six more meetings. Each session Jamal's interaction in his sandtray stories grew as did his communication with me. Mom would come in after the teleplay session and Jamal had an option to share his tray. His wishes were respected and thus encouraged him to develop communication, personal strength, and resilience.

Each sandtray session, built upon the last, miniatures were added, and more action entered the tray. For example, circle of Minecraft characters, turned into lined of characters, trees and mountains where added. On the fifth session a battle theme emerged: one character, *Enderman*, was being snowed on and taken by *Drowned* to the drowned pool in the sandtray. Eventually, this character was noted to be a bully that hurt others. The solution provided by Jamal was not to look at this bully and to avoid the bully's wrath. After this session, Jamal identified the bully as his older sister. He expressed his strategy that if he remains small, inconspicuous, and silent, no one will bother him. This issue was explained to the parents; they confirmed this was a concern of theirs. We worked on strategies and shared psychoeducational material on bullying as well as options for coping with the bullying behavior which included referring the sister to play therapy.

In addition, connections were made with the parents regarding culture, parenting styles, and the family's generational experiences regarding immigration and racism. The father recognized that his parenting style often ends in yelling when Jamal withdraws. He was hopeful for a renewed relationship with his son.

Our goal with Jamal's mother was to help her remain supportive while encouraging Jamal to develop personal strength and boundaries. Teleplay commenced with them doing the *Where Do I Feel?* intervention. They shared their drawings, where they labeled their feelings by color on the body drawings and shared what they drew and where on their body they felt these feelings.

With Jamal and his mother, I introduced the *Bilateral Scribbling Intervention: Neurosequential Art Approach*. I had them sit face-to-face – each having a plain white paper and two different colored crayons. Using both hands at the same time, Mom led, and Jamal followed by mirroring her scribbles. Then, Jamal led, and Mom followed the same pattern. This activity develops mirroring, attachment, and downregulation helpful for Jamal's neurodevelopmental trauma.

Next, we engaged in the intervention *Groove Like Me!* Mom and Jamal took turns playing a song on mom's phone and we all took turns following dance movements and mirroring them back. We chose to all dance Jamal's movement sequence together as a group. After *Groove Like Me!* and taking time to breathe, we processed what they felt in their bodies by looking at their initial *Where Do I Feel?* intervention. This brings the activity full circle. Jamal was energized yet calm and his mother was smiling. Both were engaged with looking at their *Where Do I Feel?* handout. Mom decided to add to her *Where Do I Feel?* handout in her arms and legs but not Jamal, he was ready to end the teleplay, as swimming was next, and he was ready to go!

With the father and son, my goal was to promote a stronger bond and develop the father's understanding that his son has his own capabilities, specifically with gaming and computers. This provided an opportunity for me to use the *Virtual Sandtray*®© Application with its remote play option. One of the most exciting elements was watching the son and the father communicate and relate. Dad was learning how to connect the VSA with Jamal. Jamal was learning how to choose objects to put in the VSA from Dad. I observed; watching their relational play. I found this to be a pivotal teleplay session as the son had limited interaction with his father before. In this tel-etherapy session, I saw Dad and son smile, laugh, and solve problems together.

Jamal completed 15 teleplay sessions. His symptoms – communication issues, tantrums, and withdrawal – decreased markedly. School remained challenging; however, a new resource aid helped improve communication for Jamal. Dad reported more ease in his relationship with Jamal and Mom reported improvement in Jamal's participation in communicating and participating in the family. "He's playful and funny!" They will continue to monitor the sibling relationship. At termination, during an at-home cupcake party, Jamal stated quietly that "therapy wasn't so bad!" He stated that "it was fun to play!" Lastly, he reported he might come back if he needs help in the future.

Conclusion

Ultimately, expressive therapies in telemental health play therapy provide efficacy in the treatment for a multitude of issues for youth. Understanding the pros and cons of telemental health play therapy and how to pivot from tradition application of expressive play therapy to the use of expressive teletherapy is crucial for successful outcomes with youth. By applying both the Therapeutic Powers of Play: 20 core agents of change and the Expressive Therapies Continuum into teletherapy sessions, clinicians can better understand how to develop treatment plans and help a client process through expressive therapy interventions. Understanding the ethics in the application of telemental health play therapy is essential from confidentiality and informed consent to digital asset management and more. If done ethically, deliberately, and intentionally, telemental health play therapy provides an opportunity to reach youth safely and can assist them, using expressive therapies modalities, to reach their appropriate developmental trajectories in this current pandemic climate and beyond.

References

Baker, L. (2019). Therapy in the digital age. In J. Stone (Ed.), *Integrating technology into modern therapies: A clinicians guide to developments and interventions* (pp. 37–47). New York: Routledge.

Burns, R. C., & Kaufman, S. H. (1970). *Kinetic family drawings (K-F-D): An introduction to understanding children through kinetic drawings*. Brunner/Mazel.

Chapman, L. (2014). *Neurobiologically informed trauma therapy with children and adolescents: Understanding mechanisms of change (Norton series on interpersonal neurobiology)*. W. W. Norton & Company.

Csikszentmihalyi, M. (1990). *Flow: The psychology of optimal experience*. Harper & Row.

Gil, E. (2016). *Play in family therapy* (2nd ed.). Guilford Publications.

Google, LLC. (2019). *Just a line – draw in AR*. App Store. https://apps.apple.com/us/app/just-a-line-draw-in-ar/id1367242427

Hill, K. E., & Lineweaver, T. T. (2016). Improving the short-term affect of grieving children through art. *Art Therapy, 33*(2), 91–98. https://doi.org/10.1080/07421656.2016.1166414 https://www.tandfonline.com/doi/pdf/10.1080/07421656.2016.1166414?needAccess=true

Kaduson, H. G., Cangelosi, D., & Schaefer, C. E. (2019). *Prescriptive play therapy: Tailoring interventions for specific childhood problems*. Guilford Publications.

Kolodny, P. (2020a) The evolution of trauma therapy and its relevance to art therapy. In P. Quinn (Ed.), *Art therapy in the treatment of addiction and trauma* (pp. 89–114). London, and Philadelphia: Jessica Kingsley Publishers.

Kolodny, P. (2020b) Healing addiction and trauma with the expressive therapies continuum and a neurosequential art approach. In P. Quinn (Ed.), *Art therapy in the treatment of addiction and trauma* (pp. 115–134). London, and Philadelphia: Jessica Kingsley Publishers.

Lowenfeld, M. (2005). *Understanding children's Sandplay: Lowenfeld's world technique*. Sussex Academic Press.

Lusebrink, V. B. (1991). A systems-oriented approach to the expressive therapies: The expressive therapies continuum. *The Arts in Psychotherapy, 18*(5), 395–403. https://doi.org/10.1016/0197-4556(91)90051-b

MacKinnon, L. (2012). The Neurosequential model of therapeutics: An interview with Bruce Perry. *Australian and New Zealand Journal of Family Therapy, 33*(03), 210–218. https://doi.org/10.1017/aft.2012.26

Malchiodi, C. A. (2006). *Expressive therapies*. Guilford Press.

Malchiodi, C. A. (2008). *Creative interventions with traumatized children* (1st ed.). Guilford Press.

Malchiodi, C. A. (2020). *Trauma and expressive arts therapy: Brain, body, and imagination in the healing process*. Guilford Publications.

Perry, B. D. (2006). Applying principles of neurodevelopment to clinical work with maltreated and traumatized children: The neurosequential model of therapeutics. In N. B. Webb (Ed.), *Social work practice with children and families. Working with traumatized youth in child welfare* (pp. 27–52). The Guilford Press.

QuiverVision. (n.d.). QuiverVision. https://quivervision.com/products

Schaefer, C. E., & Drewes, A. A. (2013). *The therapeutic powers of play: 20 core agents of change*. John Wiley & Sons.

Siegel, J., Iida, H., Rachlin, K., & Yount, G. (2016). Expressive arts therapy with hospitalized children: A pilot study of co-creating healing sock creatures©. *Journal of Pediatric Nursing, 31*(1), 92–98. https://doi.org/10.1016/j.pedn.2015.08.006

Slayton, S. C., D'Archer, J., & Kaplan, F. (2010). Outcome studies on the efficacy of art therapy: A review of findings. *Art Therapy, 27*(3), 108–118. https://doi.org/10.1080/07421656.2010.10129660

Southwell, J. (2016). Using 'Expressive therapies' to treat developmental trauma and attachment problems in preschool-aged children. *Children Australia, 41*(2), 114–125. https://doi.org/10.1017/cha.2016.7

Stoll, J., Sadler, J. Z., & Trachsel, M. (2020). The ethical use of Telepsychiatry in the COVID-19 pandemic. *Frontiers in Psychiatry, 11*. https://doi.org/10.3389/fpsyt.2020.00665

Stone, J. (2015). The Virtual Sandtray App®. https://www.sandtrayplay.com/Press/VirtualSandtrayArticle01.pdf

14 Nature Play Therapy and Telemental Health: How Green Time and Screen Time Play Well Together

Jamie Lynn Langley

Time spent in nature can be such a powerful experience for healing, comfort, and connection. Even more, play in nature offers children endless opportunities to explore and discover. These playful adventures in nature often lead to feelings of wonder and awe, which are far too often in short supply. As children spend more time indoors there has been a more prevalent disconnection from nature. There are concerns, backed by growing research, that this lack of play outdoors and in nature is contributing to a decline in emotional and physical wellness (Louv, 2008). The response to these concerns has been implementation of programs on local, national, and international levels to increase the awareness of the need for "green time". For children, this is often aligned with having opportunities to play outside in nature. This has also inspired therapists to include nature in provision of play therapy.

Traditional play therapy theories generally involve carefully selected toys, a playroom or play space, and a trained play therapist to hold the space for the client to play to express and explore feelings and issues (Landreth, 2012). Nature Play Therapy is a modality in which the play therapist can go outside with the child and utilize nature's toys and a natural playground for the therapeutic play or when items from nature can be brought into the playroom. The Therapeutic Powers of Play, as first identified by Drs. Charles Schaefer in 1993 and then later expanded upon by Schaefer and Drewes (2014), include the agents of change which are inherent in play therapy. These change agents can be activated indoors or outside. A play therapist can apply theoretical applications to nature play therapy which can be offered on a spectrum of structure needed from non-directive to directive just as in traditional play therapy. Given this, there may be times that a child is directing the play outside in nature or inside using nature items, with the play therapist following the child's lead. At other times, nature-based activities may be suggested by the play therapist, most often in a prescriptive or intentional practice.

COVID-19 brought in a new set of challenges in many areas, one such being translating activities involving nature while doing therapy over a screen. This chapter will explore how nature play therapy can be adapted

DOI: 10.4324/9781003166498-14

and utilized in telemental health to continue to meet the diverse needs of children and families in challenging situations such as a pandemic health crisis and beyond.

Research and Support

Ecotherapy, also referred to as "nature therapy" and "green therapy", is the umbrella for mental health therapies involving nature (Buzzell & Chalquist, 2009). From its emergence in the mid-1990s, it has been an increasingly growing movement. Introducing nature as part of play therapy followed soon after. As such it is not new, although it has recently gained a resurgence of awareness. As Dr. Kaduson recently stated in the book *Play Therapy Theories and Perspectives*: "Nature is part of play therapy because it is in all of us". (Kaduson, 2020, p 103). Despite these practices, the utilization of nature in play therapy has historically not been included in traditional play therapy trainings and writings.

Research has indicated that participating actively in nature is often associated with a decrease in anger, stress, and anxiety along with an increase in optimism and self-esteem (Buzzell & Chalquist, 2009). The roots of nature play therapy thrive on the benefits of nature for humans of all ages and stages, especially for children. Richard Louv is a journalist and naturalist who "sounded an alarm", so to speak, by correlating the decreasing time for children to be outside in nature with the growing concerns of their diminishing mental and physical wellness. In 2005, he identified this disparity as "Nature Deficit Disorder" in the first edition of his book: *Last Child in the Woods: Saving Our Children from Nature Deficit Disorder* (Louv, 2008). This designation essentially ignited a child and nature movement around the world with significantly more research conducted in this area over the last 15 years. The Children & Nature Network, co-founded by Louv, currently lists over a thousand research studies involving children and the benefits of nature.

The studies that are particularly impactful for play therapists are those which have indicated play in nature positively impacts coping mechanisms such as resilience, creative thinking, and executive functioning, and include focus and regulation (Ernst & Burcak, 2019). Dr. Jacqueline Shank has led research regarding children and nature via Nature-Based Child-Centered Play Therapy done either with bringing nature objects inside as the play materials (Swank et al., 2020) or by going outside using these nature elements as play materials. Separate studies found encouraging results including the improvement of attention (Swank & Smith-Adcock, 2018) and self-esteem (Swank & Shin, 2015a.) There has also been a study about Nature-Based Child-Centered Group Play Therapy which indicated that time in nature improved on-task behaviors and decreased problematic behaviors (Swank et al., 2017).

Drs. Janet Courtney and Joyce Mills are both play therapists who have referred to nature as their "co-therapist" in healing practices (Courtney 2020; Courtney 2017; Courtney & Mills, 2016). As can be seen from the review of studies and literature, this modality has been referred to under various titles such as Nature-Based Play Therapy, as well as including specific theoretical-based approaches such as Nature-Based Child-Centered Play Therapy (Swank & Shin, 2015b) and Nature-Based Child-Centered Group Play Therapy (Swank et al., 2017). Several play therapists including this author are now referring to this intentional modality of including nature and/or nature items in play therapy as Nature Play Therapy (Langley, 2019).

Transition to Telemental Health

Despite the growing interest in nature play therapy, the COVID-19 pandemic posed some interesting challenges. While there were a few therapists doing telemental health before the pandemic, they were more the exception than the rule. As many play therapists quickly changed to telemental health services to meet the needs of clients, they were also looking for ways to adapt their practices to virtual translations. For play therapists wanting to continue providing nature-based activities, there were initial concerns if this could even happen over a screen.

At this same time, families were finding themselves being together within the confines of their home more than ever before. A response to being inside so much and away from normal activity for some was to find ways to get outside. Children and families began experiencing nature near to them in their backyards, courtyards, or neighborhoods. This provided some opportunities to naturally bring in more nature-based activities.

Implementing nature play therapy over telemental health does include a few challenges. First, access to nature is a strong consideration. There may be limited availability to nature, particularly during certain weather conditions. In addition, the child or adolescent may need time to be out in nature and for some this will require a parent or caregiver close by. This may include taking devices outside which involves a potential risk to such devices. Other considerations are that clients may need preparation time to gather items from nature to include in telemental health sessions. Therapists also need to be prepared for the adventures they may be taken on. This may include being rocked in a swing, jumped alongside on a trampoline, or being taken along for a nature walk or game. There are times a child may play something adventuresome or risky that could concern a play therapist not in a position to be able to necessarily provide a safe environment from the confines of being on a screen rather than in person. Reviewing safety measures with parents and caregivers is often necessary, to discuss possible risks and to explore safety precautions.

Before exploring specific interventions, it is good to review the inherent therapeutic values for a child of simply going outside to play, especially in nature. This "green time" can be highly therapeutic – especially given recent circumstances of a global pandemic. Children and adolescents are spending much more time inside for both learning and playing, often while sitting, usually focused on a screen of some type. Large numbers are doing virtual learning at home while parents and caregivers are also working from home. This usually entails more rules to navigate these circumstances, which often lead to less movement and more volume-control. In addition, clients are often tasked with keeping their hands continually washed and having sanitizer in proximity for anything touched. Between more confinement and rules, children need free play now more than ever. Thankfully, they can go outside and be loud! They can touch the dirt, sticks, and trees and have free play. In the outdoors they can get dirty, roll around on the ground, make mud pies, and just literally unwind with this wonderful messy play. Much stress can be alleviated with this natural non-directed play, especially when parents and caregivers can step back and allow this free play to happen. Children often then get to experience awe, wonder, and delight which encompasses the positive emotional experience that can be a significant therapeutic power of play. In addition, a therapist and child can experience these positive nature play opportunities together, forging a stronger child–therapist relationship.

There is an unexpectedness that can happen with play therapy conducted outside in nature, which is different from the predictability of an indoor playroom. A worm may be seen on the ground, a butterfly may perch on a flower, a bird may begin to sing, or the wind may blow something away. It is particularly affirming to see the most attention-challenged child naturally become focused on a crawling insect – especially when equipped with a magnifying glass. Already in this scenario the child is experiencing self-regulation, positive emotions, and potentially empathy within this exploratory play. This unexpectedness may also at times change the course of an activity. A play therapist utilizing outdoor nature experiences needs to be prepared for change and even at times interruption due to these diversions. Having appropriate weather attire is another instrumental piece to successful nature interventions.

Putting together a nature play kit is also advantageous prior to conducting any nature-based activities. What has been found to work well is a drawstring bag that holds items useful for nature play and exploration including binoculars, a magnifying glass, tweezers, insect net, small shovel, compass, whistle, and sunglasses. Other additions may include paper, crayons, colored pencils, a journal, and a camera.

Nature Play Therapy Activities and Interventions

When considering applications for nature-based activities and interventions, a play therapist needs to understand the theoretical basis for doing so. Nature play therapy can be utilized both as a client-centered modality or along a more directive continuum. As a prescriptive play therapist, this author uses a variety of applications along this continuum of structure depending upon the need of the client at that point in time. As a child's needs change, this prescriptive approach can be reflective of that (Schaefer, 2003). There are times a client may need to lead their own play, as well as other times when a play therapist may ascertain a particular therapeutic activity is suitable for a particular need or issue. Clinical sight is always on the child, even when applying a directive intervention, so the play therapist continues to be child focused. All nature play therapy activities are grounded in the therapeutic powers of play and often several nature-based activities can be brought into play, depending upon the clinical needs of the client.

Nature-Based Creative and Expressive Arts Activities

Children and adolescents can be highly creative when given the opportunity. With nature as a play space, these opportunities for creativity are truly endless. In a standard playroom, children often play in a traditional way with the toys provided. Nature's playground, however, is free from those types of expected play. As an example, a stick is easily nature's most imagination-inspired "toy" in that it can be a magic wand, a canoe paddle, a sword, a writing instrument, a horse- and whatever else the child imagines. A play therapist can follow the child's play, facilitating when needed, even while over a screen. This free play provides the child or adolescent to have a sense of independence that lends itself to several therapeutic powers of play such as self-expression, creative problem-solving, self-esteem building, and enhancing positive emotions.

There are many additional capacities to be creative with nature both indoors and outside. One of the best ways to accomplish this is with "loose parts play" using nature items. Loose parts play is more well known in Europe, especially in England. It is based upon the premise: "In any environment, both the degree of inventiveness and creativity, and the possibility of discovery, are directly proportional to the number and kind of variables in it". (Nicholson, 1971). In other words, it can be all types of loose things: big and small, natural, or synthetic. These parts are not toys per se, but instead various items brought together to be creative with. When using selections from nature for this type of creative play, one could think of them as like nature's LEGO®s, in that all kinds of things can be built and created from the items. The gathering of the items can be done during a telemental health session outside or could be selected by the client ahead of time and then brought in, or a combination thereof. Nature items chosen could include leaves, twigs, stones, acorns, flowers, feathers, shells, pieces of bark, blades of grass, pinecones, and similar. If the play is remaining outside, larger items could be included. There are no directions for this type of play the child or adolescent creates using only their imagination as a guide. Some children may also choose to put their selected items in dirt as part of their outdoor play experience. In this case the play often becomes much like a sand tray activity, utilizing the items in the dirt in symbolic ways as well as regulating activities like sifting and smoothing the dirt. As in sand therapy, this type of play can provide access to the unconscious as another therapeutic power of play utilized. As the client is playing and creating, a play therapist can continue to observe, as well as interact, by offering facilitative comments as appropriate. This type of creative play also often involves therapeutic powers of play such as positive emotions, self-esteem building, creative problem-solving, self-regulation, and resilience.

These nature items can also be utilized with creating mandalas. Nature mandalas are a personal favorite, as in addition to creativity they also involve self-regulation which many youth can benefit from. A mandala is a circle with a center, known as a bindu, often referencing wholeness. The words "mandala" and "bindu" are from an ancient Sanskrit language, indicating that mandalas have been utilized for centuries in various cultures and religions (Turner-Bumberry, 2015). Mandalas are present throughout nature from flowers such as daisies and sunflowers to spider webs, circular seashells and even the sun. A client can be introduced to mandalas in nature using the resource *The Mandala Book: Patterns of the Universe* by Lori Cunningham (2020). The client can take a mandala walk in nature and look for mandalas. Children are usually enthused to locate them, bringing in the sense of wonder and awe with those discoveries. Their digital devices can be brought along for the therapist utilizing telemental health to accompany them on this discovery walk. Pictures of mandalas found can be taken with the device or camera or they can be drawn. These can then be placed in a nature journal that can be shared in a telemental health session.

The creation of a mandala is frequently associated with mindfulness and is popular within expressive therapies. A nature mandala can be created outdoors or nature items can be brought indoors. Children and adolescents alike enjoy making these nature mandalas and often ask to make new ones each session. When doing these sessions indoors over telemental health, calming nature music can be played as the mandala is being formed by the client. This often provides a more relaxed experience, allowing the creator to take the time needed to make the mandala. At times younger children will tend to rush through an activity and may need to be guided to slow down for more of a therapeutic effect of the experience. In whatever way nature mandalas are incorporated, they can include several therapeutic powers of play such as self-regulation, self-esteem building, and creative problem-solving. When nature mandalas are made as part of a group or family therapeutic activity, then additional therapeutic powers of play can include social competence and attachment. Children and adolescents alike often want to take a picture of their mandala creation which can be shared virtually as well as made a part of the client file when using electronic records.

There are also simple expressive art activities that can be utilized with nature items involving similar therapeutic powers of play. Taking leaves and placing under paper, and then using crayons to make leaf rubbings is both creative and calming. Designs can be made by specific placement of leaves under the paper. The play therapist can participate as well in a parallel play type of experience. This helps to achieve more connectedness in the relationship over a screen. Near this author's desk sits a basket of nature items, upon which selections can be made for any such parallel play activities. A few other creative options for activities using nature items is by dipping twigs, leaves, and other items in paint and painting pictures with them. Other nature items such as pinecones and acorns can be painted as well.

Additional creative activities with nature items include making creatures, critters, and dolls. Depending upon the therapeutic need, these interventions may be guided by the play therapist, so these may have a little more structure involved. For example, the therapist may be working with a child who is anxious and suggests making a comfort critter out of the nature items. Clay or playdough can be included in these and other formations. An example of this therapeutic activity could be working with a child who is fearful of insects. Having the child make a representation of the insect can provide a projective opportunity to play about and with the object of concern in a safe way. This involves the therapeutic power of play of counterconditioning fears. Creatures, animals, and people can also be made by gluing leaves and twigs to construction paper. One such favorite is making nature monsters out of rocks and leaves. A monster face can be drawn on stones and then have various leaves glued on the top part of the stones. The nature monsters can be adapted as needed as worry monsters, angry monsters, and more for a variety of directive therapeutic activities that can be adapted for telemental health.

Dolls or puppets can be made with sticks and twine by both client and therapist providing further narrative play opportunities over telemental health. There have also been opportunities where acorns have been used to make family members as they already come with a hat! Then it can be as simple as adding a face to the acorn with a marker. Sets can be created for nature backdrops, one such being a fairy house, which can be put together inside with supplies or outside in discovered areas. Progressive storytelling is one example of a narrative way to utilize the nature dolls. It is constructed by client and therapist taking turns back and forth to see where the direction of the story goes. This is also a time to let the child be in the driver's seat, directing how they want to use the dolls and what type of stories or play to do. This further enhances their creativity and may then delve into areas as needed. This type of play can involve additional therapeutic powers of play such as catharsis and abreaction when scenarios are played out and experienced in a projective, and thus safer, way for the client.

Rocks can be easily found and used for expressive art activities. In addition to building and creating with them, rocks can be painted with colors to represent feelings and can have favorite words or affirmations written or painted on them. Such painted rocks make great bindus for nature mandalas as well. Rocks provide a sense of grounding just by being held – giving a child a pleasurable experience with touch, which is beneficial and needed (Courtney, 2020).

Nature-Based Games and Connection Activities

Many game play activities can be held outdoors using elements of nature, as well as by bringing nature items to play with inside. These activities may also involve some creative thinking, but additional purposes include connection, trust, and at times cooperation, as with typical game play. Often the therapeutic powers of play incorporated with these types of games and activities include positive emotions, stress management, therapeutic relationship, attachment, social competence, empathy, creative problem solving, moral development, accelerated psychological development, self-regulation, self-esteem, and other therapeutic powers of play (Stone 2020Stone & Schaefer 2020). No wonder play therapists often like to utilize games! Most of these games and activities are also very adaptable for groups and families, including siblings.

A quick and easy nature-based game example is Tic-Tac-Toe. Sticks or twigs can be made to form a Tic-Tac-Toe game board, and then elements such as rocks, shells, or leaves serve as the "X's" and "O's". This is easily accomplished outdoors or inside, and over telemental health the client could make the board and the therapist indicate where their nature tokens would go. This simple game of back-and-forth play builds trust and connection between client and therapist while building self-esteem and positive emotions. It is also a great beginning game to help clients who are not as used to being outside with becoming more comfortable in doing so due to the simple nature and brevity of both the creation and play of this activity.

Follow-The-Leader is another easy game to do outside in nature. Having the child as the leader is an affirming position for the child, as they do not have many opportunities to be in control, particularly over adults. This works well with only a child and therapist, but also with a child and parents, siblings, and/or other adult caregivers. Children often particularly enjoy when they can do something an adult cannot, such as cartwheels. When this occurs, the therapist or adult can make the cartwheel motion with their hands, to indicate following the child but not able to do the activity. (Children love this and often laugh about this experience.) The client can bring the device outside to do their activities, and those therapists who can take their devices outside can join with them that way or adapt indoors as able. Another way to use this with telemental health is to be the observer and at times referee for families playing this game.

Nature scavenger hunts have been a favorite activity for several years, especially with families. (They were a fast favorite when play therapists first began telemental health as well!) Items being sought can be adapted for seasons, sensory experiences, colors, shape, and more. These scavenger hunts are easily conducted outside, but items can also be gathered and then brought inside for indoor play therapy or over telemental health. An alternative to collecting the nature items is to take pictures of found items. These scavenger hunts can be used additionally to have groups, families, and siblings address communication and cooperation as they work together to gather needed items which can also assist with connection to one another. They also assist executive function skills of focus and concentration. An adaption that promotes these latter skills even more is choosing a set number of nature items and displaying for one minute. Then cover them up and have the child see how many they can remember and go find them. This memory game works particularly well over telemental health, as the therapist can display the items over a screen and then the client can go locate in their area. It also can work the other way as well, with the child coming up with nature items for the play therapist to remember and find.

Nature I-Spy is another fun activity that can be easily incorporated as part of a nature walk. Sometimes younger children grow restless along a nature walk and having them "spy" or look out for a particular color, shape, or sound adds a fun element that is also sensory based. This adds to the regulation of the activity as well as executive function skills of focus and attunement. Having the nature play kit is especially helpful for this fun element of nature walks – where they can become more like nature adventures or missions. What child can resist the sound of that? Looking for those awe-inspiring occurrences in nature and often do not take long to find. Children and teens love to take pictures and videos. With a tablet or phone they can utilize them to keep track of items found and discovered along the way. (And a great way to pair some of the desired screen time with green time.) For any pictures taken or drawn, they can be added in a nature journal or scrapbook. Nature walks and adventures work for both one-on-one sessions as well as group and family sessions.

A final activity to mention is one that can be used indoors over the telemental health platform: a window walk. Have the client go from window to window and at each one state what they see, hear, and even smell (if the window can be opened). There are different views of nature from different windows and this activity invites self-regulation by viewing nature. They can show the play therapist their window views as well.

Ethical Considerations

Telemental health sessions require an informed consent before being practiced. The parameters of electronic platforms being used, as well as HIPAA compliance, need to be included. In addition, when outdoor sessions are an option, there are considerations to include for issues such as risk for going outside that need to be identified as well as any limits to confidentiality. The benefits of both telemental health and nature play therapy can be included in these informed consents as well.

In addition, play therapists should explore with a client and their parents/guardians regarding comfort level for being outside. For telemental health sessions, this would also include a review of what nature space is available, the security of the space, as well as parental approval for clients to take devices outside. This is also a good time to review ways for parents to be safely present but at more of a distance – thereby allowing a child freer play in nature (Sampson, 2015). Conducting sessions outside over telemental health may provide an element of felt safety when the therapist is present over the screen to interact and observe, but this is also limited in that the therapist presence is not an actual in-person physical presence. For younger children it is recommended a caregiver be within view of the child but far enough away for private dialogue between client and therapist. These safety considerations are necessary to review with parents and caregivers prior to conducting sessions outside. It is also discussed with the client to insure their understanding of limitations of the therapist while over a screen.

"Nature Ethics" are also necessary considerations. With this is the expectation that one should "leave no trace", meaning our presence is not to add or take away from natural surroundings. This is especially important when gathering items for the creative activities. Explaining to the client that one can "pick up" items that have fallen rather than "picking" items is an easy way to safely select nature items. In addition, limiting the amount of what is selected is advised as some objects such as acorns may be food sources, or others may be shelters for animals. Also advised is a "catch and release" practice in that materials no longer or not used are returned to their natural environment following the activity.

Case Example

Danny is a nine-year-old male whose parents reported an increased depressed mood and lethargy since the onset of the pandemic. He was doing virtual learning and indicated missing his friends from school. His parents were concerned about his lack of physical activity along with a growing amount of screen time with playing video games in addition to the virtual learning. Danny was hesitant when I suggested about going outside, as he indicated he did not like to play sports. I explained that going outside meant more than playing sports and called it "green time". My suggestion (with parental agreement) was that we could begin with an amount of green time that he could trade in for screen time with social video game play. He agreed and we began taking nature walks and then adventures. Since he participated in telemental health with a tablet, he was able to easily take this outside so that I could "accompany" him. We began with looking for colors and then shapes and later sounds. I would have him do nature scavenger hunts to find sensory things like something prickly or smooth. He began wanting to draw different things that he would see and discover. These can be done with drawing apps on the tablet as well. Since he enjoyed electronic devices, I also suggested he take pictures or videos with his phone of things he discovered. He also found that he liked to make mandalas both inside and outdoors. He would often have me make one and then he later would have me join his creations by asking me what I would want to place and where. I was able to direct my choice to him over the screen. This led to other types of creative play with drawing outside of sessions and sharing these during our session time. He also began taking his younger sister on some "nature missions" and planned a nature scavenger hunt for a family session.

The therapeutic powers of play involved were self-esteem, therapeutic relationship, creative problem solving, positive emotions, catharsis, stress management, and direct teaching. As these sessions were conducted over several months, Danny's depressed mood significantly decreased. He was also reporting more energy and was involved in more creative activities in his free time. Thus, our telemental health screen time and green time via nature play therapy played well together for the emotional benefit of the client.

Nature play therapy is a "dynamic duo" in that it combines nature's capacities for healing with the therapeutic powers of play. As described throughout this chapter, Nature Play Therapy is a modality that is very adaptable. It can be conducted indoors by bringing nature items in or be held outside where nature itself is the play space. In addition, nature play therapy can be as directive or non-directive as needed for the client and/or theoretical orientation of the play therapist. We have learned through necessity that nature play therapy can be conducted over telemental health, introducing nature to more children, adolescents, and their families. This access to nature for coping and healing has likely never been more important than during the COVID-19 pandemic. It will continue to be needed for the future as well.

References

Buzzell, L., & Chalquist, C. (Eds.) (2009). *Ecotherapy: Healing with nature in mind.* Counterpoint Publishing.

Courtney J. A., & Mills, J. C. (2016). Utilizing the metaphor of nature as co-therapist in StoryPlay. *Play Therapy, 11*(1), 18 – 21.

Courtney, J. A. (2017). The art of utilizing the metaphorical elements of nature as "co-therapist" in ecopsychology play therapy. In A. Kopytin & M. Rugh (Eds.) *Environmental expressive therapies: Nature-assisted therapy and practice* (pp. 100–122). Routledge.

Courtney, J. A. (2020). *Healing child and family trauma through expressive and play therapies: Art, nature, storytelling, body, mindfulness.* W. W. Norton & Co.

Cunningham, L. B. (2020). *The mandala book: Patterns of the universe.* Sterling.

Ernst, J., & Burcak, F., (2019). Young children's contributions to sustainability: The influence of nature play on curiosity, executive function skills, creative thinking, and resilience. *Sustainability, 11*(15), Art. no. 4212, doi:http://dx.doi.org/10.3390/su11154212

Kaduson, H. G. (2020). How do you incorporate nature in play therapy treatment? In R. Grant, Stone, J., & C. Mellenthin (Eds.), *Play therapy theories and perspectives* (p. 103). Routledge.

Landreth, G. L. (2012). *Play therapy the art of the relationship* (3rd ed.) New York, NY: Routledge.

Langley, J. L. (2019). Nature play therapy: When nature comes into play. *Playground*, Spring/Summer, 20–24. https://cacpt.com/wp-content/uploads/2019/04/Playground-Spring-2019.pdf

Louv, R. (2008). *Last child in the woods: Saving our children from nature-deficit disorder*. Algonquin Books.

Nicholson, S. (1971). How not to cheat children: The theory of loose parts. *Landscape architecture, 62*(1), 30–34.

Sampson, S. (2015). *How to raise a wild child: The art and science of falling in love with nature*. Houghton Mifflin Harcourt.

Schaefer, C. E. (2003). Prescriptive play therapy. In C. E. Schaefer (Ed.). *Foundations of play therapy* (pp. 306–320). Wiley.

Schaefer, C. E., & Drewes, A. A. (2014). *The therapeutic powers of play: 20 core agents of change* (2nd ed.). Wiley.

Stone, J., & Schaefer, C. E. (2020) *Game play: Therapeutic use of games with children and adolescents* (3rd ed.). Wiley.

Swank, J. M., Cheung, C., Prikhidko, A., & Su, Y. W. (2017). Nature-based child-centered group play therapy and behavioral concerns: A single-case design. *International Journal of Play Therapy, 26*(1), 47–57. https://doi.org/10.1037/pla0000031

Swank J. M., & Shin S. M. (2015a). Garden counseling groups and self-esteem: A mixed methods study with children with emotional and behavioral problems, *The Journal for Specialists in Group Work, 40*(3), 315–331. doi: https://doi.org/10.1080/01933922.2015.1056570

Swank J. M., & Shin S. M. (2015b). Nature-based child-centered play therapy: An innovative counseling approach. *International Journal of Play Therapy, 24*(3), 151–161. doi: http://dx.doi.org/10:1037/a0039127

Swank J. M., & Smith-Adcock, S. (2018). On task behavior of children with attention deficit and hyperactivity disorder: Examining treatment effectiveness of play therapy interventions. *International Journal of Play Therapy*. 27(4), 187–197. doi: http://dx.org/10.1037/pla0000084

Swank, J. M., Walker, K. L. A., & Shin, S. M. (2020). Indoor nature-based play therapy: Taking the natural world inside the playroom. *International Journal of Play Therapy, 29*(3), 155–162. https://doi.org/10.1037/pla0000123

Turner-Bumberry, T. (2015). *Finding meaning with mandalas: A therapist's guide to creating mandalas with children*. Turner Phrase Publishing.

15 The Universe of You: Using Remote VR to Improve Psychoeducation Through Spatial Presence, Attention Allocation, and Interaction

Ryan Kelly

Virtual Reality (VR) is arguably *the* innovative medium of tomorrow. VR related approaches to therapy have been repeatedly found to improve upon standard therapeutic interventions and education. Similarly, experts believe that psychoeducation, an essential component of the therapeutic process, should involve state-of-the-art technology where applicable. Research suggests that, in today's world, such "state-of-the-art technology" should include teletherapeutic applications and VR to capitalize on the benefits of spatial presence, involvement, and attention allocation. This chapter discusses the unique benefits of incorporating these technologies into telemental health therapy, including a descriptive, novel approach designed by the author called "The Universe of You", a (neuro) psychoeducational approach within VR which may be done in person or remotely. A case example and ethical considerations are included.

An inherent component of evidence-based therapy is psychoeducation, defined amply by Lukens and McFarlane (2004) in their article *Psychoeducation as Evidence-Based Practice: Considerations for Practice, Research and Policy*:

> "Psychoeducation is a professionally delivered treatment modality that integrates and synergizes psychotherapeutic and educational interventions. Many forms of psychosocial intervention are based on traditional medical models designed to treat pathology, illness, liability, and dysfunction. In contrast, psychoeducation reflects a paradigm shift to a more holistic and competence-based approach, stressing health, collaboration, coping, and empowerment (Dixon, 1999; Marsh, 1992). It is based on strengths and focused on the present. The patient/client and/or family are considered partners with the provider in treatment, on the premise that the more knowledgeable the care recipients and informal caregivers are, the more positive health-related outcomes will be for all."
> (page 206)

Psychoeducation may be in the form of skill training, communication styles, or personal discoveries, however, the clinician is ultimately a psychological guide holding a map and compass which derives from empirical studies. Whether the client is seeking guidance on how to better capitalize on their strengths or manage their clinically significant weaknesses, including psychoeducation regarding the brain and its functional manifestations through one's mind (i.e. feelings and thoughts) is essential; in fact, psychoeducation has been repeatedly found to be among the most effective of the evidence-based practices that have emerged in both clinical trials and community settings (Lukens & McFarlane, 2004). Successful psychoeducation depends largely on goodness of fit with the therapist, the ability and desire to pay attention, and a comprehensible and immersive learning experience. That being said, many studies on the positive effects of psychoeducation highlight the need for innovation in this area and the increased use of more emergent, state-of-the-art methods to integrate into therapy. In an age of virtual reality (VR), the use of such immersive technology is essential as a medium for capitalizing on "spatial presence" and the client's non-selective and selective attention.

VR can be defined as "the sum of the hardware and software systems that seek to perfect an all-inclusive, sensory illusion of being present in another environment" (Biocca & Delaney, 1995). In VR, a user utilizes some head-mounted display (HMD) ranging from something cheap and simple like a Google Cardboard (a cardboard box with VR lenses that one places their smart phone into) to something more expensive and complex like a wireless HTC-Vive Pro. Within the virtual environment, the user can see a 3D, 360-degree image around them to be perceived and oriented as if they were physically in the environment. Depending on the VR program, the environment may be traversable (i.e. it is an environment that you can fully explore through locomotion or teleportation) and interactive (e.g. you can interact with virtual items within the world as if they were real) like a VR video game, or simply a spectacle to experience like watching a live concert from the comfort of your home. Over the last 35 years, VR has been increasingly used in fields like real estate, gaming, medicine, and psychology, and continues to expand into other fields and manner of utility. For a more comprehensive review on the use and state of VR, read *Experience on Demand: What Virtual Reality Is, How It Works, and What It Can do* (Bailenson, 2018).

Presence

Ryan (2015) and Walsh and Pawlowski (2002) state that core characteristics of VR technologies include spatial presence, immersion, and interactivity. Spatial presence refers to the sense of "being there", even if experienced remotely through a "primary egocentric reference frame" (i.e. "this world is real and I am in it"), which VR has been shown to successfully be able to do neuropsychologically in place of a real environment (Witmer & Singer, 1998; Khenak et al., 2018). Interactivity can be described as the degree to which a user can modify the VR environment in real-time (Steuer, 1995). Together, through the use of VR, these components can improve the client's attention allocation, engagement, and retention of psychoeducation, which may improve related interventions. For a more comprehensive review on the benefits of using VR in therapy, read *Virtual Reality for Psychological and Neurocognitive Interventions* (Rizzo & Bouchard, 2019) and *Integrating Technology Into Modern Therapies: a Clinician's Guide to Developments and Interventions* (Stone, 2019).

Attention Allocation

Attention allocation is a fundamental prerequisite of any perception, as it determines what one processes from their environment for understanding their present state and future utilities. In other words, whatever is non-selectively or selectively chosen to be "perceived" is all that exists for the client. Attention allocation has be shown to be improved if the individual finds the information to be novel, surprising, complex (involuntary), interesting, and relevant (voluntary), which improves their experience and learning (Darken et al., 1998). VR has been used to improve traditional education for this reason and has even been described as the learning aid of the 21st century (Rogers, 2019).

Studies have often found that students retain more information, better apply what they've learned, have greater motivation, and have greater comprehension after participating in VR exercises compared to traditional educational methods (Krokos et al., 2019; Wang et al., 2018). Furthermore, in studies looking at VR in the learning context, research has found multiple characteristics of VR (e.g. animation routines, movement, simulations, multisensory input) that are particularly useful for certain subjects. Relevant to this chapter, Chavez and Bayona (2018) discovered that when learning about medicine (i.e. learning about the reaction of one's body or brain), "movement" is vital for learning, while "immersion interfaces" are more important as a way to learn through "lived experiences". Similar to previous studies, they also found 17 other positive effects of VR, including greater connection between conceptual understanding and reality, improved skills, and greater intrinsic motivation.

Interaction – A Unique Method for VR Psychoeducation and Intervention

With all of this information in mind, this author has created a unique approach to neuropsychoeducation through the use of virtual reality which may be used in person or remote, that may improve the clients' interest, attention, and recall. Ultimately, this may improve the client's learning about their brain (including affecting their thoughts, feelings, and behaviors) and the therapeutic effects of future related interventions. The psychoeducation and intervention requires at least 8x8 feet of space (both for safety and to capitalize on the evidence-based learning gains of "movement" with medical education) and some specific hardware and software as mentioned below:

Hardware

1. A clinician's unibody head-mounted display device (e.g. Oculus Quest 2, HTC Vive, Valve Index, etc.)
2. A client's unibody head-mounted display device (preferred, but optional)
3. For the VR users, a PC capable of supporting all features (e.g. 16 GB RAM+, Nvidia 1060+, i5 9600K+), otherwise any computer that can run video conferencing apps
4. A camera for use in telemental health, as in the camera used for telemental health sessions (for both parties)
5. A Bluetooth heart rate monitor like the Polar H10 (optional)
6. A Bluetooth EEG monitor like the MUSE EEG Headband (optional)

Software

1. **Google's Tilt Brush (required):** Tilt Brush lets you paint in 3D space with virtual reality. Clients can express themselves creatively with three-dimensional brush strokes, stars, light, fire, sculpting, and more. The environment and lighting of the "canvas" is customizable for better artistic expression. It is available for free on computer-based set-ups as well as in the Oculus store at a price of $19.99 for console play. Unfortunately, it does not hold a multiplayer function; however, it features the ability to import any number of still, moving, or 3D images, and allows you to create, save, and upload works into the "Poly Library" to share with or download from the community.
2. **Discord (optional):** Discord is a group-chatting platform originally built for gamers, but which has since become a general use platform for all sorts of communities. It is divided into servers, each of which has its own members, topics, rules, and channels. Discord also allows users to voice- and video-chat, as well as livestream games and other programs from their computers. ★Please refer to any applicable HIPAA compliance/confidentiality requirements before using any chat feature with clients.
3. **LIV (optional):** LIV is a leading mixed reality software to capture one's self, or their favorite avatar, in VR, and the highest performing live streaming chat & alerts utility app on Steam. Essentially, LIV allows for you to put yourself into the game for others to view in real-time or later in a recording.

4. **OVR Toolkit (required):** OVR Toolkit is a utility application designed to make viewing the desktop in VR simple and fast. It allows for viewing the desktop within VR, placing desktop windows around the world, mouse inputs, typing with a virtual keyboard, and quickly switching between windows. Within the context of this intervention, OVR Toolkit allows you to speak with (and see) your client while viewing through your headset in any VR program. It is available on Steam.
5. **A Video Conferencing App (required):** Apps like Zoom, Discord, Google Hangout, Theraplatform etc. *that allow screen sharing.* ★Please refer to any applicable HIPAA compliance/confidentiality requirements before using any telemental health platform with clients.
6. **Open Broadcast Software (OBS) (optional):** OBS is a free and open-source cross-platform streaming and recording program that allows you to record what is being displayed on your screen.

This book focuses on the telemental health remote use of VR; so, although in person is the preferred approach, this chapter will focus on interventions that can be done remotely. This intervention can be done in two ways. If the client has their own VR system at home, then have them download *Google Tilt Brush* and the *OVR toolkit*. At this point, you will have contacted this author and downloaded one of the pre-constructed brains to use and give the client access to it as well. For the example in this chapter, the pre-constructed brain used will be of an "anxious" brain, including the most relevant structures and pathways of a neurological stress response, perseveration, and general anxiety. After connecting with the client over your preferred secure face-to-face therapy app (e.g. *Zoom*), have them launch *OVR toolkit* and *Google Tilt Brush*. Walk the client through opening the brain image and setting up the OVR so that they may see and hear you while inside the game. You will be able to see them through their camera (watching them wearing the VR) and within the game (this can be done by the client sharing their screen through *Zoom* or an alternate app like *Discord* simultaneously). You will guide them remotely from your computer. If they agree to allow you to record the session for video-modeling (requires audio/video (AV) waiver and precautions to ensure the video is secure), you may do so using *OBS*, though this may begin to stretch the capabilities of their computer if it is an entry level PC or Mac.

If they do not have VR, I recommend that you switch roles. Assume the client's role as mentioned above, while they assume yours and watch you navigate through the brain "universe" on their computer. In this case, you may record yourself through *OBS* so that they may refer back to the video later, similar to the video-modeling. For either of these approaches, the LIV compositor may be used to "insert" the VR user into the application so that it looks like they are inside the world with the brain. In other words, during the observation or recording of the user interacting with the brain, the actual person will be visible in the virtual world rather than just the headset and controls.

VR Psychoeducation (Neuropsychology of Anxiety)

When entering the brain file, the VR user will find themselves on a virtual planet with a view of outer space above them, watching a massive translucent 30 foot long brain with eyes, ears, olfactory bulb, peripheral nervous system, and heart being drawn in the sky roughly 40 feet in front of and 30 feet above them. These primary structures appear opaque within the translucent structure, and include animation routines of neural pathways (e.g. sensory information flowing from sensory hardware, pulsing tubes connecting communicating structures, etc.) consistent with research. The clinician should begin with an explanation of this world similar to the following:

> *"Welcome to the Universe of You. You are standing on a planet with a never-ending horizon beneath the cosmos. Above you is everything you have ever and will ever experience. The cosmic bodies and nebulas gasses represent your memories, your potential futures, your loved ones, your enemies, your inner thoughts, your outer actions, your fears, your dreams, your successes, your failures, the trillions of permutations of your perceptions of yesterday, today and tomorrow across multiple iterations of your lifeline. Floating in front of you at about 30 feet long is your brain – a powerful force that has processed and adapted to this Universe for an eternity. For millions of years, beginning as a single-celled organism, it has withstood drought, famine, disease, predators, intense heat, intense cold, disaster, decay and entropy. It is the greatest source of power here, second only to you.*
>
> *As you stand here, you are the God of this Universe – the 'metacognitive architect' that creates and controls all of this as a mental representation of your consciousness. You greatly value the advice from your brain, the wise demi-god; however, the brain is imperfect. It wants to help, but sometimes it gives bad advice. It speaks to you through feelings using ancient structures, electrical functions and neurochemicals, though it is unable to fully understand what is happening around it. It depends on the <insert client's age> of interactions you've had with it through your own thoughts and behaviors. When it makes you feel anxious, it looks for validation by seeing if you respond with anxious thoughts and behaviors. If you validate it, it will likely give you the same message in the future under similar circumstances. If you do not, it will be less likely. Ultimately, you are in control. You are the engineer."*

At this point, have them shrink the brain so that it is roughly 5–10 feet long and have them walk around and within the brain. Teach them about how raw information enters their brain through our sensory structures and how it is processed though their prefrontal cortex (PFC) and limbic system, including the thalamus, hypothalamus, hippocampus, amygdala, locus coeruleus, and adrenal glands. These structures stand out in the translucent structure as opaque sculptures. Include how the brain identifies threats through emotional (thalamus to amygdala) and logical (thalamus to higher cortical areas and PFC loop) pathways, how that response makes us *feel* (i.e. cortisol and noradrenaline raising our heartrate, breathing, blood pressure, etc.), how those feelings affect our *thoughts* (e.g. worrisome perseverations) and *actions* (e.g. withdrawal, panic), and how those thoughts and actions may in turn increase the *feelings* of anxiety.

Psychoeducation-Based Intervention

Now you are going to take advantage of the 3D art mechanics within the game. If the client has clinical anxiety, you have taught them that their fight or flight response to a perceived threat (e.g. walking through a cafeteria) or overreaction (e.g. catastrophizing a B on a test) has both tainted and inhibited the PFC. Instead of filtering out irrational emotions through logical thought and emotional regulation, it is now indulging cognitive distortions. To guide this imagery, have them take the recolor tool, choose a color that represents fear to them (usually red), and have them recolor the green "logical" pathway to red. This represents that it is "tainted" with nonreactive anxiety. Now have them select the fire brush to draw a pathway from the locus coeruleus to the medulla of the adrenal glands, followed by selecting the electricity brush and drawing a path toward the heart structure. Direct them to the PFC. Have them create a cube guide and expand it across the PFC so that they may write on it like a wall. Have them think about something that recently made them feel anxious or panicked and have them write down the thoughts they had in that moment. For instance, perhaps they felt anxious because of approaching a group of peers, and may have had thoughts like "they'll think I'm stupid", "they're going to make fun of me", "I'm not good enough", or other cognitive distortions that worsen the anxiety. This is where the immersive CBT intervention begins.

Guide them to the fight or flight response between the thalamus and amygdala (appears as a short fire pathway pulsing red. Teach them about square breathing and how it can inhibit the stress response (and therefore inhibit the release of cortisol and noradrenaline). As they deep breathe in real life, have them choose the fog brush and a color that they feel is calming (usually blue or green) and instruct them to color over the pathway between the amygdala and thalamus, covering up that pathway. Then have them delete the fire pathway from the locus coeruleus to the adrenal gland as well as the electrical pathway to the heart. Now all that remains of the anxiety is the perseverating loop between the thalamus and the PFC. If this does not get managed, then that calming fog will disappear, and the amygdala will reactivate. Have them approach the PFC, grab the bad thoughts that they previously wrote there, and throw them into the void of space. Those thoughts will vanish. Have them write-in new rational thoughts to replace the distortions, such as "there's no reason they'll think

I'm stupid because I'm not", "these people have not made fun of me before so I have no evidence to think that they would now", "I am deserving of approval and am good enough", etc. Lastly, have them pick that same calming color from the fog brush and recolor the perseverating pathway back to a rational state.

As the metacognitive engineer of their own universe, they have successfully managed the anxiety. At this point, I encourage using a bit of art therapy in a fun way. Perhaps have them shrink the brain to 12 inches long beneath them, orienting it so it looks like it's looking up at them submissively. Have them draw or choose empowering images from the poly library (e.g. A.T.A.T's from Star Wars they can control, Pikachu, etc.) to place beside them as if to give them more power, and have them create a calming environment around that brain (e.g. a willow tree, "ember" brush to make it feel magical). This author has a yoga mat that the client can lay on, looking up through their calm space while listening to a song of their choice (or "weightless" by Marconi Union, which is clinically proven to reduce anxiety in adult samples), and instruct them to write the message "I am in control" with the "light" brush above them.

Case Example

Eliseo is a 15-year-old male (tenth grade) reportedly suffering from clinical anxiety and depression. For the initial 60-minute session, I met with his parents virtually for a comprehensive intake including (not exhaustive) primary referral concerns, family history, school and medical documents, and background information. Per parents' report, Eliseo had minor to moderate issues with school avoidance and internalizing symptoms freshman year, which had worsened since school went virtual due to COVID-19. His school avoidance had generalized into other public areas (e.g. grocery story), he was overwhelmingly behind in schoolwork, he generally withdrew and immersed himself into video games (PS4, PC, and Oculus Rift) or sleep, and he was having more self-degrading comments with some mild suicidal ideation.

The second session (45 minutes) was just with Eliseo and was aimed at developing rapport. This session was done in-person with phase III COVID-19 protocols. We began in my office walking around the facilities, discussing interests, and introducing him to the therapeutic process (including VR). After that, I offered letting him try VR in my 16 × 20 foot VR room. As a note, I use the HTC Vive Pro with a wireless adapter through a moderately powerful gaming computer. He excitedly agreed. The game of choice was Richie's Plank Experience, where I map in a 12 foot by 8-inch plank of wood into the game, allowing the client to walk across it while the game simulates a cityscape with the plank 16 stories high. As he was getting affiliated with the VR system, I spoke of spatial presence and how our brains are not always accurate, using evidence that his heartrate went up 45 bpm standing on the plank. We discussed how his brain was suggesting anxiety as a helpful response because it was hearing and seeing virtual threats it believed to be real, despite him knowing he was only 2 inches above the ground. We talked briefly about other threats that are not real that his brain believes are, in which he mentioned social settings. I taught him square breathing and a few introductory techniques to show that he could lower his heart rate and inhibit his anxiety response, which he did successfully.

The third session was done virtually. I had sent information in between about how to set up his Oculus Rift with *Tilt Brush*. In this case, he had played around with it before our third session and was familiar with the basics. I began the psychoeducation as mentioned above, getting through the structures, pathways, and physiological ways to reduce anxiety (e.g. muscle relaxation, deep breathing). He wasn't sure what music to play, so I played "Flight of the Bumblebee" by Rimsky Korsakov for the anxious state and "Weightless" by Marconi Union for the relaxed state through zoom. I directed him to turn on the "audio wave" feature, making some of the brush strokes react to the music and emulate the state of mind according to the music. I then had him explain to me what he learned, which he did with great accuracy.

The fourth session was done in the same way as the third, but focused on the CBT component (e.g. writing negative distorted thoughts, replacing with positive realistic ones). The anxiety he chose was going to the grocery store. The primary cognitive distortions he was experiencing were catastrophizing (e.g. "someone's going to yell at me and I'm going to have a panic attack at the store"), overgeneralization (e.g. "I suck, I can't even go to a stupid store"), jumping to conclusions (e.g. mind reading), and emotional reasoning (i.e. "this anxiety is valid"). We went through the intervention as described, and followed up by having him write down the positive replacement thoughts (e.g. "no one is going to yell at me, I'll be fine"; "I do not suck, I'm great at many things, this is just a bit hard for me right now"; "I'm projecting my own insecurities onto others, they know nothing about me and are not having harmful thoughts towards me"; "this feeling of anxiety is not real, it's just my brain giving me bad advice, and I can reengineer it"). We went through a few circumstances of how he could use these replacement thoughts at the grocery store and set a SMART goal that involved him going to the store for ten minutes with a family member each day. He was to bring a card with those replacement thoughts written down and go through a serious of self-regulation and cognitive techniques (including visualizing himself as the metacognitive architect) while at the store, checking the ones he used each time and rating the anxiety out of 10 at the start, during and after.

Session five involved a review of his progress. He did amazing and had already upped his SMART goal to include going on any short trip a family member took (e.g. going to get gas, food, etc.). He also said that he enjoyed revisiting the brain in *Google Tilt Brush* and reenacting those moments of stress, which went above and beyond what I requested. Session six involved meeting with the family to discuss a formal reintroduction to virtual school (though it involved two days in person at this point) and requesting a 504 from the school with some accommodations.

Ethical Considerations

A few things need to be considered when using VR in this way.

1. The clinician should ensure that any telepresence or recording is done with HIPPA compliance (in some cases like in the use of video-modeling, this may require an AV waiver).
2. Any intervention that involves balancing like Richie's Plank Experience should be accompanied by some mobile assistance apparatus (i.e. I use a waist band with grips on it used for geriatric populations and occupational therapy, etc.)
3. Age and state of mind should be strongly considered – young children (3–8 years old), the elderly, and those with dissociative or delusional conditions are at-risk of having a negative VR experience, predominately due to simulation sickness (dizziness, etc.).
4. The clinician should do frequent check-ins with the client to ensure they are having a physically and mentally comfortable experience. It should be noted that since this method involves very little simulated locomotion, this author has yet to have a negative report.
5. Any use of in-person materials should be disinfected thoroughly between use and used in accordance to CDC recommendations.

Conclusion

Virtual reality is the innovative medium of tomorrow, and related approaches to therapy are repeatedly being found to improve upon standard therapeutic interventions. Specifically, psychoeducation should be included in the therapeutic process and should involve state-of-the-art technology where applicable. Research has found that psychoeducation in some forms improve remarkably with the use of VR, which comes as no surprise, given that VR has often been described as "the learning aid of the 21st century" (Rogers, 2019). The benefits of increasing spatial presence, involvement, and attention allocation are clear, and should be pursued in a multitude of ways. One way is the method covered within this chapter – "The Universe of You" neuropsychoeducation and therapy – which may be done in person or remotely. Ethical considerations should be taken in accordance to research, including using HIPAA compliant devices and software and being mindful of the unique psychological demands of VR.

References

Bailenson, J. (2018). *Experience on demand: What virtual reality is, how it works, and what it can do*. W. W. Norton & Company.

Biocca, F., & Delaney, B. (1995). Immersive virtual reality technology. In *Communication in the age of virtual reality* (pp. 57–124). Lawrence Erlbaum Associates, Inc.

Chavez, B., & Bayona, S. (2018). *Virtual reality in the learning process: Trends and advances in information systems and technologies* (pp. 1345–1356). Springer International Publishing.

Darken, R. P., Allard, T. & Achille, L. B. (1998). Spatial orientation and wayfinding in large-scale virtual spaces. *Presence: Teleoperators and Virtual Environments*, 7(2), 101–107.

Dixon, L. (1999). Providing services to families of persons with schizophrenia: Present and future. *Journal of Mental Health Policy and Economics*, 2, 3–8.

Khenak, N., Vézien, J. M., Thery, D., & Bourdot, P. (2018). Spatial presence in real and remote immersive environments and the effect of multisensory stimulation. *PRESENCE: Virtual and Augmented Reality*, 27(3), 287–308.

Krokos, E., Plaisant, C., & Varshney, A. (2019). Virtual memory palaces: Immersion aids recall. *Virtual Reality*, 23(1), 1–15.

Lukens, E. P., & McFarlane, W. R. (2004). Psychoeducation as evidence-based practice: Considerations for practice, research, and policy. *Brief Treatment and Crisis Intervention*, 4, 205–225.

Marsh, D. (1992). Working with families of people with serious mental illness. In L. VandeCreek, S. Knapp, & T. L. Jackson (Eds.), *Innovations in clinical practice: A sourcebook* (pp. 389–402). Professional Resource Press.

Rizzo, A., & Bouchard, S. (Eds.). (2019). *Virtual reality for psychological and neurocognitive interventions*. Springer.

Rogers, S. (2019). *The learning aid of the 21st century*. Forbes.

Ryan M. L. (2015). *Narrative as virtual reality 2: Revisiting immersion and interactivity in literature and electronic media* (Vol. 2). JHU Press.

Steuer J. (1995). Defining virtual reality: Dimensions determining presence. *Communication in the age of virtual reality* (pp. 33–56). Lawrence Erlbaum Associates, Inc.

Stone, J. (Ed.). (2019). *Integrating technology into modern therapies: A clinician's guide to developments and interventions*. Routledge.

Walsh, K. R., & Pawlowski, S. D. (2002). Virtual reality: A technology in need of IS research. *Communications of Association for Information Systems*, 8(1), 20.

Wang, P., Wu, P., Wang, J., Chi, H.-L., & Wang, X. (2018). A critical review of the use of virtual reality in construction engineering education and training. *International Journal of Environmental Research and Public Health*, 15(6), Art. no. 1204.

Witmer, B. G., & Singer, M. J. (1998). Measuring presence in virtual environments: A presence questionnaire. *Presence*, 7(3), 225–240.

Conclusion

Jessica Stone

Borne out of the immediate and lingering needs of play therapy providers everywhere, *Play Therapy and Telemental Health: Foundations, Populations, and Interventions* aims to meet a number of lofty goals:

1. Release within a short amount of time so clinicians can immediately begin to incorporate the contents into their play therapy practice.
2. Provide a strong foundation for the play therapist to conceptualize and understand the underpinnings of their work regardless of the medium.
3. Provide important concepts to consider and integrate into case formulation and treatment planning.
4. Inform the reader of the history and research regarding the use of telemental health and how that translates into the incorporation of the history and foundation of play therapy and case conceptualization into telemental health play therapy.
5. Explore the importance of culture and its broadened definition so the play therapist may understand their clients and themselves and how each is affected by cultural components, particularly in a telemental health environment.
6. Provide specific telemental health play therapy information, guidelines, and interventions for particular populations.
7. Provide specific telemental health play therapy information, research, and guidelines for specific telemental health play therapy interventions.

On behalf of all the amazing authors involved, we hope you have enjoyed this book and will return to it over and over again even after the COVID-19 pandemic has rescinded.

The ability for continuity of care through technological means and advances has created a markedly different experience than any other time in history. Play therapists of today have been part of this amazing transformation and this will forever shape the future of play therapy and mental health treatment all over the world. We have all been part of something amazing; resilience is demonstrated through our perseverance to serve our clients throughout all we have faced. Who better than play therapists to adopt fundamentals to such a remarkable time in history and then carry it forward to better services for generations to come.

> *Play therapists understand play. Of any group of psychologically focused professionals, play therapists know more about the intricacies, nuances, fundamentals, and processes of play than anyone else. The therapeutic powers of play, fueled and guided by a trained professional, can drastically alter a child's understanding of themselves, their place in this world, and aspects of interpersonal interactions. (Stone, 2020, p. 1)*

Reference

Stone, J. (2020). *Digital play therapy: A clinician's guide to comfort and competence.* Routledge.

Index

Adler, Alfred 7
anime 156, 160–163, 165–167
Autism Spectrum Disorder 130, 136, 139
AutPlay Therapy 131–133, 135, 137, 140

bibliotherapy 76–77, 90, 92, *209*

case conceptualization 7, 13, 15–16, 28–30, 37–38, 240; and treatment planning *see* treatment planning
creative activities 223, 226–227
culture: cultural humility 29, 68

digital: age 17, 40, 202; art 156, 165, 167; assest(s) 201, 210, 214; divide 57; format 160; games 189; immigrants 189; natives 58, 101, 189, 192; platform 46, 188–189, 193; puppet 94; tools 58, 60, 178–179, 187, 193–194, 204; technology ix, x, 202

Erik Erikson 9–10
ethics 80, 104, 118, 131, 133, 201, 210, 214; code of 71, 73; nature 226
expressive: arts 77, 102–103, **122**, 194, 208–*209*, 221; therapies 201–214

family systems 15, 26, 30, 87; internal model 79; theory 14, 31
fan-fiction 156, **161**, 163–164, 166–167
Freud, Anna 5–6, 9

game(s) 36, 94, 106, 127, 137, 140, 182, 193–194, 197, 207; board 137–138; boundary 90; interactive 195; livestream 226; making up 153; nature-based 224; video 61, 91, 178, 226
green time 218, 220, 225–227

iGeneration 188

Jung, Carl 7–8

Klein, Melanie 5, 6, 16

Lowenfeld, Margaret 5–6, 8

Mahler, Margaret 5–6

neurobiology 17, 87
neuropsychoeducation 231, 238

online 79, 90, **134**, 188, 211; bullying 166; environment x; interventions 196–197; learning 100, 162, 187; literature 163; play room 102; platform 105, 159–160; relationship 210; schooling 64, 92; setting 116; session 126, 134, 181, 184; spaces 197; therapeutic services 105; trauma therapy 128; video- conferencing 132; webinar 88; working with clients 112–114

Parents as Partners 87, 92–93
play therapy: Adlerian **7**, 14, **27**, 36–37; Attachment Centered 103; Child Centered 33, 38; Cognitive Behavioral 36; developmental 35; digital x, 60–63, 192–193; Digital ™ 60, 114, 187; directive 7, 11, 13–14; Ecosystemic 37; Gestalt 37–38; historical theories 27, 36; integrative 141; interventions; 14, 38, 76, 133, 137, 179, 188, 201, 240; Jungian Analytical 34; Nature 217–221, 226–227; non-directive 7, 9, 12–14; online 3, 116–117, 198; Object

Relations 35; prescriptive 13–14, 27, 38; theories; trends in 16–17
psychoanalytic: model 5; movement 7–8; process 5; theory 5–6
psychoanalysis 3, 5–7, 9–10
psychoeducation 36, 195, 229–232, 235, 237–238; family 211; for parents 93; school 212–213; VR 234

Rank, Otto 8–9

telemedicine xiv, 47–51, 64
teleplay xiv, **120**, 209–210, 213; assessment 106; creation of 179; expressive 203; family-based 104; interventions 205; therapy services 74, 80; sessions 160, 210, 214; technique 165
theoretical orientation 3, 4, 16, 26–27, 30, 32–33, 35–36, 38, 40
therapy: cognitive behavioral 11, 26, 95; conjoint family therapy 15; family therapy 31, 102; parent-child therapy; *see* play therapy
theory(ies): Adlerian 7, 27, 36; Child Centered Play Therapy 12, **27**, 34; cognitive behavioral **27**; Child Centered Play Therapy 33; directive 33; object relations 6; importance of 25
TraumaPlay™ 87–97
treatment planning 14, 16, 31, 38; case conceptualization and 10, 18, 27, 33, 35, 47, 240; goal-directed 25, 32–33, 36

universe of you 229, 234, 238

Virtual Sandtray (App) ®© xii, 94, 114, **120**, 173, 177–178, 205, 214
virtual playroom 187–190, 192–199
virtual reality 60, 93, 229–234, 238

Printed in the United States
by Baker & Taylor Publisher Services